Theor Test for Drivers of Large Vehicles

The **official questions** and **answers** for **goods vehicles**, **bus** and **coach drivers**

C000257076

Produced by AA Publishing.

ISBN: 978-0-7495-6730-9

Published by AA Publishing (a trading name of AA Media Limited, whose registered office is Fanum House, Basing View, Basingstoke, Hampshire RG21 4EA; registered number 06112600).

Visit AA Publishing at theAA.com/shop

Colour separation by Keene Group, Andover
Printed and bound by G. Canale & C. s.p.a., Torino, Italy

Image credits
Front cover: © Mikael Damkier/Alamy
Back cover: © Richard Naude/Alamy

A04484

While every effort has been made to include the widest possible range of questions available at the time of printing, the Government may from time to time change, add or remove questions, and the publisher cannot be held responsible for questions that may appear on a Theory Test which were not available for inclusion in this book.

Get 10% off marked prices*
On AA Road Atlases
and Street by Street

Simply visit **theAA.com/shop** and enter the promo code **DRIVERS1** at the checkout to claim your discount, terms and conditions apply.

Get 10% off marked prices*
On AA Car Essentials

Keeping you prepared on the road

Simply visit **theAA.com/shop** and enter the promo code **DRIVERS2** at the checkout to claim your discount, terms and conditions apply.

Contents

Introduction

About the Theory Test

The Theory Test is divided into two parts: multiple choice questions and hazard perception clips. You don't have to take both tests at the same time and can choose which order you take the tests, but you have to pass both parts to get your Theory Test certificate and be allowed to take your Practical Test.

How to use this book
This book is designed to help you prepare for your PCV (passenger carrying vehicles) and/or your LGV (large goods vehicle) Theory Test.

This book contains all the official questions and answers for LGV and PCV Theory Tests, which appear in the official question databank of the DSA. You could be tested on any of these questions when you take your touch-screen Theory Test.

The questions are arranged in topics, such as Carrying Passengers, Traffic Signs and Vehicle Loading. Each topic has its own colour band, to help you find your way around, and each question is marked as applicable to PCV drivers, LGV drivers or both. You only need to study the questions relevant to the licence you require – either PCV or LGV.

The questions have multiple-choice answers and each one tells you how many answer(s) are required from four, five or six options.

You'll find all the correct answers to the Theory Test questions are at the back of the book, so you can easily test yourself to find what you are getting right and what you still need to work on.

Questions marked **NI** are **not** found in Theory Tests in Northern Ireland

This book also includes information on getting your licence, the CPC qualification for new drivers, how to prepare for the Theory Test and the Case Studies Test.

Getting your PCV/LGV licence
You want to get your passenger carrying vehicle (PCV) or large goods vehicle (LGV) licence and perhaps take advantage of the enhanced financial or career prospects that becoming a professional LGV or PCV driver will give you. Whether you intend to drive commercially or not, it is an important step, because you will be responsible for a vehicle weighing up to 40 tons and for the safety of its load or passengers as well as making sure

that your driving does not endanger your load, passengers or any other road users.

Acquiring knowledge of the rules of the road, gaining experience of driving and manoeuvring a large goods or passenger vehicle and knowing *The Highway Code* are only a small part of becoming a large vehicles driver. Key elements in your success, both in getting your licence and on the road, should be taking the right attitude and being a courteous and considerate driver to other road users.

This book is designed to help you take the first step towards achieving your goal – preparing for your Theory Test so that you can take the next step – the Practical Test – towards attaining your licence.

Certificate of Professional Competence (CPC) for new drivers

The CPC qualification was introduced from September 2008 for all drivers of public carrying vehicles and from September 2009 for all large goods vehicles drivers working in the EU. The purpose of the qualification is to ensure that professional drivers maintain high driving standards and levels of road safety.

Existing PCV drivers who have held a vocational licence from before 10 September 2008 and LGV drivers who have held a vocational licence from before 10 September 2009 do not have to take the initial CPC qualification because they are considered to have 'acquired rights'. Although existing PCV/LGV drivers do have to undertake 35 hours of periodic training within five years, and every five years thereafter, of being granted 'acquired rights' in order to maintain their Certificate of Professional Competence.

New drivers wanting to drive commercially need to pass the Driver CPC Case Studies and Driver CPC Practical Test in addition to passing the Theory and Practical tests required to get a PCV/LGV driving licence.

Introduction

Who needs the CPC qualification?

You need to take the CPC qualification, if you intend to earn a living from driving a large goods or passenger vehicle:

- want to drive a lorry over 3.5 tonnes
- plan to drive a minibus with nine seats or more

The CPC qualification for new LGV/PCV drivers is divided into four parts

Part 1 Theory Test (multiple-choice questions and hazard perception)

Part 2 Case Studies

Part 3 Practical Test

Part 4 Driver CPC Practical Test

Licence Requirements Summary

For non-commercial drivers wanting to drive a passenger vehicle with eight seats or less or a large vehicle under 3.5 tonnes , you'll need to pass Parts 1 and 3. You have to pass the Theory Test (Part 1) before you can apply to take your Practical Test (Part 3).

To drive a large vehicle commercially, a passenger vehicle with nine seats or more or a vehicle over 3.5 tonnes, you'll need to pass parts 1, 2, 3 and 4. You will need to pass your Theory Test first (Part 1), but you can then take the Case Studies test (Part 2) and your Practical Test (Part 3) in any order. However, you must pass your Case Studies (Part 2) and your Practical Test (Part 3) before being able to take your Driver CPC Practical Test (Part 4).

To stay qualified, LGV and PCV drivers have to undertake 35 hours of periodic training within five years of passing their inital CPC qualification.

For more information on earning your living from driving a large and passenger carrying vehicle and the initial CPC qualification visit www.drivercpc.org and www.businesslink. gov.uk/transport.

Six steps to getting your PCV/LGV licence

1. Get your provisional licence

The first step in getting your licence is to apply for a provisional HGV/PVC licence. To be eligible you must:

- be aged over 21 years
- have a full driving licence
- meet the eyesight and medical requirements
- hold the relevant provisional licence of the vehicle you want to drive

Before you can apply for your licence you will need to have a medical carried out by a doctor to ensure that your eyesight and health meets the standards required to drive a large goods or passenger vehicle. The doctor will complete a medical report form. Submit this form with your completed application form available from Traffic Area Offices or the

Driver Vehicle Licensing Authority (DVLA) or Driver and Vehicle Agency (DVA) in Northern Ireland. You must also disclose any criminal convictions when applying for a PCV licence.

Take care when completing all the forms. Many licences cannot be issued because of errors or omissions on the application forms. Make sure you supply all the documents required. Send your form to the DVLA or DVA in Northern Ireland.

Once you have received your provisional licence and have checked that all the details are correct you will be able to apply to take your Theory Test. You will also be able to start driver training, provided that you are supervised by a person who holds a current licence for the relevant category of vehicle and display L-plates at the front and rear of your vehicle. If you are in Northern Ireland, you will also need to display LGV or PCV plates at the front and rear of your vehicle. You can get list of the DSA's Register of instructors by calling 0115 936 6502.

2. Know your Highway Code

The Highway Code is essential reading for all drivers and road users and sets out all the rules for good driving, as well as the meaning of traffic signs and road markings. Take particular care to learn the signs that show restrictions for large goods or public transport

vehicles. When you have learned the rules you will be able to answer many of the questions in the Theory Test and be ready to start learning the driving skills you will need to pass your Practical Test. However, you will only find the answers to some questions by talking to your instructor and learning about good driving practice on the road.

3. Get Practical Experience

To attain your LGV/PVC licence you'll need to take a Theory Test and a Practical Test (Parts 1 and 3). Once you have your provisional licence you may take the Theory Test at any time, but you must pass it before you are allowed to apply for the Practical Test.

It is important that you don't take your Theory Test too early in your course of driver instruction, because you need the experience of driving a large goods or public transport vehicle to learn how it differs from a smaller vehicle. A qualified instructor will be able provide lots of guidance and tuition along with a demonstration if required. Driving with a qualified instructor and hands-on experience of driving are vital in passing not only your Practical Test(s) (Parts 3 and 4) but also the multiple-choice questions and the hazard perception parts of the Theory Test (Part 1) and the Case Studies (Part 2) if you plan to earn your living from driving a passenger carrying or large vehicle.

In addition, you are strongly recommended to prepare for the Theory Test at the same time as you develop your skills behind the wheel for the Practical Test(s). Obviously there are many similarities between the tests and you need the experience of meeting real hazards and traffic scenarios.

4. Book your Theory Test

You can book your Theory Test by post, by calling or online. Application forms are available from Theory Test centres or your instructor. Your application form should be sent to address given on the form with a cheque, postal order, credit or debit card details. You will need a credit or debit card to apply by phone or online but you will get your test date immediately. If you apply by post, you'll usually receive your test date within ten working days.

Phone 0300 200 1122
Online www.dvani.gov.uk

The Theory Test

The Theory Test is divided into two parts: multiple choice questions and hazard perception clips. You don't have to take both tests at the same time. You can choose which order you take the tests, but you have to pass both parts to get your Theory Test certificate and be allowed to book your Practical Test.

Don't Forget

You'll need to take the following original documents with you to the Theory Test centre or you won't be allowed to take your Theory Test and will lose your exam fee and have to rebook your test.

- Your signed photo card licence and paper counterpart

or

- Your signed driving licence and passport

5. Take the Practical Test

Once you have passed both parts of your Theory Test, you will receive a test certificate showing your Theory Test number. You need this number to book your Practical Test. You must pass your Practical Test within two years of the date of passing the first part of your Theory Test; otherwise you will have to take one or both parts of the Theory Test again.

6. Get your initial CPC qualification

If you decide that you want to undertake your CPC qualification then you will also need to pass parts 2 then 4 of the CPC qualification. When you have passed all four modules you will be sent a Driver Qualification Card. Make sure that you carry this card when you are driving and inform the DSA if your card is lost, stolen or damaged.

Introduction

The PCV/LGV Theory Test is in two parts multiple-choice questions, which you answer using a touch-screen computer, and hazard perception film clips, which you view on a computer and use a mouse to indicate your responses.

The Theory Test questions

You will have 115 minutes to answer 100 multiple-choice questions in the test, using a touch-screen to select your answers. The questions are drawn from a bank of more than 1000 questions. In order to pass the test you must answer a minimum of 85 questions correctly within the given time. The Government may change the questions and the pass mark from time to time. Your instructor or the DSA will be able to tell you if there has been a change.

The questions appear on the screen one at a time and you can return to any of the questions within the 115 minutes to re-check or alter your answers. This means that you can answer the questions in any order you choose by moving forwards and backwards through the questions. You can also change your answer/s if necessary and flag questions you're unsure about, then go back to them later in the test. Your remaining time is shown on the screen throughout the test.

Study each question carefully and all the possible answers, making sure you understand

what it is asking you. Look carefully at any diagram, drawing or photograph. Before you look at the answers given, decide what you think the correct answer(s) might be. You can then select the answer(s) that matches the one you had decided on. If you follow this system, you will avoid being confused by answers that appear to be similar.

Each question has four, five or six possible answers. You must mark the boxes with the correct answer(s). Each question tells you how many answers to mark. Don't worry about accidentally missing marking an answer because you'll be reminded that you haven't ticked enough boxes before moving on to the next question.

Useful Tips

You have the option to have a 15-minute practice session using the computer before your real test starts.
If you have enough time at the end of the test, you will be able to use the review button to check all your answers before finishing the test.

Preparing for the Theory Test questions

As you start to work through the questions you will soon discover that similar questions on the same topic may appear in different sections. Don't be put off by this, but read each question and the choice of answers very carefully. Similar questions may be asked in a slightly different way to test your knowledge. Make a note of any questions that you don't understand and ask your instructor to explain the answer.

Avoid the pitfalls!
- Don't try too many questions at once.
- Don't try to learn the answers by heart.
- The order of the questions in this book may be different from how they are arranged in the actual test – so don't try to memorise the order.
- The questions in your 'real test' will come from a range of topics.
- Make a note of any questions that you don't understand and ask your instructor to explain the answer they will also be able to tell you where you can find reference to these questions

Hazard perception test

The hazard perception clips part of the Theory Test lasts for about 25 minutes. Before you start you will be given some instructions explaining how the test works; you'll also get a chance to practise with the computer and mouse before you start the test.

Next you will see 19 film clips of real street scenes with traffic such as cars, pedestrians, cyclists, etc. The scenes are shot from the point of view of the driver. You will have 10 seconds to observe the road situation before the film clip starts.

You have to notice potential hazards that are developing on the road ahead – that is, problems that could lead to a collision. As soon as you see a hazard developing, click the mouse a couple of times. You will have plenty of time to see the hazard, but the sooner you notice it, the more marks you'll score.

Each of the 19 clips has at least one hazard in it and there are 20 hazards in total. You have to score a minimum of 67 out of 100 to pass, but the pass mark may change so check with your instructor or the DSA before your test.

Important Note
- The computer has checks built in to show anyone trying to cheat – for example someone who keeps clicking the mouse all the time.
- Be aware that, unlike the Theory Test questions, you will not have an opportunity to go back to an earlier clip and change your response, so you need to concentrate throughout the test.

Preparing for the hazard perception test
Who do you think have the most collisions – newly qualified or experienced drivers? New drivers have just been trained, so they should remember how to drive safely, but in fact new drivers have the most collisions.

LGV/PCV drivers need training in anticipation and planning, which is the key to spotting hazards, because they are often so busy thinking about the vehicle's controls, their load, their timetable or their passengers that they forget to watch the road and traffic. Losing concentration for even a second in a large vehicle could prove fatal to you, your passengers and other road users.

Training in anticipation and planning can help you to recognise more of the hazards that you will meet when driving and to spot those hazards earlier. It will also help you recognise the additional hazards involved when carrying a loaded vehicle or passengers. So you are less likely to have or cause a collision.

Your instructor has been trained to help you develop your anticipation and planning skills, which will in turn increase your hazard perception skills. During driver instruction you will get plenty of practise in what to look out for when driving, how to deal with hazards, and what action to take to deal with hazards of all kinds.

You won't be able to practise with the real video clips used in the test, but training books and practice videos are widely available.

Passing your Theory Test

When you have passed both parts of the Theory Test you will be sent a letter showing your pass certificate number. You need to pass your Practical Test within two years of the date of your pass certificate or you'll have to retake your Driving Test Theory again.

Top: Real road scenes feature in the film clips in the hazard perception test

Centre and bottom: Click the mouse when you spot potential hazards – the pedestrian crossing the side road and the cyclist approaching a parked vehicle (ringed in yellow). Click again as the hazard develops when the cyclist (ringed in red) moves out to overtake the parked vehicle.

Introduction

About the Case Studies

If you want to get your CPC (Certificate of Professional Competence) qualification and earn a living from driving a large vehicle or passenger vehicle then you will also need to pass the Case Studies, as well as your Practical Test and then, finally, your Driver CPC Practical Test. (See page 8 for more information about who needs the CPC qualification.)

Like the multiple-choice and hazard perception parts of the Theory Test, this is a computer-based test and can be taken at the same test centre as your Theory Test. Studying for your Theory Test, taking practical driving instruction and getting professional instruction from a skilled PCV/LGV trainer will help you to prepare you for the Case Studies exam.

The Case Studies syllabus is designed to test your knowledge of topics such as safe and fuel efficient driving, rules and regulations, health and safety issues as well as service and logistics. The Case Studies are designed to test your knowledge of the skills and technical expertise that you require to work as a PCV or LGV driver. It's all about making you a safer driver and ensuring that you understand the risks, both to yourself and to others, as the driver of a large vehicle.

To find out what topics will be covered in the Case Studies see a summary of the syllabus (right). Each topic is marked as relevant to PCV drivers, LGV drivers or both.

- Controlling and operating your vehicle (PCV/LGV)
- Driving to optimise fuel consumption (PCV/LGV)
- Loading your vehicle and transporting goods safely (LGV)
- Driving to ensure passenger safety and comfort (PCV)
- Working with different types of passengers and understanding their various needs (PCV)
- Showing knowledge about the rules governing working hours (PCV/LGV)
- Understanding the regulations governing the transport of goods (LGV) or passengers (PCV)
- Understanding the risks of working as a commercial driver (PCV/LGV)
- Preventing theft, criminal activity and trafficking in illegal immigrants (LGV)
- Awareness of health and safety issues in the workplace (PCV/LGV)
- Maintaining your physical and mental health (PCV/LGV)
- Dealing with emergency situations (PCV/ LGV)
- Working to enhance the image of your company by adopting appropriate service levels and behaviour (PCV/LGV)
- Understanding the economic environment of passenger service or road haulage operators and the business organisation (PCV/LGV)

Source: Official Journal of the European Union

What to expect in the Case Studies

Your Case Studies test could be based on any driving situation with questions taken from a range of topics.

The test is made up of seven case studies. Each case study is based on a different, traffic or workplace scenario and may be accompanied by an image. Each of the seven case studies has six to eight questions based on the scenario. You will be asked to answer questions in different ways, using a computer, mouse and keyboard, including:

- answering a multiple-choice question by clicking on the correct answer/s using the mouse
- listening to an audio clip and then answering a multiple-choice question by clicking on the correct answer(s) using the mouse
- clicking on an area of a picture using the mouse
- typing a short answer using the keyboard.

The Case Study or scenario appears on the left-hand side of the computer screen and the question, with instructions on how to answer the question, appear on the left-hand side of the screen.

You will have 90 minutes to complete the test, including some time to practise with the computer and mouse before you start the test 'for real'. You can answer the questions in any order you choose and navigate forward and backward through the case studies using the mouse. You can change your answers and choose to review your answers at the end of the test to make sure that you have provided answers for all the questions. Your remaining time is shown on the screen throughout the test.

There is a maximum of 50 questions and the pass mark for PCV drivers is currently 40 out of 50 and 38 out of 50 for LGV drivers. Please note the pass mark is to be reviewed in September 2010. Your training instructor or the DSA will be able to tell you if there has been a change. You will be given the result of your Case Studies within 10 minutes of finishing the test.

Further information

It is a good idea to obtain one of the relevant specialist publications, which cover the syllabus of the case studies in more detail and the regulations governing drivers of passenger and large goods vehicles. Books are available from all good online and high street bookshops.

See page 16 for sample case studies.

Introduction

Sample Case Studies

The following sample Case Studies (one for PCV drivers and one for LGV drivers) have been put together by the AA to demonstrate how a scenario and question may appear in the test, so you'll know what to expect. Remember each Case Study scenario in the real test will have between six and eight questions. These examples will not appear in the Case Studies test.

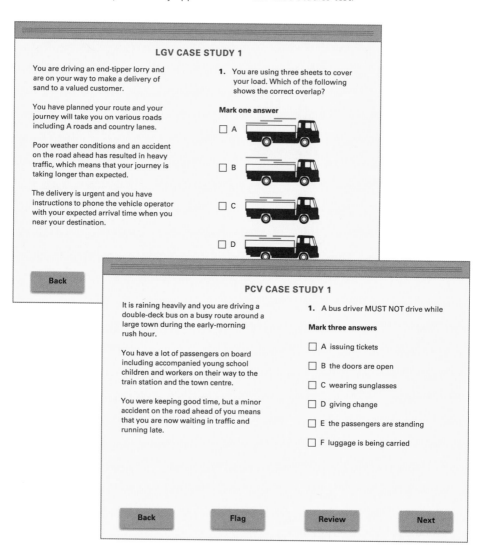

LGV CASE STUDY 1

You are driving an end-tipper lorry and are on your way to make a delivery of sand to a valued customer.

You have planned your route and your journey will take you on various roads including A roads and country lanes.

Poor weather conditions and an accident on the road ahead has resulted in heavy traffic, which means that your journey is taking longer than expected.

The delivery is urgent and you have instructions to phone the vehicle operator with your expected arrival time when you near your destination.

1. You are using three sheets to cover your load. Which of the following shows the correct overlap?

Mark one answer

☐ A
☐ B
☐ C
☐ D

Back

PCV CASE STUDY 1

It is raining heavily and you are driving a double-deck bus on a busy route around a large town during the early-morning rush hour.

You have a lot of passengers on board including accompanied young school children and workers on their way to the train station and the town centre.

You were keeping good time, but a minor accident on the road ahead of you means that you are now waiting in traffic and running late.

1. A bus driver MUST NOT drive while

Mark three answers

☐ A issuing tickets
☐ B the doors are open
☐ C wearing sunglasses
☐ D giving change
☐ E the passengers are standing
☐ F luggage is being carried

Back   Flag   Review   Next

Answers to sample Case Study questions: LGV1 A PCV1 ABD

Contents   Page

1 PCV

Fifteen passengers on your vehicle would increase the weight by about

Mark one answer

- A. 0.5 tonnes
- B. 1 tonne
- C. 2.5 tonnes
- D. 3 tonnes

2 PCV

As a guide, how many passengers equal about one tonne?

Mark one answer

- A. 15
- B. 20
- C. 25
- D. 30

3 PCV

Certain weight limit signs do not apply to buses. How would the driver know?

Mark one answer

- A. By a plate fitted beneath the weight limit sign
- B. By the colour of the weight limit sign
- C. By a plate attached to the vehicle
- D. By a certificate carried by the driver

4 PCV

You are driving a bus on a local service. You can use this lane

Mark one answer

- A. between 4pm and 6.30pm only
- B. before 4pm and after 6.30pm only
- C. at any time of the day
- D. any time except Saturdays

5 PCV

The national speed limit for buses and coaches on a dual carriageway is

Mark one answer

- A. 55mph
- B. 60mph
- C. 65mph
- D. 70mph

6 PCV

The D1 category licence allows you to drive buses with a maximum of

Mark one answer

- A. 16 passenger seats
- B. 24 passenger seats
- C. 32 passenger seats
- D. 48 passenger seats

7 PCV

A driver should know the vehicle's unladen weight. Where can this information be found?

Mark one answer

- [ ] **A.** On the dashboard of the vehicle
- [ ] **B.** On the driver's duty roster
- [ ] **C.** On the side of the vehicle
- [ ] **D.** On the depot noticeboard

8 PCV

What category of licence is required to drive an articulated bus?

Mark one answer

- [ ] **A.** D
- [ ] **B.** D + E
- [ ] **C.** D1
- [ ] **D.** D1 + E

9 PCV

The front of your bus overhangs well past the front wheels. Why should you allow for this when cornering?

Mark one answer

- [ ] **A.** The steering will become much heavier
- [ ] **B.** Your speed will become more difficult to control
- [ ] **C.** You might hit a post or fence
- [ ] **D.** You will need to brake much sooner

10 PCV

Your bus has a speed limiter fitted. What other related item must it have?

Mark one answer

- [ ] **A.** An audible warning device for the driver
- [ ] **B.** A plate in the cab showing the limited speed
- [ ] **C.** A warning sign on the back of the bus
- [ ] **D.** A manual over-ride switch for emergencies

11 PCV

You are the driver of a 1996 bus, which must be fitted with a speed limiter. At what speed is the limiter set?

Mark one answer

- [ ] **A.** 60mph (96kph)
- [ ] **B.** 62mph (100kph)
- [ ] **C.** 70mph (112kph)
- [ ] **D.** 75mph (120kph)

12 PCV

When a speed limiter is fitted to a bus, where must the setting be displayed clearly?

Mark one answer

- [ ] **A.** In the driver's cab
- [ ] **B.** On the nearside of the vehicle
- [ ] **C.** On the rear of the vehicle
- [ ] **D.** On the driver's side at the front of the vehicle

13 PCV

Maximum authorised mass refers to the weight of

Mark one answer

- [ ] **A.** your vehicle with passengers but no luggage
- [ ] **B.** your vehicle without passengers or luggage
- [ ] **C.** your vehicle with luggage but no passengers
- [ ] **D.** your vehicle with both luggage and passengers

14 PCV

Speed limiters are fitted to most modern buses and coaches. They normally work by

Mark one answer

- [ ] **A.** applying the service brake
- [ ] **B.** applying the secondary brake
- [ ] **C.** reducing fuel supplied to the engine
- [ ] **D.** changing to a lower or higher gear

15 PCV
The 'turning circle' is the

Mark one answer

- **A.** number of turns of the steering wheel between locks
- **B.** amount of space needed for the vehicle to turn
- **C.** amount by which the vehicle overhangs kerbs
- **D.** amount by which a vehicle cuts corners

16 PCV/LGV
What does this sign mean?

Mark one answer

- **A.** No entry for two-axled trailers
- **B.** No entry for vehicles with two-speed axles
- **C.** Maximum gross weight of 2 tonnes
- **D.** Axle weight limit of 2 tonnes

17 PCV/LGV
What does this sign mean?

Mark one answer

- **A.** Slippery road
- **B.** Double bend
- **C.** Overhead electrified cable
- **D.** Cable laying ahead

18 PCV/LGV
This sign means

Mark one answer

- **A.** no vehicles over 14 feet 6 inches wide
- **B.** no vehicles over 14 feet 6 inches high
- **C.** road humps 14 feet 6 inches apart
- **D.** weight limit of 14.6 tonnes

19 PCV/LGV
This sign warns of

Mark one answer

- **A.** low bridge ahead
- **B.** accident ahead
- **C.** tunnel ahead
- **D.** accident blackspot ahead

20 PCV/LGV
This sign means

400 yds

Mark one answer
- [ ] **A.** length of tunnel
- [ ] **B.** length of low bridge
- [ ] **C.** distance to tunnel
- [ ] **D.** distance to low bridge

21 PCV/LGV
You are driving a vehicle higher than 3.0 metres (10 feet). Extra care must be taken when driving

Mark three answers
- [ ] **A.** through arched bridges
- [ ] **B.** through road tunnels
- [ ] **C.** near airports
- [ ] **D.** near overhead cables
- [ ] **E.** up steep hills
- [ ] **F.** over narrow bridges

22 PCV/LGV
What is the minimum height of an unmarked bridge?

Mark one answer
- [ ] **A.** 4.5 metres (15 feet)
- [ ] **B.** 4.7 metres (15 feet 6 inches)
- [ ] **C.** 4.8 metres (16 feet)
- [ ] **D.** 5.0 metres (16 feet 6 inches)

23 PCV/LGV
Your vehicle collides with a bridge. You must report it to

Mark one answer **NI**
- [ ] **A.** the police
- [ ] **B.** the local authority
- [ ] **C.** your local garage
- [ ] **D.** the fire brigade

24 PCV/LGV
Your vehicle has collided with a railway bridge. You must telephone the railway authority to inform them of the

Mark three answers
- [ ] **A.** damage caused
- [ ] **B.** type of bridge
- [ ] **C.** vehicle height
- [ ] **D.** bridge number
- [ ] **E.** vehicle number
- [ ] **F.** bridge location

25 PCV/LGV
Bells hanging across the road warn of

Mark one answer
- [ ] **A.** a weight restriction
- [ ] **B.** trams crossing ahead
- [ ] **C.** overhead electric cables
- [ ] **D.** a railway level crossing

26 PCV/LGV
What does this sign mean?

Mark one answer

- **A.** The width of the road is 6 feet 6 inches (2 metres)
- **B.** No vehicles over 6 feet 6 inches (2 metres) wide
- **C.** No vehicles over 6 feet 6 inches (2 metres) high
- **D.** Trailer length must not exceed 6 feet 6 inches (2 metres)

27 PCV/LGV
This sign on a motorway means

Mark one answer

- **A.** 11 tonnes weight limit
- **B.** stop, all lanes ahead closed
- **C.** leave the motorway at the next exit
- **D.** lane ahead closed

28 PCV/LGV
You are driving on a motorway. You see this sign. It means end of

Mark one answer

- **A.** restriction
- **B.** crawler lane
- **C.** weight limit
- **D.** hard shoulder

29 PCV/LGV
You are driving a long vehicle. Your main concern at this hazard is your vehicle's

Mark one answer

- **A.** height
- **B.** width
- **C.** weight
- **D.** length

30 PCV/LGV
In which of the following places might vehicles over a certain length be restricted?

Mark three answers
- [ ] A. On ferries
- [ ] B. At freight terminals
- [ ] C. In road tunnels
- [ ] D. On dual carriageways
- [ ] E. On motorways
- [ ] F. On level crossings

31 PCV/LGV
At this roundabout you intend to take the fourth exit. On this road there is a limit on

```
            Cobham A 245
                              ⚠ 13'6"
  Chertsey                Old Woking
  A 320                   (B 382)
  M 25
                          Woking
  Cobham                  A320
  (A 3046)
```

Mark one answer
- [ ] A. height
- [ ] B. weight
- [ ] C. width
- [ ] D. length

32 PCV/LGV
When using passing places on narrow roads you will MOST need to be aware of your vehicle's

Mark one answer
- [ ] A. length
- [ ] B. roof height
- [ ] C. ground clearance
- [ ] D. weight

33 PCV/LGV
You are driving on a motorway. Your stopping distance can increase by up to ten times if the road surface is

Mark one answer
- [ ] A. bumpy
- [ ] B. icy
- [ ] C. worn
- [ ] D. wet

34 PCV/LGV
You are driving on the motorway in icy conditions. Your stopping distance can increase by up to

Mark one answer
- [ ] A. 2 times
- [ ] B. 4 times
- [ ] C. 10 times
- [ ] D. 20 times

35 PCV/LGV
When towing a trailer the maximum speed allowed on a motorway is

Mark one answer
- [ ] A. 40mph
- [ ] B. 50mph
- [ ] C. 60mph
- [ ] D. 70mph

36 PCV/LGV
Having just overtaken a motorcyclist on a motorway you MUST always check the

Mark one answer
- [ ] A. speedometer
- [ ] B. left mirror
- [ ] C. right mirror
- [ ] D. road ahead

37 PCV/LGV
A large vehicle is most stable when driven in a straight line under

Mark one answer
- A. harsh acceleration
- B. gentle braking
- C. gentle acceleration
- D. harsh braking

38 PCV/LGV
What does this sign mean?

Mark one answer
- A. Warning of lorry crossing a one-way road
- B. No entry for vehicles over 32 feet 6 inches (10 metres) long
- C. No entry for vehicles over 32.6 tonnes
- D. Warning of lorry straight ahead

39 PCV/LGV
You are driving a long vehicle. You want to turn right. There is a painted mini-roundabout. What should you do?

Mark one answer
- A. Make sure none of your wheels touch the roundabout
- B. Avoid going over the roundabout if possible
- C. Go ahead, and turn right at the next junction
- D. Carefully mount the left-hand kerb to make more room

40 PCV/LGV
When planning your route which of the following should be taken into consideration?

Mark three answers
- A. Any weight restrictions
- B. Any height restrictions
- C. Any speed restrictions
- D. Any parking restrictions
- E. Any width restrictions

41 PCV/LGV
Your vehicle is more than 3 metres (9 feet 10 inches) high. Where is this information usually displayed?

Mark one answer
- A. On the tax disc
- B. On the weight plate
- C. In the driver's cab
- D. In the engine bay

42 PCV/LGV
The height of your vehicle is 4.2 metres (14 feet). What action should you take on the approach to this bridge?

Mark one answer
- A. Keep to the centre of the arch and give way to oncoming traffic
- B. Drive through slowly, keeping to the left of the marked limits
- C. Keep to the centre of the arch and take priority over oncoming traffic
- D. Drive through quickly, keeping to the left of the marked limits

43 PCV/LGV
Unless otherwise shown, the headroom under bridges in the UK is at least

Mark one answer
- A. 4.0 metres (13 feet)
- B. 4.1 metres (13 feet 4 inches)
- C. 5.0 metres (16 feet 6 inches)
- D. 5.5 metres (18 feet)

44 PCV/LGV
In which one of these places may you park large vehicles at night without lights on?

Mark one answer
- A. In an off-road parking area
- B. On a road with a 20mph speed limit
- C. At least 10 metres (32 feet) away from any junction
- D. In most lay-bys

45 PCV/LGV
You are driving a vehicle fitted with a speed limiter. You should allow for its effects when

Mark one answer
- A. cornering
- B. braking
- C. overtaking
- D. changing gear

46 PCV/LGV
You must be aware of the effect a speed limiter has on your vehicle, especially when you intend to

Mark one answer
- A. brake
- B. change gear
- C. overtake
- D. reverse

47 PCV/LGV
You are driving on a motorway in a vehicle fitted with a speed limiter. You should be aware of

Mark one answer
- A. the lower running costs
- B. the smoother ride
- C. the limited power available when overtaking
- D. the increased fuel consumption

48 PCV/LGV
What does this sign mean?

Mark one answer
- A. Humpback bridge
- B. Risk of grounding
- C. Uneven road
- D. Road liable to subsidence

49 PCV/LGV
As you approach this sign your main concern should be your vehicle's

Mark one answer
- A. height
- B. width
- C. weight
- D. length

50 PCV/LGV
You are driving a long vehicle on a two-lane road. You want to turn left into a narrow road. What should you do?

Mark one answer
- A. Keep well to the left on the approach
- B. Move out to the right immediately before turning
- C. Keep to the left and turn later than normal
- D. Straddle the lanes to make more room for the turn

51 PCV/LGV
The repair of a speed limiter must be carried out at

Mark one answer
- A. an authorised Speed Limiter centre
- B. any Vehicle Inspectorate site
- C. your nearest Service Centre
- D. the depot by a mechanic

52 PCV/LGV
The information for the legal axle weight limits can be found on the

Mark one answer
- A. vehicle plate
- B. operator's licence
- C. tax disc
- D. weighbridge printout

53 LGV
This sign means no entry for goods vehicles

Mark one answer
- A. under 7.5 tonnes maximum authorised mass
- B. over 7.5 tonnes maximum authorised mass
- C. over 7.5 metres overall height
- D. under 7.5 metres overall height

54 LGV
Your lorry is over 7.5 tonnes maximum authorised mass. This sign means you may use

GET IN LANE
ANY VEH
800 yds

Mark one answer
- A. either the left-hand or middle lane
- B. only the left-hand lane
- C. only the middle lane
- D. any of the lanes

55 LGV
What is the national speed limit on a single carriageway road for a rigid lorry weighing more than 7.5 tonnes maximum authorised mass?

Mark one answer
- A. 30mph
- B. 40mph
- C. 50mph
- D. 60mph

56 LGV
You are driving a lorry over 7.5 tonnes maximum authorised mass. On a three-lane motorway you can only use the right-hand lane

Mark one answer
- A. to overtake slower lorries
- B. when the left-hand lane is closed
- C. if you do not go faster than 60mph
- D. if you are not towing a trailer

57 LGV
When driving a low loader you should be aware of grounding on

Mark three answers
- A. level crossings
- B. traffic calming humps
- C. yellow rumble strips
- D. hatched road markings
- E. humpback bridges

58 LGV
You are driving a low loader. You see this sign. Your main concern is

Mark one answer
- A. the ground clearance
- B. the weight limit
- C. the height limit
- D. the load

59 LGV
You are driving a vehicle that is over 17 metres (55 feet) long. What should you do at a level crossing?

Mark one answer
- A. Cross over using your horn and hazard warning lights
- B. Stop before the crossing and phone the signal operator
- C. Increase your speed to clear the crossing quickly
- D. Stop before the crossing and look both ways before going on

60 LGV
What types of fastenings or restraints should you use when carrying a heavy load of steel?

Mark one answer
- A. Chains
- B. Straps
- C. Ropes
- D. Sheeting

61 LGV

You are driving a lorry carrying a load which is 4.5 metres (14 feet 9 inches) wide. What is your maximum allowed speed on a motorway?

Mark one answer

- A. 10mph
- B. 20mph
- C. 30mph
- D. 40mph

62 LGV

What is the maximum speed limit on a dual carriageway for a lorry carrying a load which is 4.5 metres (14 feet 9 inches) wide?

Mark one answer

- A. 15mph
- B. 25mph
- C. 35mph
- D. 45mph

63 LGV

Markings are required on the rear of lorries over 7.5 tonnes maximum authorised mass. What colour are these?

Mark one answer

- A. Red/white
- B. Red/yellow
- C. Black/yellow
- D. Black/white

64 LGV

When this vehicle turns, the overhang of the top deck will swing through

Mark one answer

- A. a greater arc than the cab
- B. a lower arc than the cab
- C. a smaller arc than the cab
- D. the same arc as the cab

65 LGV

You are the driver of an articulated car transporter. When turning corners, you should be aware that the overhang of the top deck swings through a

Mark one answer

- A. smaller arc than the cab
- B. shorter arc than the cab
- C. lower arc than the cab
- D. greater arc than the cab

66 LGV

The driver of a car transporter must be most aware of the trailer front-overhang when

Mark one answer

- A. overtaking
- B. turning
- C. loading
- D. braking

67 **LGV**
You are scheduled to make a delivery. You arrive at your destination during the morning rush hour. The road is edged with double red lines. You should

Mark one answer
- [ ] A. unload only within a 'white box' area
- [ ] B. unload only within a 'red box' area
- [ ] C. delay your delivery until after the rush hour
- [ ] D. limit your stop to a maximum of 30 minutes

68 **LGV**
You are driving a lorry with a maximum authorised mass of more than 7.5 tonnes. What is the national speed limit on a dual carriageway?

Mark one answer
- [ ] A. 40mph
- [ ] B. 50mph
- [ ] C. 60mph
- [ ] D. 70mph

69 **LGV**
You are driving a petrol tanker. 'Roll-over' is least likely to occur on vehicles fitted with

Mark one answer
- [ ] A. tandem axles with double wheels
- [ ] B. tandem axles with air suspension
- [ ] C. tri-axles with single wheels
- [ ] D. tri-axles with double wheels

70 **LGV**
You are driving a petrol tanker. The change from 'rear wheel lift' to 'roll-over' occurs

Mark one answer
- [ ] A. only at roundabouts
- [ ] B. with very little warning
- [ ] C. with plenty of warning
- [ ] D. only when fully loaded

71 **LGV**
You are the driver of a refrigerated vehicle loaded with hanging meat carcasses. You should be especially careful when turning corners because of the

Mark one answer
- [ ] A. wave effect
- [ ] B. camber effect
- [ ] C. gravity effect
- [ ] D. pendulum effect

72 **LGV**
At overnight stops many drivers park with their rear doors close to another lorry. This is to

Mark one answer
- [ ] A. keep the load safe
- [ ] B. ensure a clear path
- [ ] C. keep 'same company' lorries together
- [ ] D. stop the theft of their fuel

73 **LGV**
Which of these should be fitted to a lorry with a maximum authorised mass of more than 7500kg?

Mark one answer
- [ ] A.
- [ ] B.
- [ ] C.
- [ ] D.

74 LGV
How far can a load overhang at the rear before you must use triangular projection markers?

Mark one answer
- A. 1 metre (3 feet 3 inches)
- B. 1.5 metres (5 feet 0 inches)
- C. 2 metres (6 feet 6 inches)
- D. 2.9 metres (9 feet 6 inches)

75 LGV
You are driving a lorry with a high load. Telephone companies on the route must be told if the height is more than

Mark one answer
- A. 4.00 metres (13 feet)
- B. 4.30 metres (14 feet 2 inches)
- C. 5.00 metres (16 feet 6 inches)
- D. 5.25 metres (17 feet 6 inches)

76 LGV
How wide can a load be before you must have side markers?

Mark one answer
- A. 2.0 metres (6 feet 6 inches)
- B. 2.9 metres (9 feet 5 inches)
- C. 3.5 metres (11 feet 5 inches)
- D. 4.3 metres (14 feet 2 inches)

77 LGV
Triangular projection markers are required when your load is wider than 2.9 metres (9 feet 5 inches). What colour are these?

Mark one answer
- A. Black/yellow
- B. Red/yellow
- C. Black/white
- D. Red/white

78 LGV
How should you secure an ISO steel cargo container onto your vehicle or trailer?

Mark one answer
- A. Using battens and chocks
- B. Using straps
- C. Using twist locks
- D. Using ropes

79 LGV
You are driving an articulated lorry on a narrow road. There is a left-hand bend ahead. Why may you need to move out before going through the bend?

Mark one answer
- A. To leave more room for braking
- B. To prevent anyone from overtaking
- C. To make room for the trailer cutting in
- D. To make sure oncoming drivers see you

80 PCV

Bus operators are required to use tachographs for regular journeys. Beyond what distance does this apply?

Mark one answer
- [ ] **A.** 10km
- [ ] **B.** 20km
- [ ] **C.** 50km
- [ ] **D.** 80km

81 PCV/LGV

How many days does a drivers' smart card normally cover?

Mark one answer
- [ ] **A.** 7
- [ ] **B.** 14
- [ ] **C.** 21
- [ ] **D.** 28

82 PCV/LGV

Under EU driver's hours regulations a 45-minute break must be taken after 4.5 hours driving. This can be split into shorter breaks of

Mark one answer
- [ ] **A.** one of 10 minutes plus one of 35
- [ ] **B.** one of 15 minutes plus one of 30
- [ ] **C.** one of 20 minutes plus one of 25
- [ ] **D.** one of 40 minutes plus one of 5

83 PCV/LGV

You are driving under EU tachograph regulations and lose your smart card. You must inform the relevant authority within a maximum of

Mark one answer
- [ ] **A.** 5 days
- [ ] **B.** 7 days
- [ ] **C.** 14 days
- [ ] **D.** 28 days

84 PCV/LGV

You have a digital tachograph driver smart card. It is valid for a maximum of

Mark one answer
- [ ] **A.** One year
- [ ] **B.** Three years
- [ ] **C.** Five years
- [ ] **D.** Ten years

85 PCV/LGV

Your driver tachograph card has been lost or stolen. Which authority MUST you contact?

Mark one answer **NI**
- [ ] **A.** The police
- [ ] **B.** DVLA
- [ ] **C.** A tachograph centre
- [ ] **D.** VOSA

86 PCV/LGV

Where can you collect a replacement driver tachograph card from?

Mark one answer **NI**
- [ ] **A.** DVLA local office
- [ ] **B.** Driving Standards Agency
- [ ] **C.** Any MOT test centre
- [ ] **D.** A tachograph centre

87 PCV/LGV

A driver is convicted of obstructing an enforcement officer during the course of their duties. Under EC drivers' hours regulations what is the maximum fine they may receive?

Mark one answer
- [ ] **A.** £2000
- [ ] **B.** £3000
- [ ] **C.** £4000
- [ ] **D.** £5000

88 PCV/LGV
When are you allowed to alter your tachograph record?

Mark one answer
- A. If there are two or more drivers
- B. If your journey will exceed 50 miles
- C. At no time
- D. When you have no spare charts

89 PCV/LGV
You are driving under EU drivers' hours. Under the rules governed by these, how is a week defined?

Mark one answer
- A. A period between 0.00 hours on Monday and 24.00 hours the following Sunday
- B. Any seven day period
- C. Any period between 0.00 hours and 24.00 hours 6 days later
- D. A working period of 56 hours

90 PCV/LGV
There are various types of Digital Tachograph Cards. Which is used by an approved calibration centre when recalibrating the tachograph?

Mark one answer
- A. Control card
- B. Company card
- C. Driver card
- D. Workshop card

91 PCV/LGV
There are four types of Digital Tachograph Cards. What is the card known as that is only available to enforcement authorities?

Mark one answer
- A. Control card
- B. CPC card
- C. Company card
- D. Workshop card

92 PCV/LGV
Drivers must have a driver smart card for use in digital tachographs. Where can you collect replacement smart cards from in Great Britain?

Mark one answer NI
- A. VOSA testing station
- B. Highways Agency office
- C. DSA test centre
- D. Local Post Office

93 PCV
The driver of a bus with 18 seats on an excursion journey from London to Scotland should abide by which drivers' hours rules?

Mark one answer
- A. AETR only
- B. Domestic
- C. EC only
- D. EC and AETR

94 PCV
EC rules require that after driving continuously for the maximum period a bus driver must take a break. This must be at least

Mark one answer
- A. 15 minutes
- B. 30 minutes
- C. 45 minutes
- D. 60 minutes

95 PCV
A driver's daily rest period may be taken in a parked vehicle if

Mark one answer
- A. it is fitted with a bunk
- B. there is a smoke alarm fitted
- C. the vehicle is in an authorised coach park
- D. there are no passengers on the vehicle

96 PCV
What should you do if asked to leave your bus by an official who is not in uniform?

Mark one answer
- A. Comply with the request
- B. Ask to see a warrant card
- C. Refuse to leave the vehicle
- D. Invite the official aboard

97 PCV
When a bus is left unattended the driver MUST ensure that

Mark one answer
- A. the tachograph chart is removed
- B. the gear lever is in reverse
- C. the gear lever is in first
- D. the parking brake is applied

98 PCV/LGV
Why are drivers' hours under close control?

Mark three answers
- A. To keep to a delivery schedule
- B. For fuel economy
- C. To save wear and tear
- D. For fair competition
- E. For road safety
- F. For safe working conditions

99 PCV/LGV
Drivers who break EC tachograph regulations

Mark two answers
- A. are allowed three warnings
- B. may lose their licence
- C. will be heavily fined
- D. are let off if they are not used to tachographs

100 PCV/LGV
When using a tachograph which of the following apply?

Mark two answers
- A. You must carry enough approved charts
- B. Damaged charts can be used if they are clean
- C. Dirty charts can be used if they are undamaged
- D. All charts must be clean and undamaged

101 PCV/LGV

The tachograph on your vehicle becomes faulty. It can be repaired on return to base, if this is within

Mark one answer
- [ ] A. one day
- [ ] B. three days
- [ ] C. one week
- [ ] D. two weeks

102 PCV/LGV

Tachograph records must be available for inspection. An enforcement officer keeps one of your charts. Who should sign the back of the replacement chart?

Mark one answer
- [ ] A. You, the driver
- [ ] B. Your transport manager
- [ ] C. The vehicle owner
- [ ] D. The officer

103 PCV/LGV

When an enforcement officer keeps your tachograph records, the officer should sign the replacement chart with their

Mark two answers
- [ ] A. name
- [ ] B. telephone number
- [ ] C. home address
- [ ] D. date of birth

104 PCV/LGV

Why should you carry spare tachograph charts?

Mark one answer
- [ ] A. As a defence against a speeding prosecution
- [ ] B. To record when you have been in a traffic delay
- [ ] C. For recording extra loading duties and overtime
- [ ] D. To replace the original chart if it gets dirty

105 PCV/LGV

Under EC rules a driver must take a break after a continuous driving period of

Mark one answer
- [ ] A. 3 hours
- [ ] B. 4 hours
- [ ] C. 4.5 hours
- [ ] D. 5.5 hours

106 PCV/LGV

You have been driving non-stop since 5am. The time is now 9.30am. Under EC rules you must have a break of at least

Mark one answer
- [ ] A. 15 minutes
- [ ] B. 30 minutes
- [ ] C. 45 minutes
- [ ] D. 60 minutes

107 PCV/LGV
Under EC rules what is the maximum daily driving time allowed?

Mark one answer
- [ ] **A.** Nine hours extended to 11 hours on three days of the week
- [ ] **B.** Ten hours extended to 11 hours on two days of the week
- [ ] **C.** Nine hours extended to ten hours on two days of the week
- [ ] **D.** Ten hours extended to 11 hours on three days of the week

108 PCV/LGV
Under EC rules your minimum daily rest is 11 hours. On three days of the week this may be reduced to

Mark one answer
- [ ] **A.** seven hours
- [ ] **B.** eight hours
- [ ] **C.** nine hours
- [ ] **D.** ten hours

109 PCV/LGV
Under EC rules your daily rest can be reduced to 9 hours but NOT more often than

Mark one answer
- [ ] **A.** 1 day per week
- [ ] **B.** 2 days per week
- [ ] **C.** 3 days per week
- [ ] **D.** 4 days per week

110 PCV/LGV
Under EC rules your normal daily rest period should be at least

Mark one answer
- [ ] **A.** 8 hours
- [ ] **B.** 11 hours
- [ ] **C.** 13 hours
- [ ] **D.** 14 hours

111 PCV/LGV
Under EC rules what is the normal weekly rest that must be taken?

Mark one answer
- [ ] **A.** 40 hours
- [ ] **B.** 41 hours
- [ ] **C.** 42 hours
- [ ] **D.** 45 hours

112 PCV/LGV
When a vehicle has two drivers each driver should

Mark one answer
- [ ] **A.** share the same tachograph chart
- [ ] **B.** use a separate tachograph chart for every driving period
- [ ] **C.** use their own tachograph chart
- [ ] **D.** not use the tachograph for such duties

113 PCV/LGV
You are making a journey with a co-driver. When the other person is driving you may show some of this time as

Mark one answer
- [ ] **A.** a daily rest period
- [ ] **B.** a weekly rest period
- [ ] **C.** a break in daily driving
- [ ] **D.** driving time

114 PCV/LGV
A tachograph will record

Mark three answers
- [ ] **A.** load weight
- [ ] **B.** driving time
- [ ] **C.** fuel consumption
- [ ] **D.** rest periods
- [ ] **E.** engine temperature
- [ ] **F.** vehicle speed

115 PCV/LGV
Which one of the following symbols on your tachograph indicates your break/rest period?

Mark one answer

- [ ] A.
- [ ] B.

05089

- [ ] C.
- [ ] D.

116 PCV/LGV
What does this tachograph chart symbol mean?

Mark one answer

- [ ] A. Driver at rest
- [ ] B. Chart not required
- [ ] C. Other work
- [ ] D. Driving

117 PCV/LGV
The 'mode' switch on a tachograph is used to record

Mark three answers

- [ ] A. driving
- [ ] B. illness
- [ ] C. taking a weekly rest period
- [ ] D. other work
- [ ] E. resting

118 PCV/LGV
At the end of your working week you have driven a total of 56 hours. What is the maximum number of hours that you can drive in the following week under EC rules?

Mark one answer

- [ ] A. 34
- [ ] B. 36
- [ ] C. 38
- [ ] D. 40

119 PCV/LGV
An emergency situation has arisen. For safety reasons you will need to exceed the normal drivers' hours under EC rules. You should

Mark one answer

- [ ] A. continue with the same tachograph chart and write an explanation on the back
- [ ] B. remove the tachograph chart and make a manual record of the rest of the journey
- [ ] C. continue; there is no need to give an explanation
- [ ] D. remove the tachograph chart and inform your employer of the reason

120 PCV/LGV

In an emergency situation you need to go over your normal drivers' hours. Under EC rules you should

Mark one answer

- [ ] **A.** take no action, the tachograph chart will record this
- [ ] **B.** note the reasons on the back of the tachograph chart
- [ ] **C.** remove the chart from the tachograph before going over the hours
- [ ] **D.** note the reasons on the front of the tachograph chart

121 PCV/LGV

Which TWO of the following are most likely to cause tiredness?

Mark two answers

- [ ] **A.** Making frequent and regular stops
- [ ] **B.** Driving breaks taken on board the vehicle
- [ ] **C.** Insufficient breaks from driving
- [ ] **D.** Modern vehicles with automatic gearboxes
- [ ] **E.** The cab becoming too warm

122 PCV/LGV

When driving, you start to feel tired or unable to concentrate. You should

Mark one answer

- [ ] **A.** stop as soon as it is safe to do so
- [ ] **B.** wind down a window and carry on
- [ ] **C.** switch on the radio and complete your journey
- [ ] **D.** speed up to get to your destination sooner

123 PCV/LGV

You feel tired after driving for two and a half hours. What should you do?

Mark one answer

- [ ] **A.** Slow down to a safer speed
- [ ] **B.** Reduce your planned driving time to three and a half hours
- [ ] **C.** Stop as soon as it is safe to do so
- [ ] **D.** Take a less busy route

124 PCV/LGV

You are driving on a motorway and suddenly become tired. What should you do?

Mark one answer

- [ ] **A.** Stop on the hard shoulder and rest
- [ ] **B.** Leave by the next exit and find a place to stop
- [ ] **C.** Stop on the next slip road and rest
- [ ] **D.** Stop on the verge of the motorway and rest

125 PCV/LGV

You are feeling tired when driving on a motorway. Where can you stop?

Mark one answer

- [ ] **A.** On the hard shoulder
- [ ] **B.** At a service station
- [ ] **C.** On a slip road
- [ ] **D.** In a deceleration lane

126 PCV/LGV
You have to leave your vehicle unattended for a very short time. You should

Mark one answer
- A. avoid having to stop the engine
- B. leave keys available in case of obstruction
- C. keep the engine running but lock the doors
- D. be aware of the risks of theft or damage

127 PCV/LGV
The time is 10am. You have been driving non-stop since 6am. Under EC rules what is the longest you may now drive without a break?

Mark one answer
- A. 15 minutes
- B. 30 minutes
- C. 40 minutes
- D. 45 minutes

128 PCV/LGV
Under EC rules you may drive for up to nine hours daily. On two days of the week this may be increased to a maximum of

Mark one answer
- A. 9.5 hours
- B. 10 hours
- C. 11 hours
- D. 11.5 hours

129 PCV/LGV
Under EC rules you can drive for a maximum of nine hours daily. On how many days of the week can this be extended to ten hours?

Mark one answer
- A. One
- B. Two
- C. Three
- D. Four

130 PCV/LGV
Who is responsible for the issue of tachograph charts to a bus or lorry driver?

Mark one answer
- A. The driver's employer
- B. The local vehicle licensing office
- C. The authorised calibration centre
- D. The local MOT testing centre

131 PCV/LGV
You can find out when an analogue tachograph was last recalibrated by

Mark one answer
- A. a date on the tachograph chart
- B. contacting the vehicle's manufacturer
- C. checking the vehicle's service record
- D. a plaque on or near the tachograph

132 PCV/LGV
Under EC rules an analogue tachograph must be recalibrated every

Mark one answer
- A. 2 years
- B. 4 years
- C. 6 years
- D. 8 years

133
PCV/LGV

Your vehicle breaks down during a journey. You continue by driving in another vehicle with the same type of tachograph. What must you do with your tachograph chart?

Mark one answer

- [ ] **A.** Leave it in the broken down vehicle
- [ ] **B.** Take it with you for security, but use a new chart in the new vehicle
- [ ] **C.** Telephone the testing authority for permission to drive without a chart
- [ ] **D.** Take it with you, using it in the new vehicle

134
PCV/LGV

Under EC rules what is the maximum driving time allowed in any two consecutive weeks?

Mark one answer

- [ ] **A.** 85 hours
- [ ] **B.** 90 hours
- [ ] **C.** 100 hours
- [ ] **D.** 105 hours

135
PCV/LGV

Under EC rules an analogue tachograph must be checked at an approved calibration centre every

Mark one answer

- [ ] **A.** 1 year
- [ ] **B.** 2 years
- [ ] **C.** 5 years
- [ ] **D.** 6 years

136
LGV

Goods vehicle drivers' hours of work are controlled for three reasons. They are

Mark three answers

- [ ] **A.** vehicle sympathy
- [ ] **B.** fair competition
- [ ] **C.** fair road use
- [ ] **D.** vehicle security
- [ ] **E.** road safety
- [ ] **F.** working conditions

137
LGV

Goods vehicle drivers' hours are controlled in the interests of

Mark two answers

- [ ] **A.** fuel economy
- [ ] **B.** road safety
- [ ] **C.** traffic calming
- [ ] **D.** fair competition

138
LGV

Under the rules for domestic drivers' hours you must

Mark one answer

- [ ] **A.** keep a written record of hours worked
- [ ] **B.** only record any driving off public roads
- [ ] **C.** keep a written record of driving time only
- [ ] **D.** always use a vehicle fitted with a tachograph

139
LGV

You must have enough tachograph charts with you for your journey. You will need at least one for every

Mark one answer

- [ ] **A.** 10 hours
- [ ] **B.** 24 hours
- [ ] **C.** 36 hours
- [ ] **D.** 48 hours

140 LGV
One tachograph chart covers a period of

Mark one answer
- [ ] **A.** 24 hours
- [ ] **B.** 48 hours
- [ ] **C.** 5 days
- [ ] **D.** 7 days

141 LGV
Your tachograph chart becomes dirty or damaged. What should you do?

Mark one answer
- [ ] **A.** Continue with the same chart and enter the details in writing
- [ ] **B.** Use a spare chart and destroy the damaged chart
- [ ] **C.** Use a spare chart and attach it to the damaged one
- [ ] **D.** Continue to use the chart

142 LGV
During your break your vehicle will be moved by another person. What should you do with the tachograph chart?

Mark one answer
- [ ] **A.** Leave the chart in the vehicle and record the changes on the back
- [ ] **B.** Put in a new chart on your return to the vehicle
- [ ] **C.** Switch to rest mode to record the break
- [ ] **D.** Remove the chart and make a manual record of the break period

143 LGV
You have been driving a lorry without a break for four and a half hours. Under EC rules a break must be taken. How long must it be?

Mark one answer
- [ ] **A.** 30 minutes
- [ ] **B.** 35 minutes
- [ ] **C.** 40 minutes
- [ ] **D.** 45 minutes

144 LGV
You are driving a lorry on a motorway and you are getting drowsy. There are no service areas or exits for some distance. What should you do?

Mark one answer
- [ ] **A.** Stop on the hard shoulder and rest
- [ ] **B.** Open the window and turn the heating down
- [ ] **C.** Slow down and use the hazard warning lights
- [ ] **D.** Increase your speed to get to the next service area sooner

145 LGV
You are driving a lorry. During the journey you are feeling ill and unable to concentrate. What should you do?

Mark one answer
- [ ] **A.** Stop in a safe place and seek help
- [ ] **B.** Continue your journey and keep your windows open
- [ ] **C.** Increase your speed to finish your work earlier
- [ ] **D.** Keep stopping at regular intervals for rest

146 LGV

Which two of the following would NOT be helpful when trying to keep your load from being stolen?

Mark two answers

- A. Giving a lift to a stranger
- B. Making sure all doors and windows are locked
- C. Discussing your load with members of the public
- D. Having a kingpin or drawbar lock fitted
- E. Parking in secure well-lit places when possible

147 LGV

When leaving your vehicle for an overnight stop, it is good practice to park with the

Mark one answer

- A. rear doors close up to another vehicle
- B. rear doors well away from another vehicle
- C. front doors well away from another vehicle
- D. front doors close up to another vehicle

148 LGV

You are parking overnight with a high-value load and intend sleeping in the cab. You should

Mark three answers

- A. lock doors but leave a window open for ventilation
- B. ensure doors and windows will be secure
- C. be in a reputable, lit lorry park
- D. be in a quiet, unlit, non-residential area
- E. stay at the same location regularly
- F. block access to the rear door if possible

149 LGV

You are often involved in the carrying of high-value goods. What security measures can you adopt?

Mark three answers

- A. Vary your routes and rest stops
- B. Always discuss details of your load
- C. Give lifts to anyone for added security
- D. Park overnight in well-lit areas
- E. Remove keys when not in attendance
- F. Keep your journeys to a strict routine

150 LGV

It is necessary to leave your trailer unattended. It should be parked

Mark one answer

- A. in a public car park
- B. on the public highway
- C. on secure premises
- D. in a quiet residential area

151 LGV

Your trailer should be fitted with a kingpin or drawbar lock when

Mark one answer

- A. driving on motorways
- B. being driven abroad
- C. partly loaded
- D. left unattended

152 LGV

Only lorries above a specific maximum authorised mass need a tachograph. That weight is

Mark one answer

- A. 3.5 tonnes
- B. 5 tonnes
- C. 7.5 tonnes
- D. 10 tonnes

153 LGV

Before starting driving, which of the following should you complete on the centre field of your tachograph chart?

Mark one answer

- A. The place from which you start your day's journey
- B. Details of the goods carried
- C. The name and address of your employer
- D. The amount of daily rest taken prior to starting the shift

154 LGV

During your working day you are changing to another vehicle with the same type of tachograph. What should you do with your tachograph chart?

Mark one answer

- A. Use the chart that is already in the other vehicle
- B. Take the chart with you and use it in the other vehicle
- C. Record your driving hours in a record book
- D. Install a new chart in the other vehicle

155 LGV

A lorry driver must take care of the vehicle and load. Which of the following is NOT good practice?

Mark one answer

- A. Always parking it in a quiet area out of sight
- B. Parking with the rear doors hard up against another vehicle
- C. Avoiding using the same route and stops too often
- D. Always asking to see the identity of any officer who may stop you

156 LGV

You are driving a lorry at night. What can you do to help you keep alert?

Mark three answers

- A. Eat a heavy meal before setting off
- B. Keep plenty of cool fresh air moving through the cab
- C. Keep the cab warm and comfortable
- D. Take proper rest periods at correct intervals
- E. Drive faster to get to your destination sooner
- F. Walk around in fresh air at a rest stop

157 LGV

How can you reduce the risk of your lorry or trailer being stolen?

Mark two answers

- A. Fit an alarm and immobiliser
- B. Fit a kingpin lock to your trailer
- C. Use the same route and rest periods
- D. Park in quiet areas away from other vehicles

158 LGV

You are planning to carry high-value goods on a regular basis. You should seek advice from

Mark one answer

- A. other drivers in your area
- B. your local crime prevention officer
- C. other operators in your area
- D. your local road safety officer

159

LGV

A driver's week is defined as

Mark one answer

- [ ] **A.** 0.00 hours Monday to 24.00 hours the following Sunday
- [ ] **B.** 0.00 hours Sunday to 24.00 hours the following Saturday
- [ ] **C.** any seven consecutive days
- [ ] **D.** any 56 hours driven

160

LGV

When driving you notice your tachograph is not working. What should you do?

Mark one answer

- [ ] **A.** Stop immediately until it is repaired
- [ ] **B.** Report it to the nearest police station
- [ ] **C.** Telephone the vehicle testing authority and report the fault
- [ ] **D.** Continue your journey but make a manual record

161 PCV
What does this simplified diagram show?

Mark one answer

- [ ] **A.** Range change gearbox
- [ ] **B.** Air brake system
- [ ] **C.** Engine management system
- [ ] **D.** Two-speed axle

162 PCV/LGV
You are stationary. The air brake pressure warning light comes on. Why should you NOT release the parking brake?

Mark one answer

- [ ] **A.** Because the vehicle will suddenly roll backwards
- [ ] **B.** Because it will cause the air pressure to rise
- [ ] **C.** Because the service brake may not stop you
- [ ] **D.** Because the warning light will go out

163 PCV/LGV
You are about to drive a vehicle fitted with air-assisted hydraulic brakes. The brake pedal feels hard when pressed. What could this mean?

Mark one answer

- [ ] **A.** The vacuum pump is not working
- [ ] **B.** The pedal movement requires adjustment
- [ ] **C.** The brakes are locked on fully
- [ ] **D.** The brake fluid reservoir is empty

164 PCV/LGV
Your vehicle is fitted with an air-assisted hydraulic braking system. What would warn you that the vacuum pump is not working?

Mark one answer

- [ ] **A.** The brake pedal feels spongy when pressed
- [ ] **B.** The brake pedal has little resistance
- [ ] **C.** The brake pedal feels hard when pressed
- [ ] **D.** The brake pedal travels a long way

165 PCV/LGV
Your vehicle is fitted with hydraulic brakes. The brake pedal goes down too far when pressed. What could this mean?

Mark one answer

- [ ] **A.** There is too much fluid in the braking system
- [ ] **B.** The pedal travel requires adjustment
- [ ] **C.** The vacuum exhauster is not working
- [ ] **D.** There is not enough fluid in the braking system

166 PCV/LGV
You are driving a vehicle fitted with a hydraulic brake system. What is it important to check, specific to this, before driving away?

Mark one answer

- [ ] **A.** The hydraulic brake fluid level
- [ ] **B.** The power steering fluid level
- [ ] **C.** The cooling system fluid level
- [ ] **D.** The windscreen washer fluid level

167
PCV/LGV
Your vehicle is fitted with air-assisted hydraulic brakes. What would warn you that there is insufficient air in the system?

Mark one answer
- **A.** An increase of pressure in the air gauge
- **B.** A buzzer or light
- **C.** The exhaust brake will not work
- **D.** Brake fade

168
PCV/LGV
You are driving down a long steep hill. You will make best use of engine braking by keeping the rev counter in which coloured band?

Mark one answer
- **A.** Blue
- **B.** Red
- **C.** Amber
- **D.** Green

169
PCV/LGV
Your vehicle is fitted with air brakes. As you start the engine a brake warning light shows. What does this mean?

Mark one answer
- **A.** Low air pressure
- **B.** Increased air pressure
- **C.** The parking brake is not working
- **D.** The air reservoirs are fully charged

170
PCV/LGV
Your vehicle is fitted with air-assisted hydraulic brakes. The brake pedal becomes hard to press. What does this mean?

Mark one answer
- **A.** The brake system has a loss of vacuum
- **B.** The brake linings are worn
- **C.** The brake linings need adjusting
- **D.** The brake system requires more fluid

171
PCV/LGV
Your vehicle is fitted with a retarder. This has been activated. On which of these would wear be minimized?

Mark one answer
- **A.** The brake linings
- **B.** The catalytic converter
- **C.** The exhaust system
- **D.** The transmission

172
LGV
Changing to a lower gear can be useful in some circumstances. You should do this to help avoid

Mark one answer
- **A.** brake fade
- **B.** clutch slip
- **C.** excessive engine revs
- **D.** tyre wear

173 **LGV**
What does this simplified diagram show?

Mark one answer
- [ ] **A.** Automatic gearbox unit
- [ ] **B.** Air conditioning unit
- [ ] **C.** Air brake system
- [ ] **D.** Fuel injection system

174 **LGV**
A Jake brake is an additional method of slowing a vehicle down. It works by

Mark one answer
- [ ] **A.** altering the valve timing in the engine
- [ ] **B.** altering the number of axles in contact with the road
- [ ] **C.** operating automatically as you descend steep hills
- [ ] **D.** operating if you exceed the limit of your cruise control

175 **LGV**
You have to drive onto a muddy building site. Why should you switch on your diff-lock?

Mark one answer
- [ ] **A.** To make your steering lighter
- [ ] **B.** To improve your fuel consumption
- [ ] **C.** To increase your engine power
- [ ] **D.** To make the wheels less likely to spin

176 **PCV**
You are about to set off in your bus in very frosty weather. You notice a lack of brake air pressure. What is the likely cause of this?

Mark one answer
- [ ] **A.** Engine temperature too low
- [ ] **B.** Weak engine anti-freeze mixture
- [ ] **C.** Brake pedal needs adjustment
- [ ] **D.** Frozen moisture in the storage tanks

177 **PCV**
What could prevent the build-up of brake air pressure on a bus in frosty weather?

Mark one answer
- [ ] **A.** Lack of anti-freeze in storage tanks
- [ ] **B.** Insufficient lagging of tanks and pipes
- [ ] **C.** Low engine revolutions
- [ ] **D.** Moisture freezing in the system

178 **PCV**
An anti-lock braking system warning light fitted to a bus should go out

Mark one answer
- [ ] **A.** when the brakes are used for the first time
- [ ] **B.** immediately after the anti-lock braking system comes into operation
- [ ] **C.** when road speed is 10kph (6mph) or more
- [ ] **D.** when the secondary braking system is used

179 PCV
The MOST powerful brake on a bus is normally the

Mark one answer
- A. secondary brake
- B. anti-lock braking system
- C. endurance brake (retarder)
- D. service brake

180 PCV
When making a short stop, facing uphill, you should

Mark one answer
- A. hold the vehicle on the clutch
- B. hold the vehicle on the footbrake
- C. select neutral and apply the parking brake
- D. apply the parking brake after stopping

181 PCV
You are about to move off. Your vehicle has automatic transmission. Before you select drive (D) you must

Mark one answer
- A. put your foot on the footbrake
- B. signal to move off
- C. alter your seat position
- D. adjust your mirrors

182 PCV
Which THREE of the following are advantages of progressive braking when driving a bus?

Mark three answers
- A. Passenger safety and comfort
- B. Increased air brake pressure
- C. Lower fuel consumption
- D. Reduced tyre wear
- E. Avoidance of 'brake fade'

183 PCV/LGV
Your vehicle has anti-lock brakes. This allows you to

Mark one answer
- A. follow vehicles more closely
- B. steer while braking
- C. drive faster on wet roads
- D. brake later than normal

184 PCV/LGV
What could prevent air pressure building up in an air brake system in cold frosty weather?

Mark one answer
- A. Moisture in the air may form bubbles in the brake fluid
- B. The air will contract, reducing the pressure
- C. The dampness may cause valves to rust
- D. Moisture drawn in with the air may freeze and cause a blockage

185 PCV/LGV
The brake air pressure warning light comes on whilst driving. You should

Mark one answer
- A. stop and seek help without delay
- B. report the fault on return to your depot
- C. boost the pressure through added acceleration
- D. drain air tanks and continue normally

186 PCV/LGV
When the brake air pressure warning light is operating, you should NEVER

Mark one answer
- A. leave your vehicle
- B. release the parking brake
- C. switch your engine off
- D. engage the clutch

187 PCV/LGV
Your vehicle is fitted with an anti-lock braking system. Its main purpose is to help you to

Mark one answer
- A. drive at faster speeds
- B. brake much later than normal
- C. apply the brakes more quickly
- D. stop safely in an emergency

188 PCV/LGV
As the driver of a vehicle fitted with an anti-lock braking system, you should check it is working before each

Mark one answer
- A. service
- B. day's work
- C. week's work
- D. journey

189 PCV/LGV
'Pumping' the brake pedal in a vehicle fitted with anti-lock brakes will cause

Mark one answer
- A. increased effectiveness
- B. reduced effectiveness
- C. reduced brake wear
- D. increased brake wear

190 PCV/LGV
You are driving a vehicle fitted with anti-lock brakes. When braking in an emergency, you should

Mark one answer
- A. 'pump' the brake pedal harshly
- B. apply minimum force to the brake pedal
- C. use the exhaust brake (retarder) then the footbrake
- D. apply firm continuous pressure to the brake pedal

191 PCV/LGV
You are driving a vehicle not fitted with anti-lock brakes. How can 'wheel lock' be controlled during heavy braking?

Mark one answer
- A. By using engine braking
- B. By cadence braking
- C. By braking suddenly
- D. By using clutch and brake together

192 PCV/LGV
You have to stop quickly in an emergency. Which of the following are most likely to prevent 'wheel lock'?

Mark one answer
- A. Using the parking brake
- B. Selecting neutral
- C. Cadence braking
- D. Changing up a gear

193 PCV/LGV
What is 'brake fade'?

Mark one answer
- A. Reduction of air pressure
- B. Smooth progressive braking
- C. Reduction of braking effectiveness
- D. Low hydraulic brake fluid level

194 PCV/LGV
'Brake fade' is a loss of effectiveness of the brakes, caused by their continuous use. When would this be most likely to happen?

Mark one answer
- A. On a long journey
- B. On a long downhill gradient
- C. On the approach to hazards
- D. On a long uphill gradient

195

PCV/LGV
When driving down a steep hill the driver of a large vehicle should

Mark two answers
- **A.** partly apply the parking brake
- **B.** have changed to a lower gear
- **C.** use an endurance brake (retarder)
- **D.** put the gear lever into neutral
- **E.** use as high a gear as possible

196

PCV/LGV
Your vehicle has anti-lock brakes. When stopping in an emergency this should allow you to

Mark one answer
- **A.** brake more gently
- **B.** brake much later
- **C.** maintain steering control
- **D.** stop over a long distance

197

PCV/LGV
Your vehicle is fitted with an anti-lock braking system. When braking normally you should press the brake pedal

Mark one answer
- **A.** in the usual way
- **B.** on and off rapidly
- **C.** quickly and firmly
- **D.** later than usual

198

PCV/LGV
Your vehicle has anti-lock brakes. This means that when you brake normally you will

Mark one answer
- **A.** not need to alter the way you brake
- **B.** be able to brake much later
- **C.** need to brake more firmly
- **D.** not need to brake so early

199

PCV/LGV
You would see an escape lane

Mark one answer
- **A.** outside a fire station
- **B.** alongside a bus lane
- **C.** before a motorway exit
- **D.** down a steep hill

200

PCV/LGV
You would use an escape lane

Mark one answer
- **A.** where motorways merge
- **B.** when carrying a dangerous cargo
- **C.** when your brakes have failed
- **D.** for emergency vehicle repairs

201 PCV/LGV
On steep hills an emergency area to be used only when your brakes have failed is called

Mark one answer

A. a buffer lane
B. an escape lane
C. a rumble strip
D. the hard shoulder

202 PCV/LGV
An endurance brake (retarder) can be especially useful

Mark one answer

A. when driving down long hills
B. when driving on steep cambers
C. to reduce gear changes
D. to improve fuel consumption

203 PCV/LGV
You are driving down a long hill and want to avoid the brakes overheating. The vehicle's speed should be controlled by using the

Mark one answer

A. anti-lock braking system
B. footbrake
C. secondary brake
D. endurance brake (retarder)

204 PCV/LGV
A system for controlling the vehicle's speed without using the footbrake is

Mark one answer

A. a secondary brake
B. an endurance brake (retarder)
C. a differential lock
D. an emergency air system

205 PCV/LGV
An endurance brake (retarder) may work in which TWO of the following ways?

Mark two answers

A. Increasing engine braking
B. Using an extra transmission device
C. Sensing wheel speed
D. Using the parking brake
E. Using the secondary brake

206 PCV/LGV
An endurance brake (retarder), when not combined with the footbrake, should be used

Mark one answer

A. on motorways only
B. on long downhill slopes
C. when braking quickly
D. all the time when stopping

207 PCV/LGV
An endurance brake (retarder) should be used

Mark one answer

A. on motorways only
B. when braking quickly
C. when you stop or park
D. on long downhill slopes

208 PCV/LGV
An electromagnetic endurance brake (retarder) operates by applying resistance to the

Mark one answer
- [ ] A. hydraulic lines
- [ ] B. starter motor
- [ ] C. air lines
- [ ] D. transmission

209 PCV/LGV
Your vehicle is fully loaded. When dealing with bends all braking should be done

Mark two answers
- [ ] A. as close to the bend as possible
- [ ] B. smoothly and in good time
- [ ] C. when driving in a straight line
- [ ] D. as you start to turn the wheel
- [ ] E. when halfway round the bend

210 PCV/LGV
A lorry is overtaking you on a two-lane motorway. It does not have the speed to get past. What should you do?

Mark one answer
- [ ] A. Continue at the same speed
- [ ] B. Be prepared to reduce your speed
- [ ] C. Increase your speed and force the lorry to drop back
- [ ] D. Brake hard to allow the other driver to cut in

211 PCV/LGV
After driving through a flood what should you do?

Mark one answer
- [ ] A. Carry out an emergency stop
- [ ] B. Drive in low gear with the footbrake lightly applied
- [ ] C. Avoid braking until the brakes are dried out
- [ ] D. Pump the footbrake when approaching hazards

212 PCV/LGV
Coasting downhill could seriously affect the correct working of the

Mark one answer
- [ ] A. air brakes
- [ ] B. cooling system
- [ ] C. tachograph
- [ ] D. electrical systems

213 PCV/LGV
'Brake fade' happens when the brakes get too

Mark one answer
- [ ] A. hot
- [ ] B. cold
- [ ] C. dry
- [ ] D. wet

214 PCV/LGV
To prevent 'brake fade' you should

Mark two answers
- [ ] A. use the endurance brake (retarder)
- [ ] B. apply the parking brake
- [ ] C. select a lower gear
- [ ] D. repeatedly pump the brake pedal
- [ ] E. select neutral for a short distance

215 PCV/LGV
What causes 'brake fade'?

Mark one answer
- [ ] **A.** Continuous use of the brakes
- [ ] **B.** Repeated pumping of the brakes
- [ ] **C.** Loss of air pressure in the system
- [ ] **D.** Badly worn brake pads

216 PCV/LGV
The main cause of 'brake fade' is

Mark one answer
- [ ] **A.** the brakes overheating
- [ ] **B.** moisture in the air tanks
- [ ] **C.** oil on the brake linings
- [ ] **D.** the brakes out of adjustment

217 PCV/LGV
When using an endurance brake (retarder), extra care must be taken on

Mark one answer
- [ ] **A.** uneven roads
- [ ] **B.** slippery roads
- [ ] **C.** downhill gradients
- [ ] **D.** uphill gradients

218 PCV/LGV
What action would you take if a brake air pressure warning device comes on?

Mark one answer
- [ ] **A.** Continue to drive the vehicle
- [ ] **B.** Drain the air tanks
- [ ] **C.** Stop and get the fault put right
- [ ] **D.** Pump the brake pedal repeatedly

219 PCV/LGV
You are driving down a snow-covered hill. You should take extra care when using an independent endurance brake (retarder) because

Mark one answer
- [ ] **A.** your brakes could overheat
- [ ] **B.** your speed could increase
- [ ] **C.** compressed air could escape
- [ ] **D.** the drive-wheels could lock

220 PCV/LGV
When using an independent endurance brake (retarder) on slippery roads, you should take care to avoid

Mark one answer
- [ ] **A.** the front wheels spinning
- [ ] **B.** the drive-wheels locking
- [ ] **C.** brake pad wear
- [ ] **D.** anti-skid road surfaces

221 LGV
Your lorry does not have an anti-lock braking system fitted. You may prevent the wheels from locking under heavy braking by

Mark one answer
- [ ] **A.** pushing the brake pedal harder until you stop
- [ ] **B.** depressing the clutch pedal as you brake
- [ ] **C.** rapid pumping of the brake pedal
- [ ] **D.** changing down through the gears as you brake

222 LGV
Trailer swing is more likely to occur on a lorry and draw bar combination when

Mark three answers
- A. braking on a bend
- B. oversteering at speed
- C. the brakes are out of adjustment
- D. braking lightly several times
- E. steering at slow speed and fully loaded
- F. an endurance brake (retarder) is fitted

223 LGV
Your vehicle is fitted with a 'diff-lock'. You would normally use it when

Mark one answer
- A. driving on straight roads
- B. towing an empty trailer
- C. driving on muddy construction sites
- D. uncoupling a trailer

224 LGV
On a three-line braking system to the trailer of a lorry what colour is the auxiliary line?

Mark one answer
- A. Red
- B. Blue
- C. Green
- D. Yellow

225 LGV
The emergency line is common to both two- and three-line brake systems. What is its colour?

Mark one answer
- A. Red
- B. Blue
- C. Black
- D. Yellow

226 LGV
Air brake systems usually have two lines. What additional line is fitted on a three-line system?

Mark one answer
- A. Emergency
- B. Service
- C. Electrical
- D. Auxiliary

227 LGV
In frosty weather, what precaution could a lorry driver take to prevent moisture freezing in brake air storage tanks?

Mark one answer
- A. Drain the tanks daily
- B. Cover the tanks with a blanket
- C. Keep the engine at high revs when starting
- D. Pump the brakes

228 LGV
To help to avoid 'brake fade' lorry drivers should ensure that

Mark one answer
- A. the air tanks are drained before journeys
- B. the air pressure is correct
- C. the handbrake is applied before stopping
- D. the appropriate gears are engaged before downhill gradients

229 LGV
Exhaust brakes give greatest efficiency when used

Mark one answer
- A. at high engine speed in low gears
- B. at low engine speed in high gears
- C. on stop-start town work
- D. on high-speed motorway runs

230 LGV

The principal braking system on a lorry is called the

Mark one answer

- A. endurance brake (retarder)
- B. service brake
- C. parking brake
- D. handbrake

231 LGV

The three main braking systems fitted to lorries are known as

Mark three answers

- A. over-run
- B. cadence
- C. exhaust
- D. service
- E. secondary
- F. parking

232 LGV

You are driving a lorry and trailer. You change to a lower gear when going too fast. This could cause the

Mark one answer

- A. vehicle to jack-knife
- B. engine to stall
- C. brakes to fail
- D. trailer to uncouple

233 LGV

An articulated vehicle is more likely to jack-knife when

Mark three answers

- A. unladen
- B. manoeuvring slowly
- C. braking sharply
- D. fully loaded
- E. on a bend
- F. fitted with an endurance brake (retarder)

234 LGV

Your lorry is stuck in snow. You use the diff-lock to move off. When should you switch the diff-lock off?

Mark one answer

- A. Only after selecting top gear
- B. Once the engine has warmed up
- C. As soon as the vehicle is moving
- D. As soon as the snow has cleared

235 LGV

Your tractor unit has three air lines. You are connecting to a trailer with two air lines. What colour is the line you should NOT connect to the trailer?

Mark one answer

- A. Red
- B. Yellow
- C. Black
- D. Blue

236 LGV

On an articulated lorry which has a three-line connection, the red line is the

Mark one answer

- A. emergency line
- B. service line
- C. auxiliary line
- D. electrical line

237 LGV

You are driving a tractor unit fitted with two air lines. You want to couple up to a trailer with three air lines. How should this be done?

Mark one answer

- A. The trailer auxiliary line should be left unconnected
- B. The trailer service line should be left unconnected
- C. Only the service line should be connected
- D. Only the auxiliary line should be connected

238 LGV

The correct procedure for stopping a lorry equipped with an anti-lock braking system in an emergency is to

Mark one answer

- A. apply the footbrake firmly in a pumping action until the vehicle has stopped
- B. apply the footbrake firmly and continuously until the vehicle has stopped
- C. apply the footbrake and handbrake until the vehicle has stopped
- D. apply the handbrake only

239 PCV/LGV

You are about to drive an unfamiliar vehicle. There may be moisture in the air brake reservoir. What should you do?

Mark one answer

- A. Assume the system has automatic drain valves
- B. Find out whether you need to drain the system manually
- C. Nothing, it is the vehicle owner's responsibility
- D. Leave the engine running for a while before driving

240 PCV
The driver of a bus should wear a seat belt if one is fitted UNLESS

Mark two answers
- [ ] A. the seat belt is particularly uncomfortable
- [ ] B. the vehicle is being reversed
- [ ] C. a valid medical exemption certificate is held by the driver
- [ ] D. the belt is of the lap-only type
- [ ] E. the passengers carried are children

241 PCV
Which of the following MUST be clearly displayed on your bus?

Mark four answers
- [ ] A. Seating and standing capacity
- [ ] B. Location of all bus stops
- [ ] C. Emergency exit location
- [ ] D. The route timetable
- [ ] E. Fuel cut-off switch
- [ ] F. Electrical isolator switch

242 PCV
The nearside mirror is used for checking

Mark one answer
- [ ] A. if the driver's door is closed properly
- [ ] B. for any vehicles moving up on the left
- [ ] C. if passengers are seated
- [ ] D. for any vehicles parking in front of you

243 PCV
You are driving a bus in a built-up area. You should NOT

Mark one answer
- [ ] A. block side road junctions
- [ ] B. leave a safe stopping distance
- [ ] C. anticipate traffic ahead
- [ ] D. use the MSM routine

244 PCV/LGV
You are driving on a motorway. A moving lorry just ahead of you switches on its hazard warning lights. What does this mean?

Mark one answer
- [ ] A. There are speed cameras ahead
- [ ] B. The lorry is about to change lanes
- [ ] C. The lorry is leaving the motorway
- [ ] D. Traffic further ahead may be stopping

245 PCV/LGV
You are driving in busy traffic. You lose your way. What should you do?

Mark one answer
- [ ] A. Stop at traffic lights and ask pedestrians
- [ ] B. Shout to other drivers to ask them the way
- [ ] C. Drive on until you find a safe place to stop
- [ ] D. Check a map as you keep moving with the traffic

246 PCV/LGV
You should show extra consideration for pedestrians when driving past

Mark three answers
- [ ] A. mobile shops
- [ ] B. open moorland
- [ ] C. shopping areas
- [ ] D. ice cream vans
- [ ] E. wooded areas
- [ ] F. suspension bridges

247 PCV/LGV
Which of the following are most likely to cause danger to a group of horse riders?

Mark three answers
- [ ] **A.** Powerful brake lights
- [ ] **B.** Size of your vehicle
- [ ] **C.** Noise of your vehicle
- [ ] **D.** The hiss of air brakes
- [ ] **E.** Leaving plenty of room
- [ ] **F.** Reacting in good time

248 PCV/LGV
Which of these should you do when passing sheep on a road?

Mark three answers
- [ ] **A.** Pass quickly and quietly
- [ ] **B.** Tap your horn once
- [ ] **C.** Drive very slowly
- [ ] **D.** Allow plenty of room
- [ ] **E.** Be ready to stop

249 PCV/LGV
Your nearside mirror is most likely to endanger pedestrians when

Mark one answer
- [ ] **A.** using a crawler lane
- [ ] **B.** braking hard on a bend
- [ ] **C.** driving close to the kerb
- [ ] **D.** passing a traffic sign

250 PCV/LGV
Which of the following can prevent you from obtaining a bus or lorry licence?

Mark one answer
- [ ] **A.** heart disorders
- [ ] **B.** dyslexia
- [ ] **C.** skin problems
- [ ] **D.** stomach problems

251 PCV/LGV
Before starting your engine your seat should be adjusted for

Mark three answers
- [ ] **A.** height
- [ ] **B.** back support
- [ ] **C.** seat belt tension
- [ ] **D.** air ventilation
- [ ] **E.** distance from the controls
- [ ] **F.** leaving the cab

252 PCV/LGV
A properly adjusted head restraint will

Mark one answer
- [ ] **A.** make you more comfortable
- [ ] **B.** help you to avoid neck injury
- [ ] **C.** help you to relax
- [ ] **D.** help you to maintain your driving position

253 PCV/LGV
You may remove your seat belt when carrying out a manoeuvre that involves

Mark one answer
- [ ] **A.** reversing
- [ ] **B.** a hill start
- [ ] **C.** an emergency stop
- [ ] **D.** driving slowly

254
PCV/LGV

You are driving along this road. The red van cuts in close in front of you. What should you do?

Mark one answer

- A. Accelerate to get closer to the red van
- B. Give a long blast on the horn
- C. Drop back to leave the correct separation distance
- D. Flash your headlights several times

255
PCV/LGV

While driving you approach a large puddle that is close to the left-hand kerb. Pedestrians are close to the water. You should

Mark two answers

- A. ignore the puddle
- B. brake suddenly and sound your horn
- C. slow down before the puddle
- D. try to avoid splashing the pedestrians
- E. wave at the pedestrians to keep back

256
PCV/LGV

A long, heavily laden lorry is taking a long time to overtake you. What should you do?

Mark one answer

- A. Speed up
- B. Slow down
- C. Hold your speed
- D. Change direction

257
PCV/LGV

You are driving a slow-moving vehicle on a narrow road. When traffic wishes to overtake you should

Mark one answer

- A. take no action
- B. put your hazard warning lights on
- C. stop immediately and wave them on
- D. pull in safely as soon as you can do so

258
PCV/LGV

You are driving a slow-moving vehicle on a narrow winding road. In order to let other vehicles overtake you should

Mark one answer

- A. wave to them to pass
- B. pull in when you can
- C. show a left turn signal
- D. keep left and hold your speed

259
PCV/LGV

What should you use your horn for?

Mark one answer

- A. To alert others to your presence
- B. To allow you right of way
- C. To greet other road users
- D. To signal your annoyance

260
PCV/LGV

You are following a car driven by a learner driver. You cannot overtake it. You should

Mark two answers

- A. flash your lights so that the driver sees you
- B. be patient and stay well behind
- C. switch your hazard lights on and stay well behind
- D. be ready for mistakes made by the driver
- E. drive along the centre line of the road

261 PCV/LGV
You are signalled to stop by a police car. You should

Mark one answer
- A. brake harshly to a stop
- B. drive on until you reach a side road
- C. pull up on the left when it is safe to
- D. stop immediately wherever you are

262 PCV/LGV
A police car is following you. The police would like you to stop. They will do this by flashing their headlights and

Mark one answer
- A. signalling with the right indicator
- B. signalling with the left indicator
- C. switching their hazard flashers on
- D. switching their rear fog lights on

263 PCV/LGV
You are driving a vehicle fitted with a hand-held telephone. To answer it you should

Mark one answer
- A. find a safe place to stop
- B. reduce your speed to less than 30mph
- C. steer your vehicle with one hand
- D. be very careful when dealing with junctions

264 PCV/LGV
You have a mobile telephone fitted in your vehicle. It should only be used when you are

Mark one answer
- A. stopped in a safe place
- B. travelling slowly
- C. on a motorway
- D. in light traffic

265 PCV/LGV
A pelican crossing that crosses the road in a STRAIGHT line and has a central island must be treated as

Mark one answer
- A. one crossing in daylight only
- B. one complete crossing
- C. two separate crossings
- D. two crossings during darkness

266 PCV/LGV
At a pelican crossing the flashing amber light means you should

Mark one answer
- A. stop, if you can do so safely
- B. give way to pedestrians already on the crossing
- C. stop and wait for the green light
- D. give way to pedestrians waiting to cross

267 PCV/LGV
At a zebra crossing you should

Mark one answer

- A. rev your engine to encourage pedestrians to cross quickly
- B. park only on the zigzag lines on the left
- C. always leave it clear in traffic queues
- D. wave pedestrians to cross if you intend to wait for them

268 PCV/LGV
A coach is overtaking you. When it is safe for the coach to move back to the left you should

Mark one answer

- A. do nothing and let the driver decide
- B. switch your sidelights on and off
- C. flash your headlights once
- D. flash your headlights twice

269 PCV/LGV
Which THREE of the following emergency vehicles will use blue flashing beacons?

Mark three answers

- A. Motorway maintenance
- B. Bomb disposal team
- C. Blood transfusion
- D. Police vehicle
- E. Breakdown recovery vehicle

270 PCV/LGV
When being followed by an ambulance showing a flashing blue beacon you should

Mark one answer

- A. pull over as soon as safely possible to let it pass
- B. accelerate hard to get away from it
- C. ignore it if possible, let it pass if forced to
- D. brake harshly and immediately stop in the road

271 PCV/LGV
You see a car showing a flashing green beacon. Should you give way to it?

Mark one answer

- A. Yes, it is a doctor going to an emergency
- B. Yes, it is a fire crew support vehicle
- C. No, it is a slow-moving vehicle
- D. No, it is a breakdown vehicle

272 PCV/LGV
What type of emergency vehicle is fitted with a green flashing beacon?

Mark one answer

- A. Fire engine
- B. Road gritter
- C. Ambulance
- D. Doctor's car

273 PCV/LGV
You stop for pedestrians waiting to cross at a zebra crossing. They do not start to cross. What should you do?

Mark one answer

- A. Be patient and wait
- B. Sound your horn
- C. Drive on
- D. Wave them to cross

274 PCV/LGV
You should beckon pedestrians to cross the road at

Mark one answer
- A. pedestrian crossings
- B. no time
- C. junctions
- D. school crossings

275 PCV/LGV
You should never wave people across at pedestrian crossings because

Mark one answer
- A. there may be another vehicle coming
- B. they may not be looking
- C. it is safer for you to carry on
- D. they may not be ready to cross

276 PCV/LGV
You are driving close to the kerb in a busy shopping area. What dangers should you be most aware of?

Mark three answers
- A. Traffic lights suddenly changing to green
- B. The amount of fuel being used when driving slowly
- C. Pedestrians stepping off the edge of the pavement
- D. The nearside mirror striking the heads of pedestrians
- E. Cyclists moving up the left side of your vehicle

277 PCV/LGV
You should NOT park your vehicle or trailer

Mark three answers
- A. at an overnight service area
- B. near the brow of a hill
- C. opposite a traffic island
- D. in front of an entrance to a property
- E. in a factory yard

278 PCV/LGV
Mirrors fitted to your vehicle MUST be

Mark two answers
- A. clean
- B. properly adjusted
- C. convex
- D. tinted
- E. concave

279 PCV/LGV
As you drive past a group of school children standing close to the kerb you should

Mark one answer
- A. check your offside mirror
- B. check your nearside mirror
- C. switch on your headlights
- D. switch on your hazard lights

280 PCV/LGV
You are driving at the legal speed limit. A vehicle comes up quickly behind, flashing its headlights. You should

Mark one answer
- A. accelerate to maintain a gap behind you
- B. touch the brake pedal sharply to show your brake lights
- C. maintain your speed and prevent the vehicle from overtaking
- D. allow the vehicle to overtake

281 PCV/LGV
A vehicle pulls out in front of you at a junction. What should you do?

Mark one answer
- [ ] A. Swerve past it and sound your horn
- [ ] B. Flash your headlights and drive up close behind
- [ ] C. Slow down and be ready to stop
- [ ] D. Accelerate past it immediately

282 PCV/LGV
Which THREE of these are likely effects of drinking alcohol on driving?

Mark three answers
- [ ] A. Reduced coordination
- [ ] B. Increased confidence
- [ ] C. Poor judgement
- [ ] D. Increased concentration
- [ ] E. Faster reactions
- [ ] F. Colour blindness

283 PCV/LGV
Drinking any amount of alcohol is likely to

Mark three answers
- [ ] A. reduce your ability to react to hazards
- [ ] B. increase the speed of your reactions
- [ ] C. worsen your judgement of speed
- [ ] D. increase your awareness of danger
- [ ] E. give a false sense of confidence

284 PCV/LGV
What else can seriously affect your concentration when driving, other than alcoholic drinks?

Mark three answers
- [ ] A. Drugs
- [ ] B. Tiredness
- [ ] C. Tinted windows
- [ ] D. Contact lenses
- [ ] E. Loud music

285 PCV/LGV
How does alcohol affect your driving?

Mark one answer
- [ ] A. It speeds up your reactions
- [ ] B. It increases your awareness
- [ ] C. It improves your coordination
- [ ] D. It reduces your concentration

286 PCV/LGV
You have been convicted of driving whilst unfit through drink or drugs. You will find this is likely to cause the cost of one of the following to rise considerably. Which one?

Mark one answer
- [ ] A. Road fund licence
- [ ] B. Insurance premiums
- [ ] C. Vehicle test certificate
- [ ] D. Driving licence

287 PCV/LGV
What advice should you give to a driver who has had a few alcoholic drinks at a party?

Mark one answer

- [ ] **A.** Have a strong cup of coffee and then drive home
- [ ] **B.** Drive home carefully and slowly
- [ ] **C.** Go home by public transport
- [ ] **D.** Wait a short while and then drive home

288 PCV/LGV
A driver attends a social event. What precaution should the driver take?

Mark one answer

- [ ] **A.** Drink plenty of coffee after drinking alcohol
- [ ] **B.** Avoid busy roads after drinking alcohol
- [ ] **C.** Avoid drinking alcohol completely
- [ ] **D.** Avoid drinking alcohol on an empty stomach

289 PCV/LGV
It is eight hours since you last had an alcoholic drink. Which of the following applies?

Mark two answers

- [ ] **A.** You will certainly be under the legal limit
- [ ] **B.** You will have no alcohol in your system
- [ ] **C.** You may still be unfit to drive
- [ ] **D.** You may still be over the legal limit

290 PCV/LGV
Your doctor has given you a course of medicine. Why should you ask if it is OK to drive?

Mark one answer

- [ ] **A.** Drugs make you a better driver by quickening your reactions
- [ ] **B.** You will have to let your insurance company know about the medicine
- [ ] **C.** Some types of medicine can cause your reactions to slow down
- [ ] **D.** The medicine you take may affect your hearing

291 PCV/LGV
You have been taking medicine for a few days which made you feel drowsy. Today you feel better, but still need to take the medicine. You should only drive

Mark one answer

- [ ] **A.** if your journey is necessary
- [ ] **B.** at night on quiet roads
- [ ] **C.** if someone goes with you
- [ ] **D.** after checking with your doctor

292 PCV/LGV
You are not sure if your cough medicine will affect your driving. What TWO things could you do?

Mark two answers

- [ ] **A.** Ask your doctor
- [ ] **B.** Check the medicine label
- [ ] **C.** Drive if you feel all right
- [ ] **D.** Ask a friend or relative for advice

293 PCV/LGV
You take some cough medicine given to you by a friend. What must you do before driving?

Mark one answer

- [ ] A. Drink some strong coffee
- [ ] B. Ask your friend if taking the medicine affected their driving
- [ ] C. Check the label to see if the medicine will affect your driving
- [ ] D. Make a short journey to see if the medicine is affecting your driving

294 PCV/LGV
You are driving along a motorway and become tired. You should

Mark two answers

- [ ] A. stop at the next service area and rest
- [ ] B. leave the motorway at the next exit and rest
- [ ] C. increase your speed and turn up the radio volume
- [ ] D. close all your windows and set heating to warm
- [ ] E. pull up on the hard shoulder and change drivers

295 PCV/LGV
You are about to drive home. You feel very tired and have a severe headache. You should

Mark one answer

- [ ] A. wait until you are fit and well before driving
- [ ] B. drive home, but take a tablet for headaches
- [ ] C. drive home if you can stay awake for the journey
- [ ] D. wait for a short time, then drive home slowly

296 PCV/LGV
If you are feeling tired it is best to stop as soon as you can. Until then you should

Mark one answer

- [ ] A. increase your speed to find a stopping place quickly
- [ ] B. ensure a supply of fresh air
- [ ] C. gently tap the steering wheel
- [ ] D. keep changing speed to improve concentration

297 PCV/LGV
Your reactions will be much slower when driving

Mark one answer

- [ ] A. if tired
- [ ] B. in fog
- [ ] C. too quickly
- [ ] D. in rain

298 PCV/LGV
You are driving on a motorway. You feel tired. You should

Mark one answer

- [ ] A. carry on but drive slowly
- [ ] B. leave the motorway at the next exit
- [ ] C. complete your journey as quickly as possible
- [ ] D. stop on the hard shoulder

299 PCV/LGV
You are taking medication that could affect your driving. What should you do?

Mark one answer

- [ ] A. Seek medical advice
- [ ] B. Make short journeys only
- [ ] C. Drive only at night
- [ ] D. Drink plenty of water

300 PCV/LGV
You are driving on a motorway and feel tired. You should

Mark one answer

- A. stop on the hard shoulder for a rest
- B. carry on, but drive slowly
- C. leave at the next exit
- D. try to complete your journey more quickly

301 PCV/LGV
You have driven a long distance and feel tired. Your tachograph shows that you have not exceeded your driving hours. What should you do?

Mark one answer

- A. Park in a suitable place and rest
- B. Reduce your speed and drive more slowly
- C. Carry on driving to use up your hours
- D. Increase your speed and reduce your journey time

302 PCV/LGV
Persistent misuse of drugs or alcohol may lead to

Mark one answer

- A. better concentration
- B. better eyesight
- C. withdrawal of a driving licence
- D. faster reactions

303 PCV/LGV
You are driving a vehicle on a motorway. A front tyre bursts. You should

Mark one answer

- A. loosen your grip on the steering wheel
- B. brake firmly to a stop
- C. hold the steering wheel firmly
- D. drive to the next service area

304 PCV/LGV
Your mobile phone rings while you are driving. You should

Mark one answer

- A. stop immediately
- B. answer it immediately
- C. pull up in a suitable place
- D. pull up at the nearest kerb

305 PCV/LGV
You break down on a motorway. You need to call for help. Why may it be better to use an emergency roadside telephone rather than a mobile phone?

Mark one answer

- A. It connects you to a local garage
- B. Using a mobile phone will distract other drivers
- C. It allows easy location by the emergency services
- D. Mobile phones do not work on motorways

306 PCV/LGV
You are most likely to lose concentration when driving if you

Mark one answer

- A. use a mobile phone
- B. switch on the windscreen wipers
- C. switch on the heated rear window
- D. look at the door mirrors

307

PCV/LGV

You should not use a mobile phone whilst driving

Mark one answer

- [ ] **A.** until you are satisfied that no other traffic is near
- [ ] **B.** unless you are able to drive one handed
- [ ] **C.** because it might distract your attention from the road ahead
- [ ] **D.** because reception is poor when the engine is running

308

PCV/LGV

You should ONLY use a mobile phone when

Mark one answer

- [ ] **A.** receiving a call
- [ ] **B.** suitably parked
- [ ] **C.** driving at less than 30mph
- [ ] **D.** driving an automatic vehicle

309

PCV/LGV

Using a mobile phone while you are driving

Mark one answer

- [ ] **A.** is acceptable in a vehicle with power steering
- [ ] **B.** will reduce your field of vision
- [ ] **C.** could distract your attention from the road
- [ ] **D.** will affect your vehicle's electronic systems

310

PCV/LGV

Your vehicle breaks down on the hard shoulder of a motorway. You decide to use your mobile phone to call for help. You should

Mark one answer

- [ ] **A.** stand at the rear of the vehicle while making the call
- [ ] **B.** try to repair the vehicle yourself
- [ ] **C.** get out of the vehicle by the right-hand door
- [ ] **D.** check your location from the marker posts on the left

311

PCV/LGV

To answer a call on your mobile phone while driving you should

Mark one answer

- [ ] **A.** reduce your speed wherever you are
- [ ] **B.** stop in a proper and convenient place
- [ ] **C.** keep the call time to a minimum
- [ ] **D.** slow down and allow others to overtake

312

PCV/LGV

You are overtaking a lorry. You see the driver flash their headlights. What should you do?

Mark one answer

- [ ] **A.** Move back to the left when it is safe to do so
- [ ] **B.** Indicate left and move back slowly
- [ ] **C.** Act immediately on the other driver's signa
- [ ] **D.** Flash your rear lights on and off twice

313 PCV/LGV
A bus has stopped at a bus stop ahead of you. Its right-hand indicator is flashing. You should

Mark one answer

A. flash your headlights and slow down
B. slow down and give way if it is safe to do so
C. sound your horn and keep going
D. slow down and then sound your horn

314 PCV/LGV
You have stopped for an elderly pedestrian who is slowly crossing the road. Traffic behind you is being held up. What should you do?

Mark one answer

A. Edge forward slowly and make them hurry
B. Remain where you are and allow them to cross in their own time
C. Steer slowly around them to ease the build up of traffic
D. Get out of your vehicle and wave them across

315 PCV/LGV
You are driving a slow-moving vehicle along a narrow road. You should let other vehicles overtake by

Mark one answer

A. maintaining a steady speed
B. waving them past
C. giving a left turn signal
D. pulling in when you can

316 PCV/LGV
Your vehicle is fitted with a hands-free phone system. Using this equipment whilst driving

Mark one answer

A. is quite safe as long as you slow down
B. could distract your attention from the road
C. is recommended by *The Highway Code*
D. could be very good for road safety

317 PCV/LGV
Using a hands-free phone is likely to

Mark one answer

A. improve your safety
B. increase your concentration
C. reduce your view
D. divert your attention

318 PCV/LGV
Your mobile phone rings while you are on the motorway. Before answering you should

Mark one answer

A. reduce your speed to 40mph
B. pull up on the hard shoulder
C. move into the left-hand lane
D. stop in a safe place when you can

319 PCV/LGV
Which THREE of these are likely effects of drinking alcohol on driving?

Mark three answers

A. Less control
B. A false sense of confidence
C. Faster reactions
D. Poor judgement of speed
E. Greater awareness of danger

320

PCV/LGV

You are driving on a motorway. There has been an accident on the other side of the carriageway. You should take extra care as traffic in your lane may

Mark one answer
- [ ] A. leave at the next exit
- [ ] B. slow down to have a look
- [ ] C. pull out to overtake
- [ ] D. stop on the hard shoulder

321

PCV/LGV

You are driving on a motorway. There has been an accident on the opposite carriageway. What should you do?

Mark one answer
- [ ] A. Concentrate on your driving
- [ ] B. Slow down to look across
- [ ] C. Switch on your hazard lights
- [ ] D. Stop on the hard shoulder

322

PCV/LGV

You are driving on a motorway. There has been an accident on the opposite carriageway. Busy traffic ahead is slowing to look. You should

Mark one answer
- [ ] A. concentrate on the road ahead
- [ ] B. slow down to take a look
- [ ] C. pull up on the hard shoulder
- [ ] D. overtake using the hard shoulder

323

PCV/LGV

Your vehicle has power-assisted steering. Its main purpose is to

Mark one answer
- [ ] A. reduce tyre wear
- [ ] B. assist with braking
- [ ] C. reduce driver effort
- [ ] D. assist road holding

324

PCV/LGV

Many vehicles are fitted with power-assisted steering. You need to be aware that this

Mark three answers
- [ ] A. causes less tyre wear
- [ ] B. prevents you from oversteering
- [ ] C. makes it easier for you to steer
- [ ] D. senses when you start to turn the wheel
- [ ] E. only works at high speeds
- [ ] F. makes the steering seem light

325

PCV/LGV

A driver pulls out of a side road in front of you. You have to brake hard. You should

Mark one answer
- [ ] A. ignore the error and stay calm
- [ ] B. flash your lights to show your annoyance
- [ ] C. sound your horn to show your annoyance
- [ ] D. overtake as soon as possible

326

PCV/LGV

A car driver pulls out causing you to brake. You should

Mark one answer
- [ ] A. keep calm and not retaliate
- [ ] B. overtake and sound your horn
- [ ] C. drive close behind and sound your horn
- [ ] D. flag the driver down and explain the mistake

327 PCV/LGV
Another driver's behaviour has upset you. It may help if you

Mark one answer
- A. stop and take a break
- B. shout abusive language
- C. gesture to them with your hand
- D. follow their car, flashing your headlights

328 PCV/LGV
Another driver does something that upsets you. You should

Mark one answer
- A. try not to react
- B. let them know how you feel
- C. flash your headlights several times
- D. sound your horn

329 PCV/LGV
You are driving in fast-moving traffic along a motorway. There is a stationary queue of traffic ahead. What should you do?

Mark one answer
- A. Move to the hard shoulder
- B. Change lanes
- C. Switch on your rear foglights
- D. Switch on your hazard warning lights

330 PCV/LGV
You are turning right onto a dual carriageway from a side road. Your vehicle is too long for the central gap. How should you proceed?

Mark one answer
- A. Move forward and wait in the middle
- B. Wait until it is clear from both directions
- C. Move out blocking traffic from the right
- D. Edge out slowly so other traffic will see you

331 PCV/LGV
You want to turn left at a road junction. What is most important when deciding your position?

Mark three answers
- A. The length of the vehicle
- B. The width of the roads
- C. The camber of the road
- D. The type of road surface
- E. The angle of the corner

332 PCV/LGV ·
As well as planning your route before starting a journey, you should also plan an alternative route. Why is this?

Mark one answer
- A. To let another driver overtake
- B. Your first route may be blocked
- C. To avoid a railway level crossing
- D. In case you have to avoid emergency vehicles

333 PCV/LGV
You are making an appointment and will have to travel a long distance. You should

Mark one answer
- A. allow plenty of time for your journey
- B. plan to go at busy times
- C. avoid all national speed limit roads
- D. prevent other drivers from overtaking

334 PCV/LGV
While driving you should remain alert at all times. How can you help yourself to maintain concentration?

Mark one answer
- [ ] A. Eat sugary snacks when on duty
- [ ] B. Have regular meals and rest breaks
- [ ] C. Do not eat at all on duty
- [ ] D. Avoid meals containing bread and vegetables

335 PCV/LGV
The amount of fluid you need to drink can vary. It is influenced by the temperature in your vehicle. What is the best type of fluid to drink?

Mark one answer
- [ ] A. Bottled water
- [ ] B. Sugary canned drinks
- [ ] C. High caffeine drinks
- [ ] D. Hot chocolate

336 PCV/LGV
You have to drive through the night. What should you do to help concentration?

Mark one answer
- [ ] A. Have continual snacks whilst driving
- [ ] B. Not prepare your own food in advance
- [ ] C. Have a meal at the beginning of your shift
- [ ] D. Not eat anything during your period of work

337 PCV/LGV
A number of vehicle accidents are sleep-related. Between which times is there a particular risk?

Mark one answer
- [ ] A. 2am and 7am
- [ ] B. 11pm and 2am
- [ ] C. 6pm and 11pm
- [ ] D. 7am and 2pm

338 PCV/LGV
A number of sleep related vehicle incidents (SRVIs) are probably work related. What percentage involve commercial vehicles?

Mark one answer
- [ ] A. 20%
- [ ] B. 40%
- [ ] C. 60%
- [ ] D. 80%

339 PCV/LGV
Commercial vehicles have been shown to be involved in sleep related vehicle incidents (SRVIs). Approximately what percentage of these incidents involve commercial vehicles?

Mark one answer
- [ ] A. 40%
- [ ] B. 55%
- [ ] C. 70%
- [ ] D. 95%

340 PCV/LGV
Driving for long periods can cause fatigue. Tired drivers are normally

Mark one answer
- [ ] A. aware of their sleepiness
- [ ] B. over their permitted hours
- [ ] C. not aware of their sleepiness
- [ ] D. able to judge hazards better

341 PCV/LGV
Poor eating habits can increase your risk of long term health problems. Which THREE may result from a poor diet?

Mark three answers
- [ ] A. Deafness
- [ ] B. Obesity
- [ ] C. Lung disease
- [ ] D. Diabetes
- [ ] E. Heart disease
- [ ] F. Epilepsy

342 PCV/LGV
You have driven for a long time and are fighting sleep. What should you do?

Mark one answer
- [ ] A. Stop driving
- [ ] B. Open a window
- [ ] C. Play loud music
- [ ] D. Stretch your arms

343 PCV/LGV
Driver sleepiness most often occurs on which type of road?

Mark one answer
- [ ] A. Motorway
- [ ] B. One-way street
- [ ] C. Rural road
- [ ] D. Tourist route

344 PCV/LGV
Many sleep-related vehicle incidents (SRVIs) occur at work. Men are more likely than women to be involved. Between what ages are men most at risk?

Mark one answer
- [ ] A. 30 years and under
- [ ] B. 31–45 years
- [ ] C. 46–59 years
- [ ] D. 60 years and over

345 PCV/LGV
Your vehicle has a front wheel blow-out. What should you try to do?

Mark one answer
- [ ] A. Hold the steering wheel firmly and slow down gradually
- [ ] B. Steer to the right-hand side and brake firmly
- [ ] C. Do not use your brakes in any circumstance
- [ ] D. Brake hard and steer towards the affected side

346 PCV/LGV
Your vehicle is fitted with seat belts. You must wear them unless

Mark one answer
- [ ] A. you hold a medical exemption certificate
- [ ] B. the seat belt is too large for your use
- [ ] C. you are driving on a motorway
- [ ] D. the speed limit is 30mph or less

347

PCV/LGV

When you are driving between 2am and 7am there is a particular risk, in relation to your 'body clock'. You are more likely to

Mark one answer

- A. fall asleep at the wheel
- B. face road rage
- C. meet traffic congestion
- D. have a vehicle breakdown

348

PCV/LGV

Which of these is specifically provided to protect against neck and whiplash injuries?

Mark one answer

- A. An air-sprung seat
- B. Anti-lock brakes
- C. A collapsible steering wheel
- D. A properly adjusted head restraint

349

LGV

You are approaching a green traffic light and going straight on. Traffic in front of you is stopped and queuing just beyond the junction. What should you do?

Mark one answer

- A. Only go if your vehicle will clear the junction
- B. Drive slowly across the junction
- C. Maintain your speed and sound your horn
- D. Stop in the junction until the traffic clears

350

LGV

In rural areas why should you avoid parking on the grass verge?

Mark one answer

- A. When moving off you may leave mud on the road
- B. There may be sheep or cattle grazing in the area
- C. You will be blocking an entrance to premises or a driveway
- D. Your vehicle will probably be blown over by high winds

351

LGV

Seat belts are fitted to your lorry. The wearing of them is

Mark one answer

- A. not advisable
- B. advisable
- C. required by law
- D. not required by law

352

LGV

You are waiting to turn right in this box van. Just before turning you should

Mark one answer

- A. wave the pedestrian across
- B. check your left mirror and blind spot
- C. wave out the green car (arrowed)
- D. check your right mirror and blind spot

353 LGV

Extra skills are needed when driving at night. The MAIN problems you will have to deal with are

Mark two answers

- A. headlight dazzle
- B. other drivers speeding
- C. cold weather conditions
- D. dazzle from shop windows
- E. becoming tired

354 LGV

You are driving a lorry in a busy town. A driver pulls out in front of you. You have to brake hard. What should you do?

Mark one answer

- A. Overtake as quickly as possible
- B. Stay calm and accept the error
- C. Flash your lights to show your annoyance
- D. Sound your horn and speed up

355 LGV

Your lorry is fitted with a driver's seat belt. You MUST wear it at all times unless

Mark one answer

- A. your deliveries are less than 50 metres apart
- B. you are towing at less than 50mph
- C. you are working less than 50 hours in a week
- D. you are within 50 miles of your depot

356 LGV

You have been issued with protective clothing. Whose responsibility is it to make sure it is worn?

Mark one answer

- A. You, the driver
- B. The insurance company
- C. The Health and Safety Executive
- D. Your employer

357 PCV
As a bus driver your first consideration is to your

Mark one answer
- [ ] A. timetable
- [ ] B. passengers
- [ ] C. employer
- [ ] D. workmates

358 PCV
As a bus driver your main responsibility is

Mark one answer
- [ ] A. the safety and comfort of your passengers
- [ ] B. keeping to a strict timetable
- [ ] C. the collecting of fares
- [ ] D. the issuing of tickets

359 PCV
As a bus driver you should show care to your passengers. You can do this by

Mark two answers
- [ ] A. stopping close to the kerb
- [ ] B. reaching destinations early
- [ ] C. not speaking when taking fares
- [ ] D. giving them time to get seated

360 PCV
What is the MAIN reason for using smooth acceleration when driving your bus?

Mark one answer
- [ ] A. To reduce wear on the tyres
- [ ] B. To reduce wear on the engine
- [ ] C. To improve fuel consumption
- [ ] D. To improve passenger comfort

361 PCV
When driving a bus, your main priorities should be

Mark two answers
- [ ] A. the safety of your passengers
- [ ] B. the comfort of your passengers
- [ ] C. keeping strictly to your timetable
- [ ] D. greeting all passengers with a smile
- [ ] E. making sure passengers take their luggage

362 PCV
For the comfort of your passengers harsh braking should be avoided. You should

Mark one answer
- [ ] A. pump the brakes when approaching a bus stop or hazard
- [ ] B. use the gears to slow down
- [ ] C. use the parking brake just before stopping to avoid throwing passengers forward
- [ ] D. plan ahead and take early action on all stops and hazards

363 PCV
A bus driver brakes harshly. Passengers may be thrown towards

Mark one answer
- [ ] A. the front of the bus
- [ ] B. the rear of the bus
- [ ] C. the nearside
- [ ] D. the offside

364 PCV
How can you avoid harsh braking?

Mark one answer
- [ ] A. Gently apply the parking brake
- [ ] B. Plan ahead and take early action
- [ ] C. Slow down by using your gears only
- [ ] D. Pump the brake pedal several times

365 PCV

On which TWO occasions would passengers be most likely to notice weight transfer?

Mark two answers

- [ ] A. Braking
- [ ] B. Cornering
- [ ] C. Reversing
- [ ] D. Overtaking

366 PCV

Well ahead of you are traffic lights on green. What should you do in case the lights change to red?

Mark one answer

- [ ] A. Accelerate to make sure you can cross before they change
- [ ] B. Slow down to avoid the need to stop suddenly
- [ ] C. Accelerate, but warn your passengers you may have to stop
- [ ] D. Carry on at a constant speed, but be ready to sound your horn

367 PCV

A bus driver accelerates sharply. Passengers may be thrown towards

Mark one answer

- [ ] A. the rear of the bus
- [ ] B. the front of the bus
- [ ] C. the nearside
- [ ] D. the offside

368 PCV

A bus driver should avoid stopping harshly MOSTLY for the benefit of the

Mark one answer

- [ ] A. tyres
- [ ] B. brakes
- [ ] C. passengers
- [ ] D. suspension

369 PCV

If a bus takes a bend too fast passengers may be thrown towards

Mark one answer

- [ ] A. the outside of the bend
- [ ] B. the inside of the bend
- [ ] C. the front of the bus
- [ ] D. the rear of the bus

370 PCV

For the safety and comfort of your passengers you should

Mark three answers

- [ ] A. brake smoothly
- [ ] B. think well ahead
- [ ] C. stop close to the kerb
- [ ] D. brake hard on a bend
- [ ] E. give change on the move
- [ ] F. drive with the door open

371 PCV

Before moving off from a standstill, a bus driver should be especially aware of passengers who attempt to

Mark two answers

- [ ] A. change seats
- [ ] B. smoke
- [ ] C. ask you questions
- [ ] D. get off
- [ ] E. get on
- [ ] F. refuse to pay

372 PCV
When seat belts are fitted in a bus your passengers SHOULD wear them

Mark one answer
- [ ] A. on journeys over distances of 25km (15.5 miles)
- [ ] B. only when travelling in EC countries
- [ ] C. only when travelling on motorways
- [ ] D. at all times

373 PCV
Which of the following is a legal requirement for every bus?

Mark one answer
- [ ] A. A fire extinguisher
- [ ] B. A current timetable
- [ ] C. A mobile phone or radio
- [ ] D. A working tachograph

374 PCV
The location of which of the following MUST be clearly labelled on a bus?

Mark three answers
- [ ] A. Air vents
- [ ] B. First aid equipment
- [ ] C. Vehicle length
- [ ] D. Route timetables
- [ ] E. Fuel cut-off switch
- [ ] F. Fire extinguisher

375 PCV
If a passenger carries a white stick with a red ring painted on it this shows the person is

Mark one answer
- [ ] A. blind and deaf
- [ ] B. deaf only
- [ ] C. unable to climb steps
- [ ] D. blind only

376 PCV
A passenger is boarding your bus. They are carrying a white stick with a red ring painted on it. What does this mean?

Mark one answer
- [ ] A. They have a learning difficulty
- [ ] B. They have poor vision and hearing
- [ ] C. They have a physical disability
- [ ] D. They have a speech problem

377 PCV
A disabled passenger is boarding your bus. They tell you that getting on board is not a problem to them. You should

Mark one answer
- [ ] A. let them board without help
- [ ] B. ask a passenger to help them
- [ ] C. leave your cab and help them
- [ ] D. do nothing, you cannot leave your seat

378 PCV
As a bus driver, which of the following should you not do?

Mark three answers
- [ ] A. Signal if necessary when pulling in
- [ ] B. Drive on before people are seated
- [ ] C. Issue tickets without looking at customers' faces
- [ ] D. Use smooth acceleration and anticipate braking needs
- [ ] E. Give time to passengers and show consideration
- [ ] F. Always rush to keep to a timetable

379

PCV

While you are collecting fares you should look at passengers when speaking to them. This will

Mark three answers

- [ ] **A.** help you to recognise someone having difficulty
- [ ] **B.** show people you are in a rush to keep to a timetable
- [ ] **C.** show common courtesy and help the image of your company
- [ ] **D.** help deaf and hearing-impaired people to understand you
- [ ] **E.** help you decide whether people with a disability should get on the bus

380

PCV

When dealing with passengers who are hard of hearing it is important that you

Mark two answers

- [ ] **A.** shout as loudly as you can
- [ ] **B.** look at them when speaking to them
- [ ] **C.** hurry them to get seated
- [ ] **D.** are as helpful as possible

381

PCV

The purpose of a 'kneeling bus' is to

Mark one answer

- [ ] **A.** improve passenger comfort on bumpy roads
- [ ] **B.** help with access under low bridges
- [ ] **C.** allow the step height to be raised and lowered
- [ ] **D.** give more clearance over speed ramps

382

PCV

This sign fitted to the front and rear of a bus means that

Mark one answer

- [ ] **A.** the bus may be carrying children
- [ ] **B.** children must be accompanied by an adult
- [ ] **C.** the bus is carrying blind people
- [ ] **D.** the driver will help disabled people

383

PCV

Hazard warning lights may only be used at certain times. In addition, a bus displaying this sign may use them when

Mark one answer

- [ ] **A.** stopped at a pedestrian crossing
- [ ] **B.** stopped and children are getting on or off the vehicle
- [ ] **C.** approaching a school crossing patrol
- [ ] **D.** there is a sign warning of a school ahead

384 PCV
You are driving a bus. The bell rings four times. This means

Mark one answer
- A. continue past the next bus stop
- B. the bus is full
- C. move off when safe
- D. there is an emergency

385 PCV
Your bus has broken down at night in heavy rain. Why should you move your passengers to the front of the bus?

Mark one answer
- A. To keep the bus stable
- B. To help you see clearly out of the back window
- C. To limit injuries in case of a rear-end collision
- D. To keep them informed about the breakdown

386 PCV
You are driving a half-cab bus and have no contact with the passengers. This is only allowed if

Mark one answer
- A. it is fitted with an interior mirror
- B. there is a chain or strap across the doorway
- C. a responsible person is in charge of them
- D. you make sure no one stands on the platform

387 PCV
You are driving a coach at night with passengers on board. You should never

Mark one answer
- A. stop at service stations
- B. switch the radio on
- C. leave the interior in darkness
- D. close any curtains

388 PCV
There is a fire on the upper deck of your double-deck bus. You should

Mark three answers
- A. stop safely and quickly
- B. get everyone off the bus
- C. contact emergency services
- D. open all the windows
- E. move the passengers into the lower deck
- F. make sure passengers have their belongings

389 PCV
Kneeling buses are specifically designed to improve access for

Mark one answer
- A. the driver
- B. extra luggage
- C. elderly passengers
- D. low bridges

390 PCV
You are driving a bus carrying passengers at night. Why should you always put the interior lights on?

Mark one answer

- A. It will help you see the road ahead
- B. So that passengers can see to move around
- C. It will help passengers to see outside
- D. So that you can see your controls

391 PCV
As you move off watch out, in particular, for any passengers who attempt to

Mark one answer

- A. smoke in the lower saloon
- B. stand in the upper saloon
- C. avoid paying the correct fare
- D. board the bus

392 PCV
A passenger finds walking difficult. What could you do to help?

Mark one answer

- A. Drive quickly so that passengers will not be on for long
- B. Wait until the passenger is sitting down before moving away
- C. Make sure they have a window seat
- D. Suggest they stand near the door

393 PCV
You are the driver of a bus displaying reflective yellow signs. You are permitted to use hazard warning lights when

Mark two answers

- A. stationary and parked to take a rest period
- B. stationary and children are boarding
- C. stationary and children are getting off
- D. slowing down to find a parking space
- E. slowing down in town centre traffic queues
- F. slowing down approaching a bus stop

394 PCV
You are parking your coach at a coastal resort. Your passengers will still have access. You should make sure

Mark two answers

- A. the cab area is isolated
- B. the gear lever is in neutral
- C. the storage lockers are open
- D. a responsible person is on the coach

395 PCV
You have parked and left your bus. The public will still have access to it. You should make sure that

Mark two answers

- A. the door key is different to the ignition key
- B. the cab area is shut off
- C. a responsible person is on board
- D. all interior lights are on

396
PCV

When driving a double-deck bus on a steep camber you should be especially aware of

Mark three answers

- [ ] **A.** lamp posts
- [ ] **B.** parking meters
- [ ] **C.** parked cars
- [ ] **D.** shop awnings
- [ ] **E.** litter bins
- [ ] **F.** traffic signs

397
PCV

What is the likely weight difference between an empty bus and a bus with 75 passengers on board?

Mark one answer

- [ ] **A.** 5 tonnes
- [ ] **B.** 10 tonnes
- [ ] **C.** 15 tonnes
- [ ] **D.** 20 tonnes

398
PCV

It is important to be able to work out the weight difference between a full bus and an empty one. About how many passengers will equal 1 tonne in weight?

Mark one answer

- [ ] **A.** 8
- [ ] **B.** 15
- [ ] **C.** 25
- [ ] **D.** 30

399
PCV

It is only legal to drive an empty, half-cab bus when the passenger access has

Mark one answer

- [ ] **A.** a vertical pole
- [ ] **B.** no high steps
- [ ] **C.** no obstructions
- [ ] **D.** a chain or strap

400
PCV

You are driving a double-deck half-cab bus. Passengers can only be carried if

Mark one answer

- [ ] **A.** no one uses the upper deck
- [ ] **B.** you can see them in your mirror
- [ ] **C.** a responsible person is in charge of them
- [ ] **D.** they are all travelling to the same destination

401 PCV
While driving your half-cab bus you hear the three-bell signal from the conductor. This means

Mark one answer
- [ ] A. stop when safe
- [ ] B. bus empty
- [ ] C. bus full
- [ ] D. move off when safe

402 PCV
It is legal to drive an empty, half-cab double-deck bus, but the passenger access must have

Mark one answer
- [ ] A. a hand rail
- [ ] B. a vertical pole
- [ ] C. a chain or strap
- [ ] D. a warning notice

403 PCV
Buses and coaches used for school contract work MUST have

Mark one answer
- [ ] A. yellow reflective signs
- [ ] B. only one door
- [ ] C. a conductor
- [ ] D. a 'no overtaking' sign

404 PCV
You are driving a half-cab bus. The correct signal to move off when safe is

Mark one answer
- [ ] A. one bell
- [ ] B. two bells
- [ ] C. three bells
- [ ] D. four bells

405 PCV
A passenger comments on exhaust smoke in the vehicle. You should

Mark one answer
- [ ] A. report it as soon as you return to the depot
- [ ] B. stop and have the fault put right
- [ ] C. avoid heavy revving of the engine when stationary
- [ ] D. have the emissions checked at the next vehicle inspection test

406 PCV
What would you have to be especially aware of when driving a double-deck bus on a road with a steep camber?

Mark one answer
- [ ] A. 'Keep Left' islands
- [ ] B. A smooth road surface
- [ ] C. Pedestrian crossings
- [ ] D. Overhanging trees

407 PCV
You are driving a double-deck bus. Passenger care is important. You should

Mark two answers
- [ ] A. assist passengers with special needs
- [ ] B. provide a commentary of the route
- [ ] C. listen to passengers while driving
- [ ] D. help passengers unfamiliar with the service
- [ ] E. carry passenger's luggage upstairs

408 PCV
Your bus is fitted with lifts or ramps for the less able-bodied. The equipment should only be operated by

Mark one answer
- [ ] A. wheelchair attendants
- [ ] B. fully-trained people
- [ ] C. bus company employees
- [ ] D. accompanying nurses

409 PCV
Your conductor rings the bell twice. This means

Mark one answer
- [ ] A. carry on past the next bus stop
- [ ] B. immediately carry out an emergency stop
- [ ] C. pull in at the next bus stop
- [ ] D. move off when it is safe to do so

410 PCV
You are driving a bus. The bell rings three times. This means

Mark one answer
- [ ] A. pull in at the next stop
- [ ] B. move away when it is safe to do so
- [ ] C. an emergency on board
- [ ] D. your vehicle is full

411 PCV
What is a 'kneeling bus' designed to improve?

Mark one answer
- [ ] A. Access for the disabled
- [ ] B. Stability when cornering
- [ ] C. Passenger comfort at higher speeds
- [ ] D. Access for the driver

412 PCV
Your double-deck bus breaks down on a busy road. You should ask your passengers to move to the

Mark one answer
- [ ] A. rear of the bus
- [ ] B. top deck
- [ ] C. lower deck
- [ ] D. front of the bus

413 PCV
When you pull away from a bus stop watch out in particular for passengers who attempt to

Mark one answer
- [ ] A. avoid paying the correct fare
- [ ] B. smoke in the lower saloon
- [ ] C. alight from the bus
- [ ] D. use an expired travel pass

414 PCV
A bus driver MUST not drive while

Mark three answers
- [ ] A. issuing tickets
- [ ] B. the doors are open
- [ ] C. wearing sunglasses
- [ ] D. giving change
- [ ] E. passengers are standing
- [ ] F. luggage is being carried

415 PCV
Your bus breaks down on the motorway. You have several passengers on board. You should

Mark two answers
- [ ] A. move the passengers to the rear
- [ ] B. place a warning triangle in front of the bus
- [ ] C. stop on the hard shoulder
- [ ] D. move the passengers to the front

416 PCV
As a bus driver your main aim should be

Mark one answer
- A. to keep strictly to the timetable
- B. the safety of your passengers
- C. service to your colleagues
- D. to keep accurate details of ticket sales

417 PCV
As the driver of a bus your FIRST priority is

Mark one answer
- A. the safety and comfort of your passengers
- B. making sure that you are always on time
- C. making sure that your log book and tachograph are correctly completed
- D. making sure that your destination is clearly marked

418 PCV
You are driving a one-person-operated bus. You are at a bus stop issuing tickets. You should

Mark one answer
- A. be in gear without any signal
- B. be in gear and signalling
- C. signal only when ready to move away
- D. be in neutral but signalling to move off

419 PCV
As the driver of a one-person-operated double-deck bus you should be constantly aware of passengers on the top deck. How should you do this?

Mark one answer
- A. By counting passengers up and down the staircase
- B. By frequent checks upstairs while stopped at bus stops
- C. By listening to passengers in the upstairs gangway when approaching bus stops
- D. By making full use of the internal mirror system

420 PCV
When driving a double-deck bus, the internal mirror system is used to

Mark one answer
- A. watch for traffic on your right-hand side
- B. keep a look out for any overtaking vehicles
- C. keep a look out for passengers using the stairs
- D. watch for cyclists on your left-hand side

421 PCV
You are stopping to collect passengers from a bus stop. Where should you pull up?

Mark one answer
- A. Close to the kerb
- B. Away from the kerb
- C. After the bus stop
- D. Before the bus stop

422 PCV
You should stop your bus to allow passengers to get on or off near

Mark one answer
- A. soft grass
- B. guard rails
- C. parked cars
- D. the kerb

423 PCV
A bus stop is blocked and you cannot pull into it. Before opening the exit door what is the most important action to take?

Mark one answer
- A. Try to get the bus stop cleared
- B. Carry on to the next bus stop
- C. Check for traffic on the left
- D. Check for traffic on the right

424 PCV
Several cars have parked blocking your bus stop. Before allowing passengers to get off you should

Mark one answer
- A. move on to the next bus stop
- B. check it is clear of traffic on the left
- C. try and find the car owners
- D. check it is clear of traffic on the right

425 PCV
What should you do before allowing passengers off your bus?

Mark one answer
- A. Collect their used tickets
- B. Activate an audible warning system
- C. Check mirrors before opening doors
- D. Ask if they have luggage to collect

426 PCV
Passengers may be in a hurry to get off the bus as you approach a bus stop. What should you do to reduce any dangers?

Mark one answer
- A. Insist that passengers stay seated until the bus stops
- B. Pull up just before the stop and let passengers get off
- C. Let passengers on the bus before letting passengers off
- D. Not open the passenger doors until the bus stops

427 PCV
You are driving a half-cab bus and carrying passengers. You must have

Mark one answer
- A. a chain or strap across the doorway
- B. electrically operated doors
- C. school children only on board
- D. a responsible person in charge of them

428 PCV
You can drive a bus at night without having the interior lights on if

Mark one answer
- A. the passengers want to sleep
- B. most passengers request it
- C. there are no standing passengers
- D. there are no passengers

429

PCV

You are driving a bus in hot weather. May the passenger door be left open to let fresh air in?

Mark one answer

- A. Yes, this is normal practice
- B. No, unless all passengers are seated
- C. Yes, unless carrying school children
- D. No, this is not allowed

430

PCV

Air suspension systems give

Mark two answers

- A. increased fuel consumption
- B. uneven tyre wear
- C. increased speed
- D. even height
- E. a comfortable ride to passengers

431

PCV

A disabled person is getting on your bus. They are having problems but say they can manage. What should you do?

Mark one answer

- A. Be prepared to move off
- B. Smile and offer to help them
- C. Ask them politely to hurry up
- D. Do nothing, you can't leave your seat

432

PCV

TV and video equipment fitted to a coach must ONLY be used when

Mark one answer

- A. the coach is moving slowly
- B. it cannot be seen by the driver
- C. on long motorway journeys
- D. the coach is on tour

433

PCV

What MUST new buses be fitted with, to benefit people with disabilities?

Mark one answer

- A. Internal mirror
- B. Radio telephone
- C. Automatic transmission
- D. Priority seating

434

PCV

Priority seating on a bus is designed for passengers

Mark one answer

- A. to store heavy luggage
- B. with a weekly pass
- C. who got on first
- D. with disabilities

435

PCV

A passenger using a wheelchair wants to get on your bus. When may you need to deny them access?

Mark one answer

- A. When the wheelchair will not fit in the luggage rack
- B. When the boarding device has failed to work
- C. When the passenger must remain in a wheelchair
- D. When the heater on the vehicle is not working

436 PCV
Your bus is accessible to wheelchair users. You must always allow them access unless

Mark one answer
- A. the designated space is occupied
- B. you are running behind schedule
- C. the traffic behind you will be held up
- D. you are shortly due to take a break

437 PCV
You are driving a school bus. You MUST avoid all physical contact with school children other than

Mark one answer
- A. in a medical emergency
- B. to prevent fare dodging
- C. when carrying luggage
- D. when fastening seat belts

438 PCV
Which should you wear when making a walk-round check of your coach?

Mark one answer
- A. Ear protectors
- B. Protective goggles
- C. High-visibility vest
- D. Face mask

439 PCV
You are about to drive on a route where you will be picking up wheelchair users. To accommodate them what MUST be checked before leaving the depot?

Mark one answer
- A. Boarding device
- B. Radio
- C. Door seals
- D. Heater

440 PCV
When should you NOT allow a wheelchair user onto your bus?

Mark one answer
- A. When the lift has stopped working
- B. When the wheelchair will not fold up
- C. When the heater has stopped working
- D. When the wheelchair is too heavy to lift manually

441 PCV
You are unable to allow a person in a wheelchair to enter your bus. What would be the reason for this?

Mark one answer
- A. Passengers are standing in a wheelchair space and cannot move elsewhere
- B. You will take time to load the wheelchair and fall behind schedule
- C. The wheelchair passenger will have to stand up
- D. You cannot fold down the wheelchair

442 PCV
A bus driver should never allow passengers to

Mark one answer
- A. sit in rear facing seats
- B. stand in the aisle
- C. stow their own luggage
- D. ride on an open platform

443 PCV
You will be driving a high-floor coach. You will be going over several high bridges. Why should you check the weather forecast?

Mark one answer
- [ ] **A.** Rain can make crossing bridges very difficult for buses and coaches
- [ ] **B.** In hot weather the bridges might be closed to heavy traffic
- [ ] **C.** You won't be able to climb the bridges if it's frosty
- [ ] **D.** Some roads may be closed to certain vehicles in high winds

444 PCV
As a bus driver, what should you do when overtaking a motorcyclist in strong winds?

Mark one answer
- [ ] **A.** Sound the horn
- [ ] **B.** Pass close
- [ ] **C.** Use the nearside mirror
- [ ] **D.** Move back in early

445 PCV
You are driving a bus in strong winds. What should you do when overtaking a motorcyclist?

Mark one answer
- [ ] **A.** Pass close
- [ ] **B.** Move back early
- [ ] **C.** Give a thank you wave
- [ ] **D.** Pass wide

446 PCV
When overtaking a cyclist in heavy rain extra care has to be taken because of

Mark one answer
- [ ] **A.** spray from your vehicle
- [ ] **B.** exhaust fumes from your vehicle
- [ ] **C.** noise from your vehicle
- [ ] **D.** the height of your vehicle

447 PCV
What TWO effects will a strong side wind have on a bus?

Mark two answers
- [ ] **A.** Steering will be easier
- [ ] **B.** The bus will tend to go off course
- [ ] **C.** Braking will be affected
- [ ] **D.** Stopping distance will be increased
- [ ] **E.** Steering will be more difficult
- [ ] **F.** Stopping distance will be decreased

448 PCV
Double-deck buses are more likely than single-deck buses to be affected by

Mark one answer
- [ ] **A.** strong winds
- [ ] **B.** heavy rain
- [ ] **C.** thick fog
- [ ] **D.** dense spray

449 PCV
As a bus driver what should you do when overtaking a motorcycle in strong winds?

Mark one answer
- [ ] **A.** Pass close
- [ ] **B.** Move back early
- [ ] **C.** Pass wide
- [ ] **D.** Signal left

450 PCV
Spray suppression equipment fitted to buses is particularly useful when it is

Mark one answer
- [ ] A. raining
- [ ] B. icy
- [ ] C. foggy
- [ ] D. windy

451 PCV
With a long bus, under normal driving conditions, when is it acceptable to straddle lanes?

Mark one answer
- [ ] A. Only when joining a bus lane
- [ ] B. On all bends and corners
- [ ] C. On the approach to all roundabouts
- [ ] D. To avoid mounting the kerb

452 PCV
When parked on the road at night, buses and coaches must

Mark one answer
- [ ] A. be under street lights
- [ ] B. be within 25 metres (82 feet) of a street light
- [ ] C. have all of the interior lights switched on
- [ ] D. have their sidelights on

453 PCV
Unless there is street lighting, why could it be dangerous to overtake at night when driving a bus?

Mark one answer
- [ ] A. There may be unseen dips or bends in the road
- [ ] B. You may dazzle other drivers
- [ ] C. It is harder to concentrate
- [ ] D. It is harder to keep control in the dark

454 PCV
Why do some buses have marker lights along their sides?

Mark one answer
- [ ] A. To make them easier to overtake
- [ ] B. To help the driver when reversing
- [ ] C. To help any passengers getting on or off
- [ ] D. To make them easier to see at junctions

455 PCV
You are driving a bus. Where should you be most aware of the risk of grounding?

Mark one answer
- [ ] A. On a hump bridge
- [ ] B. On a crawler lane
- [ ] C. On a left-hand bend
- [ ] D. On a narrow road

456 PCV/LGV
Braking continuously can make brakes overheat. This will make

Mark one answer
- [ ] A. the brakes work better
- [ ] B. braking less effective
- [ ] C. the brake pedal hard
- [ ] D. the air pressure build up

457 PCV/LGV
You are driving in a high wind. What do you need to be careful of?

Mark one answer
- [ ] A. Fallen trees
- [ ] B. Poor visibility
- [ ] C. A risk of grounding
- [ ] D. Steep gradients

458

PCV/LGV

You are driving a high-sided vehicle. You are about to drive over a high suspension bridge. What in particular do you need to be aware of?

Mark one answer

- [ ] A. The swaying of the bridge
- [ ] B. The width of the lanes
- [ ] C. The effect of strong crosswinds
- [ ] D. The overhanging bridge cables

459

PCV/LGV

You are driving through the night. You notice that your steering feels lighter than normal. What could this mean?

Mark one answer

- [ ] A. That your tyres are losing pressure
- [ ] B. There is a leak in the power steering pump
- [ ] C. That there is ice or frost on the road
- [ ] D. There is not enough tread on your tyres

460

PCV/LGV

You are in the centre lane of a motorway and overtaking another vehicle. What should you do before returning to the left-hand lane?

Mark one answer

- [ ] A. Signal left then check your mirror
- [ ] B. Wait for the other driver to flash their headlights
- [ ] C. Check ahead and then your nearside mirror
- [ ] D. Check behind for fast traffic in the right-hand lane

461

PCV/LGV

When approaching a zebra crossing you should

Mark one answer

- [ ] A. stop before the zigzag lines
- [ ] B. wave pedestrians across the road
- [ ] C. sound the horn and flash headlights
- [ ] D. be prepared to stop in good time

462

PCV/LGV

You are driving a high-sided vehicle on a motorway. You should be ESPECIALLY aware of the effects of crosswinds

Mark one answer

- [ ] A. on high bridges
- [ ] B. in cuttings
- [ ] C. in tunnels
- [ ] D. when passing signs

463

PCV/LGV

You are on a motorway in a high-sided vehicle. You should be ESPECIALLY aware of the effects of crosswinds

Mark one answer

- [ ] A. when passing signs
- [ ] B. on exposed sections
- [ ] C. in contraflow systems
- [ ] D. in service areas

464 PCV/LGV

You are driving a high-sided vehicle in very windy conditions. Which of the following should you avoid if possible?

Mark one answer

- A. Suspension bridges
- B. Steep hills
- C. Country lanes
- D. Road tunnels

465 PCV/LGV

The conditions are very windy. You are driving a high-sided vehicle. Which of the following should you avoid if possible?

Mark one answer

- A. Road tunnels
- B. Steep hills
- C. Country lanes
- D. Viaducts

466 PCV/LGV

You are driving in heavy rain. Your steering suddenly feels very light. What should you do?

Mark one answer

- A. Brake very sharply
- B. Steer towards the centre line
- C. Ease off the accelerator
- D. Increase your speed

467 PCV/LGV

Why should you be especially aware of parked cars when driving at night?

Mark one answer

- A. There are more of them
- B. They are more likely to move off
- C. The drivers may be drunk
- D. They can park without lights

468 PCV/LGV

You are waiting at a T-junction. A vehicle is coming from the right with the left signal flashing. What should you do?

Mark one answer

- A. Move out and accelerate hard
- B. Wait until the vehicle starts to turn in
- C. Pull out before the vehicle reaches the junction
- D. Move out slowly

469 PCV/LGV

On a motorway what do signs showing a crawler lane suggest?

Mark one answer

- A. Advance warning for a steep downhill section
- B. Only lorries and buses are allowed to use that lane
- C. Vehicles fitted with speed limiters must use that lane
- D. There will be a long, gradual uphill gradient ahead

470 PCV/LGV
You are about to pass this car. What are the TWO main hazards you should be aware of?

Mark two answers

- **A.** Bright sunshine reflecting off the car windscreen
- **B.** The driver's side door may suddenly open
- **C.** The parked car may move off with no warning
- **D.** The narrow pavement on the right

471 PCV/LGV
You have parked your vehicle on a two-way road at night. You should

Mark one answer

- **A.** leave the lights on
- **B.** switch off all lights
- **C.** leave your lights on if you have parked on the right-hand side
- **D.** switch off your lights if you have parked underneath a street lamp

472 PCV/LGV
When driving, on which TWO occasions would you be most likely to experience weight transfer?

Mark two answers

- **A.** Reversing
- **B.** Braking
- **C.** Overtaking
- **D.** Unloading
- **E.** Cornering
- **F.** Loading

473 PCV/LGV
When driving a laden vehicle downhill, the effect of gravity will tend to

Mark three answers

- **A.** make the vehicle use more fuel
- **B.** make the vehicle's speed increase
- **C.** require more braking effort
- **D.** require less braking effort
- **E.** increase stopping distances
- **F.** reduce stopping distances

474 PCV/LGV
Long vehicles need to straddle lanes

Mark one answer

- **A.** to avoid mounting the kerb
- **B.** to avoid braking sharply
- **C.** when driving on motorways
- **D.** when coming to contraflow systems

475 PCV/LGV
When driving in windy weather, you should

Mark one answer
- [ ] A. drive in a normal manner in exposed areas
- [ ] B. anticipate how conditions may affect other road users
- [ ] C. never alter your intended route if this would lengthen a journey
- [ ] D. always overtake smaller or vulnerable vehicles quickly

476 PCV/LGV
You are driving a high-sided vehicle on a motorway. You should be especially aware of the effects of crosswinds on your vehicle

Mark one answer
- [ ] A. when travelling in cuttings
- [ ] B. after passing motorway bridges
- [ ] C. after passing motorway signs
- [ ] D. when travelling in tunnels

477 PCV/LGV
High-sided vehicles can be affected by side winds. In which TWO situations is this most likely?

Mark two answers
- [ ] A. Narrow country roads
- [ ] B. Open roads
- [ ] C. Motorway flyovers
- [ ] D. Motorway underpasses
- [ ] E. Built-up areas
- [ ] F. Roads with speed humps

478 PCV/LGV
You are driving a high-sided vehicle. Which of these places may cause you problems on a windy day?

Mark two answers
- [ ] A. Road tunnels
- [ ] B. High-level roads
- [ ] C. Dead ground
- [ ] D. Ring roads
- [ ] E. Exposed viaducts
- [ ] F. Residential roads

479 PCV/LGV
Which of the following vehicles is least likely to be affected by high winds?

Mark one answer

- [ ] A.
- [ ] B.
- [ ] C.
- [ ] D.

480 PCV/LGV
What is a 'buffer' lane?

Mark one answer
- [ ] A. A lane for large vehicles blown off course
- [ ] B. A lane for overtaking
- [ ] C. A lane to park in until the wind drops
- [ ] D. The only lane to be used in high winds

181 PCV/LGV
In high winds where would you expect to find 'buffer' lanes?

Mark one answer
- [ ] **A.** In built-up areas
- [ ] **B.** On high bridges
- [ ] **C.** On country roads
- [ ] **D.** In roadworks

182 PCV/LGV
When is a 'buffer' lane most likely to be in use?

Mark one answer
- [ ] **A.** When windy
- [ ] **B.** When raining
- [ ] **C.** When foggy
- [ ] **D.** When icy

183 PCV/LGV
How can you best control your vehicle when driving on snow in windy conditions?

Mark one answer
- [ ] **A.** By keeping the engine revs high and spinning the wheels
- [ ] **B.** By driving in your very lowest crawler gear
- [ ] **C.** By keeping the engine revs high and slipping the clutch
- [ ] **D.** By driving slowly in as high a gear as possible

184 PCV/LGV
You are driving a large vehicle in gusty conditions. Which of the following is most likely to be affected when you overtake it?

Mark one answer
- [ ] **A.** A motorcycle
- [ ] **B.** A flat-bed lorry
- [ ] **C.** A car
- [ ] **D.** A loaded tanker

485 PCV/LGV
You are driving on a motorway in high winds. You are overtaking a motorcyclist. You should be especially aware of the effects caused by

Mark one answer
- [ ] **A.** exhaust smoke
- [ ] **B.** engine noise
- [ ] **C.** buffeting
- [ ] **D.** tyre noise

486 PCV/LGV
In gusty winds on a motorway you must be aware of motorcyclists as they may

Mark one answer
- [ ] **A.** be blown into your path
- [ ] **B.** leave at the next exit
- [ ] **C.** suddenly stop on the hard shoulder
- [ ] **D.** position to turn right

487 PCV/LGV
Which road users are in the most danger from the buffeting effects of large vehicles?

Mark three answers
- [ ] **A.** Lorry drivers
- [ ] **B.** Coach drivers
- [ ] **C.** Tractor drivers
- [ ] **D.** Pedestrians
- [ ] **E.** Horse riders
- [ ] **F.** Cyclists

488 PCV/LGV
Which road users would be most affected by turbulence caused by your vehicle?

Mark four answers
- [ ] **A.** Pedestrians
- [ ] **B.** Car drivers towing caravans
- [ ] **C.** Drivers of skip lorries
- [ ] **D.** Cyclists
- [ ] **E.** Coach drivers
- [ ] **F.** Horse riders

489 PCV/LGV
Turbulence is created by large vehicles travelling at speed. This is most likely to be a danger to

Mark four answers
- [ ] **A.** low-loaders
- [ ] **B.** cyclists
- [ ] **C.** pedestrians
- [ ] **D.** motorcyclists
- [ ] **E.** tankers
- [ ] **F.** caravans

490 PCV/LGV
You are overtaking a motorcycle in windy conditions. Why should you always check your nearside mirror?

Mark one answer
- [ ] **A.** To check your road position
- [ ] **B.** To see if the rider is still in control of the motorcycle
- [ ] **C.** To see if other vehicles have been affected
- [ ] **D.** To check if it is properly adjusted

491 PCV/LGV
Which THREE of the following are most likely to be affected by high winds?

Mark three answers
- [ ] **A.** Slow-moving vehicles
- [ ] **B.** Cyclists
- [ ] **C.** Vehicles towing caravans
- [ ] **D.** Curtain-sided vehicles
- [ ] **E.** Track-laying vehicles
- [ ] **F.** Front-wheel drive vehicles

492 PCV/LGV
You are driving a high-sided vehicle on a motorway. You should be especially aware of the effects of crosswinds on your vehicle when

Mark one answer
- [ ] **A.** travelling in cuttings
- [ ] **B.** travelling through tunnels
- [ ] **C.** driving across viaducts
- [ ] **D.** passing motorway signs

493 PCV/LGV
On a motorway the surface is still wet after rain. You should take extra care when overtaking because

Mark one answer
- [ ] **A.** wet roads may create more buffeting
- [ ] **B.** other vehicles will have their lights on
- [ ] **C.** vehicles may be parked on the hard shoulder
- [ ] **D.** the road may still be slippery

494 PCV/LGV
The road is wet. Why might a motorcyclist steer around drain covers on a bend?

Mark one answer

A. To prevent the motorcycle skidding
B. To avoid puncturing the tyres
C. To help steer around the bend
D. To avoid splashing pedestrians

495 PCV/LGV
In heavy rain what is the least amount of space you should allow for braking?

Mark one answer

A. The normal distance
B. Twice the normal distance
C. Three times the normal distance
D. Five times the normal distance

496 PCV/LGV
You are driving on a motorway. Your view ahead is poor due to heavy spray. Which THREE of the following should you do?

Mark three answers

A. Move into the lane on the right
B. Use the four-second rule
C. Switch on your dipped headlights
D. Switch on your full-beam headlights
E. Reduce your speed

497 PCV/LGV
When overtaking on motorways in very wet weather, what is the main danger that can affect your vehicle?

Mark one answer

A. Your engine may get flooded
B. Your braking distance may be reduced
C. Your steering may become heavy
D. Your tyres may lose grip

498 PCV/LGV
Overtaking on a motorway in heavy rain needs extra care because of

Mark one answer

A. slippery manhole covers
B. spray from traffic
C. reduced braking distances
D. bright reflections

499 PCV/LGV
Visibility can be worse when driving at higher speeds in wet weather because

Mark one answer

A. drivers always bunch together
B. headlights will dazzle you more easily
C. of people driving at different speeds
D. more spray is thrown up

500 PCV/LGV
You intend to overtake a large vehicle that is throwing up spray. You should

Mark one answer

A. get much closer before moving out
B. wait until the other driver gives a left signal
C. move out earlier than normal
D. wait for the other vehicle to slow down on a hill

501 PCV/LGV

Your vehicle is fitted with spray suppression equipment. What effect will this have on other drivers if it is NOT in good working order?

Mark one answer

- [ ] **A.** Their vision will be increased
- [ ] **B.** Their vision will be reduced
- [ ] **C.** They will be able to overtake quickly
- [ ] **D.** They will be able to follow closely

502 PCV/LGV

The purpose of the brushes fitted to this vehicle is to

Mark one answer

- [ ] **A.** clear mud from the tyres on building sites
- [ ] **B.** remove objects from the tyre tread
- [ ] **C.** stop snow building up behind the wheel
- [ ] **D.** reduce spray and increase visibility

503 PCV/LGV

You should check your vehicle's spray suppression equipment

Mark one answer

- [ ] **A.** only when you will be using a motorway
- [ ] **B.** before setting out on a journey
- [ ] **C.** only at the start of winter as a pre-winter check
- [ ] **D.** yearly before the MOT test

504 PCV/LGV

In wet weather, following drivers will be able to see better if your vehicle is fitted with

Mark one answer

- [ ] **A.** spray reducers
- [ ] **B.** side-panel skirts
- [ ] **C.** wind deflectors
- [ ] **D.** a catalytic converter

505 PCV/LGV

This vehicle is fitted with spray suppression equipment. This will be most useful when it is

Mark one answer

- [ ] **A.** raining
- [ ] **B.** snowing
- [ ] **C.** windy
- [ ] **D.** foggy

506 PCV/LGV

When driving through deep water you should drive

Mark one answer

- [ ] **A.** slowly in a low gear with engine speed high
- [ ] **B.** slowly in a high gear with engine speed low
- [ ] **C.** as quickly as possible to cause less delay
- [ ] **D.** at normal speed if you have spray reducers fitted

507 PCV/LGV
You are approaching a working snow plough on a motorway. You should not overtake because

Mark one answer

- A. it is illegal to overtake snow ploughs
- B. snow ploughs are left-hand drive only
- C. your speed could cause snow to drift behind
- D. there may be deep snow ahead

508 PCV/LGV
You are driving in heavy rain. Why is there a need to increase your distance from the vehicle in front?

Mark three answers

- A. To prevent rain entering the vehicle's braking system
- B. The tyres will have less grip on the road surface
- C. Spray from traffic will make it difficult to see ahead
- D. To reduce the risk of water spraying into filters
- E. Normal stopping distances could be doubled

509 PCV/LGV
You are driving a large vehicle on a motorway. Why should you slow down when the roads are very wet?

Mark one answer

- A. To force other drivers to act properly and slow down
- B. To reduce the amount of spray thrown up
- C. To prevent water entering the braking system
- D. To stop the electrics getting wet

510 PCV/LGV
You are driving on a motorway in heavy rain. When would you be allowed to use high-intensity rear fog lights?

Mark one answer

- A. When visibility is more than 100 metres (328 feet)
- B. Only when the national speed limit applies
- C. Only when you are being followed closely by other traffic
- D. When visibility is reduced to 100 metres (328 feet) or less

511 PCV/LGV
You are driving on a motorway in heavy rain. What could cause your steering to be less responsive?

Mark one answer

- A. Water reducing the tyre grip on the road
- B. Tyres becoming hotter in the bad weather
- C. Braking gently and in good time
- D. Water entering the braking system

512 PCV/LGV
What causes extra danger when overtaking in rain?

Mark one answer

- A. Other vehicles driving slowly
- B. Vehicles wandering across lanes
- C. Increase in vehicle noise
- D. Spray from large vehicles

513 PCV/LGV
A vehicle travelling downhill will

Mark three answers

- [ ] **A.** need more engine power
- [ ] **B.** need more braking effort
- [ ] **C.** take longer to stop
- [ ] **D.** need a shorter stopping distance
- [ ] **E.** require less braking effort
- [ ] **F.** increase speed quickly

514 PCV/LGV
The road is wet. Why should you slow down as you approach this pedestrian?

Mark one answer

- [ ] **A.** Because there are no road markings
- [ ] **B.** To avoid splashing them
- [ ] **C.** Because they have priority
- [ ] **D.** To encourage them to cross

515 PCV/LGV
Tailgating another vehicle is dangerous because

Mark two answers

- [ ] **A.** your job could be at risk
- [ ] **B.** your braking time is increased
- [ ] **C.** your view to the rear is reduced
- [ ] **D.** your view ahead is reduced
- [ ] **E.** your room for braking is reduced

516 PCV/LGV
Hazard warning lights may be used while moving when

Mark one answer

- [ ] **A.** you have just overtaken another vehicle
- [ ] **B.** you need to reverse for some distance
- [ ] **C.** traffic ahead is slowing quickly on a motorway
- [ ] **D.** one of your lights has failed

517 PCV/LGV
You are driving in town and see these lights flashing. What would you expect to see ahead?

Mark one answer

- [ ] **A.** Contraflow system
- [ ] **B.** Uneven road surface
- [ ] **C.** Children crossing the road
- [ ] **D.** Roadworks ahead

518 PCV/LGV
Where are these lights found?

Mark one answer

☐ A. On approach to a level crossing
☐ B. Near a fire station
☐ C. On approach to a motorway
☐ D. Near a school

519 PCV/LGV
You are allowed to use hazard warning lights while moving when

Mark one answer

☐ A. towing another vehicle
☐ B. an overtaking lorry has cleared the front of your vehicle
☐ C. being towed by another vehicle
☐ D. traffic ahead on a motorway is slowing down quickly

520 PCV/LGV
What extra problems may you have when driving at night?

Mark three answers

☐ A. Increased overtaking distances
☐ B. An increase in traffic
☐ C. Reduced visibility
☐ D. Reduced braking distances
☐ E. Dazzle from other vehicles
☐ F. Becoming tired

521 PCV/LGV
You should take extra care when overtaking at night because

Mark one answer

☐ A. every driver will normally be tired
☐ B. large vehicles are subject to a 10% speed reduction
☐ C. speed and distance are harder to judge
☐ D. most towns are not adequately lit

522 PCV/LGV
You are driving along a motorway in thick fog at night. The reflective studs are red on your left and white on your right. You are driving

Mark one answer

☐ A. in the right-hand lane
☐ B. on the hard shoulder
☐ C. in the left-hand lane
☐ D. in the middle lane

523 PCV/LGV
You are driving on a three-lane motorway. You are about to move into the middle lane to overtake a slower vehicle. You should check

Mark one answer

☐ A. for traffic in the right-hand lane returning to the middle lane
☐ B. for traffic which is intending to leave at the next exit
☐ C. the nearside mirror before pulling out
☐ D. for any traffic behind that is trying to pass you on the left

524 PCV/LGV
Before overtaking or changing lanes on a motorway you should always

Mark one answer

- A. check your mirrors carefully
- B. change to a lower gear
- C. look over your left shoulder
- D. increase your speed gently

525 PCV/LGV
You are driving at the maximum speed limit for your vehicle on a clear motorway. You should keep to

Mark one answer

- A. any one of the lanes
- B. the middle lane
- C. the right-hand lane
- D. the left-hand lane

526 PCV/LGV
You are driving in the left-hand lane of a motorway. You see another large vehicle merging from a slip road. It is travelling at the same speed as you. You should

Mark one answer

- A. try to race and get ahead of it
- B. leave the other vehicle to adjust its speed
- C. stay at the maximum speed allowed for your vehicle
- D. be ready to adjust your speed

527 PCV/LGV
When driving in the left-hand lane of a motorway you see merging vehicles travelling at the same speed as you. You should

Mark two answers

- A. try and accelerate past them
- B. move to the next lane if safe
- C. allow the traffic to merge by adjusting your speed
- D. expect the traffic to let you pass

528 PCV/LGV
You should take extra care before moving into the centre lane of a three-lane motorway because

Mark three answers

- A. the centre lane is narrower
- B. another vehicle might be planning to use the same lane
- C. other drivers need time to react
- D. car drivers might not know they must give way to large vehicles
- E. the bridge height clearance will be less in that lane
- F. traffic from behind may be travelling much faster than you

529 PCV/LGV

Normally, vehicles over 7.5 tonnes maximum authorised mass may use the right-hand lane of a motorway only when

Mark one answer

- A. it is a three-lane motorway
- B. there are vehicles on the hard shoulder
- C. it is a two-lane motorway
- D. other vehicles are turning right

530 PCV/LGV

You have just overtaken another vehicle on a motorway. When moving back to the left you should avoid

Mark one answer

- A. cutting in
- B. increasing your speed
- C. changing gear
- D. signalling

531 PCV/LGV

What is a crawler lane for?

Mark one answer

- A. To enable other traffic to overtake on the nearside
- B. To enable large vehicles to pull over and park out of the way
- C. To enable slow-moving traffic to move further over to the left on uphill gradients
- D. To enable emergency vehicles to get to the scene of an accident quicker

532 PCV/LGV

You see this sign on a motorway. It means you are coming to a

Mark one answer

- A. long downhill slope
- B. long uphill slope
- C. 'lorries only' lane
- D. service area

533 PCV/LGV

You should use a crawler lane

Mark one answer

- A. to let faster traffic overtake you
- B. when turning right from major roads
- C. for parking when having a break
- D. when slowing down for a motorway exit

534 PCV/LGV

Before overtaking you should

Mark one answer

- A. flash your headlights to oncoming traffic
- B. look ahead for right-turn lane markings
- C. drive very close to the vehicle in front
- D. make a final check in your left mirror

535 PCV/LGV
You should not overtake when

Mark three answers
- [ ] A. there are signs and road markings that allow you to
- [ ] B. you are unable to see clearly ahead
- [ ] C. you would have to break the speed limit
- [ ] D. your view of the road ahead is clear
- [ ] E. approaching motorway exits or slip roads
- [ ] F. other road users would have to slow down

536 PCV/LGV
After overtaking another large vehicle how would you know when it was safe to move back to the nearside lane?

Mark one answer
- [ ] A. By waiting for the driver you have just overtaken to flash the headlights
- [ ] B. By checking your nearside mirror
- [ ] C. By using your hazard warning lights as a signal
- [ ] D. By moving over to the nearside in the hope that the other vehicle will slow down

537 PCV/LGV
You are driving on a dual carriageway and intend to overtake the vehicle ahead. Behind there is a car approaching quickly in the right-hand lane. You should

Mark one answer
- [ ] A. keep behind the slower vehicle
- [ ] B. signal and move out
- [ ] C. move up closer to the slower vehicle
- [ ] D. stay on the left, large vehicles cannot use the right-hand lane

538 PCV/LGV
What should you do after overtaking on a dual carriageway?

Mark one answer
- [ ] A. Move back to the left as soon as possible
- [ ] B. Indicate left then right
- [ ] C. Wait until the other driver flashes their headlights
- [ ] D. Switch your rear lights on and off

539 PCV/LGV
You are turning right at a roundabout driving a long vehicle. You need to occupy the left-hand lane. You should check mirrors and

Mark one answer
- [ ] A. signal left on approach
- [ ] B. signal right on approach
- [ ] C. avoid giving a signal on approach
- [ ] D. signal right after entering the roundabout

540 PCV/LGV
Long vehicles need to straddle lanes

Mark one answer
- [ ] A. to avoid braking sharply
- [ ] B. when driving on motorways
- [ ] C. to avoid mounting the kerb
- [ ] D. when coming to contraflow systems

541 PCV/LGV
When approaching these roadworks, you should NOT

Mark two answers

- A. start to overtake
- B. increase speed
- C. flash your headlights
- D. give any signals

542 PCV/LGV
It is very windy. You are about to overtake a motorcyclist. You should

Mark one answer

- A. allow extra room
- B. overtake slowly
- C. sound your horn as you pass
- D. keep close as you pass

543 PCV/LGV
You are driving behind two cyclists. They are approaching a roundabout in the left-hand lane. What should you expect them to do?

Mark one answer

- A. Go in any direction
- B. Turn left
- C. Turn right
- D. Go straight ahead

544 PCV/LGV
You should never attempt to overtake a cyclist

Mark one answer

- A. on a roundabout
- B. before you turn left
- C. before you turn right
- D. on a one-way street

545 PCV/LGV
You are about to overtake a lorry. You should

Mark one answer

- A. look well ahead for uphill gradients
- B. check your position in the left mirror
- C. quickly change to a higher gear
- D. close right up before pulling out

546 PCV/LGV
You are in the left-hand lane on a three-lane motorway. Before you overtake you should check for any vehicles in the right-hand lane that might be about to

Mark one answer

- A. move to the right
- B. move back to the left
- C. cut in sharply behind you
- D. accelerate briskly in front of you

547
PCV/LGV
Normally white lights on a vehicle at night show you that the vehicle is

Mark three answers
- [ ] A. moving away from you
- [ ] B. moving towards you
- [ ] C. ahead of you and braking
- [ ] D. stationary facing you
- [ ] E. stationary and facing away from you
- [ ] F. reversing towards you

548
PCV/LGV
When driving at night you should make sure all your lights are clean and working correctly. Why is this?

Mark three answers
- [ ] A. To enable you to see ahead properly
- [ ] B. To prevent the battery from overcharging
- [ ] C. So that other road users can see the size of your vehicle
- [ ] D. So that the intensity of street lighting can be reduced
- [ ] E. To allow following drivers to use dipped headlights
- [ ] F. So that other road users are aware of your direction of travel

549
PCV/LGV
High-intensity rear fog lights should be used when visibility is less than

Mark one answer
- [ ] A. 100 metres (328 feet)
- [ ] B. 200 metres (656 feet)
- [ ] C. 300 metres (984 feet)
- [ ] D. 400 metres (1312 feet)

550
PCV/LGV
You should switch off fog lights when visibility is more than

Mark one answer
- [ ] A. 10 metres (32 feet)
- [ ] B. your stopping distance
- [ ] C. your separation distance
- [ ] D. 100 metres (328 feet)

551
PCV/LGV
You should switch off rear fog lights when visibility is more than

Mark one answer
- [ ] A. 10 metres (32 feet)
- [ ] B. 50 metres (164 feet)
- [ ] C. 75 metres (246 feet)
- [ ] D. 100 metres (328 feet)

552
PCV/LGV
In fast traffic a two-second gap from the vehicle in front may be enough only when conditions are

Mark one answer
- [ ] A. dry
- [ ] B. wet
- [ ] C. damp
- [ ] D. foggy

553
PCV/LGV
When driving in traffic on a motorway you see a lorry too close behind. You should

Mark one answer
- [ ] A. increase your distance from the vehicle in front
- [ ] B. touch the brake pedal sharply to show your brake lights
- [ ] C. briskly accelerate away from the vehicle behind
- [ ] D. switch your rear fog lamps on and off

554 PCV/LGV
Another vehicle has overtaken you and has pulled in too close in front. You should

Mark one answer

A. slow down

B. drive on close behind

C. overtake the vehicle

D. flash your headlights

555 PCV/LGV
At 50mph (80kph) what gap should you leave behind the vehicle in front on a dry, level road?

Mark one answer

A. One vehicle length

B. Two vehicle lengths

C. A minimum one-second gap

D. A minimum two-second gap

556 PCV/LGV
You are behind a large vehicle. How can you improve your view ahead?

Mark one answer

A. Stay further back

B. Move over to the right

C. Move over to the left

D. Overtake as soon as you can

557 PCV/LGV
You should overtake at night only when

Mark two answers

A. you can see well ahead

B. you can do so without cutting in

C. there is an overtaking lane

D. you are outside built-up areas

E. the road is well lit

558 PCV/LGV
When driving in snow, stopping distances may be increased by up to how many times, compared with a dry road?

Mark one answer

A. Two

B. Four

C. Five

D. Ten

559 PCV/LGV
When required to slow down or stop on an icy road you should make sure that

Mark one answer

A. braking is gentle and in good time

B. retarders are always used

C. downward gear changes are made

D. the parking brake is used in a rapid on-and-off movement

560 PCV/LGV
You are driving a vehicle in icy weather. All braking must be done

Mark two answers

A. suddenly

B. by 'pumping' the brakes

C. gently

D. by using the gears first

E. over longer distances

561 PCV/LGV
You should use the 'two-second rule'

Mark one answer

- [ ] A. before restarting the engine after it has stalled
- [ ] B. to keep a safe distance from the vehicle in front
- [ ] C. before using the 'Mirror–Signal–Manoeuvre' routine
- [ ] D. when emerging on wet roads

562 PCV/LGV
Following a large goods vehicle too closely is dangerous because

Mark one answer

- [ ] A. your field of vision is seriously reduced
- [ ] B. slipstreaming will reduce wind effect
- [ ] C. your engine will overheat
- [ ] D. your brakes need a constant cooling effect

563 PCV/LGV
You are following a vehicle on a wet road. You should leave a time gap of at least

Mark one answer

- [ ] A. one second
- [ ] B. two seconds
- [ ] C. three seconds
- [ ] D. four seconds

564 PCV/LGV
The entrances to roundabouts are often slippery when wet. You should always

Mark one answer

- [ ] A. keep in the left-hand lane
- [ ] B. brake in good time
- [ ] C. use the handbrake
- [ ] D. stop before emerging

565 PCV/LGV
You become stuck in snow. What might help you to move off?

Mark one answer

- [ ] A. Trolley jack
- [ ] B. Can of de-icer
- [ ] C. Wheel brace
- [ ] D. Shovel

566 PCV/LGV
What might help you to move off when you are stuck in snow?

Mark one answer

- [ ] A. Trolley jack
- [ ] B. Cloth sacks
- [ ] C. Wheel brace
- [ ] D. Can of de-icer

567 PCV/LGV
Before braking in wet conditions you should make sure, as far as possible, that

Mark one answer

- [ ] A. the gear lever is in neutral
- [ ] B. all spray suppression equipment is working
- [ ] C. there is no mist on your rear-view mirrors
- [ ] D. your vehicle is travelling in a straight line

568 PCV/LGV
You are driving a fully laden vehicle. You are approaching an uphill gradient as you are overtaking another vehicle. Which of the following is NOT correct?

Mark one answer

- [ ] A. You will be able to get past quicker
- [ ] B. The extra weight will make you slower
- [ ] C. It will take you longer to get past
- [ ] D. You will need more power from the engine

569 PCV/LGV
You are driving at night in a built-up area. To ensure that you can be seen you should use

Mark one answer

- [ ] **A.** dipped beam headlights
- [ ] **B.** main beam headlights
- [ ] **C.** sidelights only
- [ ] **D.** front fog lights only

570 PCV/LGV
You are on a motorway and there is a strong crosswind. Which of these vehicles is particularly at risk?

Mark one answer

- [ ] **A.** A motorcycle
- [ ] **B.** A taxi
- [ ] **C.** A sports car
- [ ] **D.** A road tanker

571 PCV/LGV
You are driving at a speed of 50mph (80kph) in good, dry conditions. What distance should you stay behind the vehicle in front?

Mark one answer

- [ ] **A.** At least 20 metres (66 feet)
- [ ] **B.** At least 30 metres (98 feet)
- [ ] **C.** At least 40 metres (131 feet)
- [ ] **D.** At least 50 metres (164 feet)

572 PCV/LGV
You are on a motorway just after heavy rain. Spray is being thrown up causing poor visibility. What should you do?

Mark one answer

- [ ] **A.** Keep a two-second gap
- [ ] **B.** Use sidelights only
- [ ] **C.** Remove spray suppression equipment
- [ ] **D.** Leave a greater separation distance

573 PCV/LGV
Spray is causing poor visibility on the motorway. What should you do?

Mark one answer

- [ ] **A.** Use a two-second gap
- [ ] **B.** Use sidelights only
- [ ] **C.** Slow to a safe speed
- [ ] **D.** Remove spray suppression equipment

574 PCV/LGV
You are driving in snow. Care should be taken when using the endurance brake (retarder) because it may cause

Mark one answer

- [ ] **A.** additional brake wear
- [ ] **B.** an increase in speed
- [ ] **C.** the drive-wheels to lock
- [ ] **D.** compressed air to escape

575 LGV
You overtake a cyclist on a two-way road. What should you do?

Mark one answer

- [ ] A. Pass closely staying about 1 metre (3 feet 3 inches) from the kerb
- [ ] B. Go past quickly and move back to the left sharply
- [ ] C. Leave plenty of room and check your nearside mirror before returning
- [ ] D. Use a right-turn signal after pulling out

576 LGV
Your lorry has a curtain-side body. Your route will take you over several high-level bridges. Why is it particularly important to check the weather forecast?

Mark one answer

- [ ] A. Rain can make crossing bridges very difficult for large vehicles
- [ ] B. In hot weather the bridges might be closed to heavy traffic
- [ ] C. You won't be able to climb the bridges if it's frosty
- [ ] D. Some routes may be closed to certain vehicles in high winds

577 LGV
You want to join a motorway. Traffic is flowing freely on the motorway. What should you do?

Mark one answer

- [ ] A. Keep to a low speed until you see a gap on the motorway
- [ ] B. Build up your speed on the slip road before joining the motorway
- [ ] C. Stop at the start of the slip road and move off when there is a gap
- [ ] D. Use the hard shoulder if necessary, to build up speed

578 LGV
Before driving your lorry in high winds, you should always

Mark one answer

- [ ] A. check your wind deflector
- [ ] B. check your spray suppression equipment
- [ ] C. plan your journey well in advance
- [ ] D. only half load your lorry

579 LGV
You are overtaking another lorry. Due to an uphill gradient you start to lose speed. You should

Mark one answer

- [ ] A. continue at the same speed and position
- [ ] B. try to force the vehicle you were overtaking to drop back
- [ ] C. try to force the vehicle you were overtaking to speed up
- [ ] D. ease off and drop behind the vehicle you were trying to overtake

580 LGV

When driving an empty curtain-sided vehicle, how could you reduce crosswind problems on exposed bridges?

Mark one answer

- [ ] A. Tie just one curtain side back and lock open the rear doors
- [ ] B. Leave both curtain sides closed
- [ ] C. Tie both curtain sides at one end of the vehicle
- [ ] D. Tie the curtain sides halfway back

581 LGV

A high-sided vehicle will be MOST affected by crosswinds when it is

Mark one answer

- [ ] A. stationary
- [ ] B. travelling loaded
- [ ] C. reversing
- [ ] D. travelling empty

582 LGV

You are driving an empty curtain-sided vehicle. Why might you consider tying the curtains open?

Mark one answer

- [ ] A. To use less fuel
- [ ] B. It is a legal requirement
- [ ] C. To prevent the curtains tearing
- [ ] D. To reduce the effect of crosswinds

583 LGV

A box van will be MOST affected by crosswinds when it is

Mark one answer

- [ ] A. travelling empty
- [ ] B. stationary
- [ ] C. travelling loaded
- [ ] D. reversing

584 LGV

In high winds, drivers of lorries approaching high bridges or viaducts should expect

Mark three answers

- [ ] A. lower speed limits
- [ ] B. minimum speed limits
- [ ] C. no restrictions for loaded vehicles
- [ ] D. lane closures
- [ ] E. no restrictions for lorries
- [ ] F. diversions

585 LGV

Which of these vehicles is MOST at risk from high crosswinds?

Mark one answer

- [ ] A. A laden lorry with box body
- [ ] B. An unladen lorry with box body
- [ ] C. An unladen lorry with platform body
- [ ] D. A laden lorry with platform body

586 LGV

Which vehicle is most at risk when being driven in strong crosswinds?

Mark one answer

- [ ] A. A box van carrying light goods
- [ ] B. An unladen lorry with platform body
- [ ] C. A container vehicle with a heavy load
- [ ] D. A low-loader carrying heavy machinery

587 LGV
In strong winds an overtaking lorry can affect other road users. Which vehicle is most at risk?

Mark one answer
- [ ] **A.** A car
- [ ] **B.** A furniture van
- [ ] **C.** A motorcycle
- [ ] **D.** A coach

588 LGV
Which TWO types of vehicle are most at risk in windy conditions?

Mark two answers
- [ ] **A.** High-sided lorries
- [ ] **B.** Saloon cars
- [ ] **C.** Unladen vans
- [ ] **D.** Single-deck buses
- [ ] **E.** Tractor units

589 LGV
When are air deflectors most effective?

Mark one answer
- [ ] **A.** When there is a crosswind
- [ ] **B.** When there is a headwind
- [ ] **C.** When reversing
- [ ] **D.** When there is a strong tailwind

590 LGV
You are driving your lorry on the motorway. Visibility is reduced by heavy rain and spray. You should

Mark two answers
- [ ] **A.** maintain a constant speed
- [ ] **B.** use main beam headlights
- [ ] **C.** double your dry weather separation distance
- [ ] **D.** stay in the left-hand lane
- [ ] **E.** obey advisory speed limit signs

591 LGV
Before driving your lorry from a wet construction site at the side of a motorway, you should

Mark one answer
- [ ] **A.** inform the local council
- [ ] **B.** hose down the road
- [ ] **C.** hose down the wheels
- [ ] **D.** inform the lorry operator

592 LGV
You are driving a lorry from a wet construction site onto a motorway. You must take extra precautions before driving because

Mark one answer
- [ ] **A.** your lorry will be unladen and liable to 'bounce'
- [ ] **B.** it is an offence to emerge from a works site straight onto a motorway
- [ ] **C.** your lorry's spray suppression equipment will be inoperative
- [ ] **D.** it is an offence to deposit mud on a road

593 LGV
Before raising the body of a tipper lorry you should make sure the ground is

Mark one answer
A. soft and level
B. soft and downhill
C. solid and uphill
D. solid and level

594 LGV
You are driving a lorry weighing more than 7.5 tonnes maximum authorised mass. You may only use the right-hand lane to overtake on a motorway with

Mark one answer
A. two lanes
B. three lanes
C. a 50mph speed limit
D. a 40mph speed limit

595 LGV
You are driving on a motorway. You look in your mirrors and see smoke coming from your rear tyres. What should you do?

Mark one answer
A. Reduce speed for the rest of your journey
B. Drive on the hard shoulder until the smoke stops
C. Stop as soon as it's safe to do so
D. Ignore it, this is normal when driving at speed

596 LGV
You are on a wet level road. At 50mph what gap should you leave from the vehicle in front?

Mark one answer
A. One second minimum
B. Two seconds minimum
C. Three seconds minimum
D. Four seconds minimum

597 LGV
You are driving an articulated lorry on a three-lane motorway. When can you drive in the right-hand lane?

Mark one answer
A. When overtaking a slow-moving car in the middle lane
B. When the escort vehicle of an oversized load signals you to pass
C. If no speed limiter is fitted to your lorry
D. If your lorry is unladen

598 LGV
You are driving on a motorway after heavy rain. Visibility is low because of spray being thrown up by other lorries. You should

Mark one answer
A. use dipped headlights
B. use sidelights only
C. remove spray suppression equipment
D. use the two-second rule

599 PCV
You are driving a coach carrying elderly people. You arrive at the scene of an accident. The emergency services have already arrived. You should

Mark one answer
- A. ask your passengers to find out what is happening
- B. not tell passengers anything in case you upset them
- C. leave the passengers on the bus and see what is happening yourself
- D. tell the passengers what is happening without upsetting them

600 PCV
Your bus and other vehicles have been involved in an accident. You should

Mark one answer
- A. switch off their headlights
- B. switch off the fuel supply
- C. turn vehicles the right way up
- D. always pull casualties out of their vehicles

601 PCV
Your bus has hit a parked vehicle. The owner cannot be found. You must report the accident

NI

Mark one answer
- A. to the police within seven days
- B. to the owner as soon as possible
- C. to the owner within seven days
- D. to the police within 24 hours

602 PCV
You are treating a passenger who is in shock. You should

Mark one answer
- A. give them liquids
- B. keep them moving
- C. encourage them to sleep
- D. keep them warm

603 PCV
A passenger on your bus has stopped breathing. You help them by giving mouth to mouth resuscitation. When should you stop doing this?

Mark one answer
- A. When they can breathe on their own
- B. When you think the passenger has died
- C. When their skin colour has turned blue
- D. When you think the ambulance is coming

604 PCV
Your bus is involved in an accident. You have a passenger who is unconscious but still breathing. What should you do?

Mark one answer
- A. Get medical help
- B. Check their pulse
- C. Give them liquid
- D. Lie them on their back

605 PCV
Your bus is stopped at the scene of an accident. Why should you consider moving your passengers to the front of the bus?

Mark one answer
- A. To improve weight distribution
- B. To reduce the risk of injury from behind
- C. To be nearer emergency exits
- D. To be witnesses of the accident

606 **PCV**
Your bus hits a low railway bridge. Nobody is injured. You should report the accident

Mark one answer **NI**

- [ ] **A.** immediately to your employer
- [ ] **B.** within 24 hours to the railway authority
- [ ] **C.** within seven days to the police
- [ ] **D.** immediately to the railway authority

607 **PCV**
While going through a tunnel your coach catches fire. It cannot be driven any further. What should you do?

Mark one answer

- [ ] **A.** Move the passengers to the rear of the coach
- [ ] **B.** Get the passengers off, keeping them together
- [ ] **C.** Make sure the passengers stay in their seats
- [ ] **D.** Move the passengers to the front of the coach

608 **PCV**
You are driving a loaded school bus. Looking in your mirror you see smoke from the engine compartment at the rear. You must

Mark two answers

- [ ] **A.** stop as quickly and safely as possible
- [ ] **B.** open the engine covers to investigate
- [ ] **C.** drive to the bus station for a replacement vehicle
- [ ] **D.** get everyone off the bus quickly
- [ ] **E.** move the passengers to the front away from danger

609 **PCV**
You are driving in a tunnel. Your bus catches fire and you cannot drive out. After stopping, what should you do?

Mark one answer

- [ ] **A.** Move the passengers to the nearest tunnel exit
- [ ] **B.** Use the extinguisher to put out the fire
- [ ] **C.** Keep the passengers together in front of the vehicle
- [ ] **D.** Stand behind your vehicle and warn other drivers

610 **PCV/LGV**
In the UK the headroom under bridges, unless otherwise shown, is AT LEAST

Mark one answer

- [ ] **A.** 4.8 metres (16 feet)
- [ ] **B.** 5 metres (16 feet 6 inches)
- [ ] **C.** 6 metres (19 feet 8 inches)
- [ ] **D.** 8 metres (26 feet 3 inches)

611 **PCV/LGV**
You are approaching a bridge that has NO height restriction on it. The height of the bridge will be at least

Mark one answer

- [ ] **A.** 3.6 metres (11 feet 10 inches)
- [ ] **B.** 4.4 metres (14 feet 5 inches)
- [ ] **C.** 4.8 metres (16 feet)
- [ ] **D.** 5 metres (16 feet 6 inches)

612 **PCV/LGV**
A laminated windscreen is one which

Mark two answers

- [ ] **A.** will not shatter
- [ ] **B.** does not mist up
- [ ] **C.** has a plastic layer
- [ ] **D.** cuts down on glare

613 PCV/LGV

You are the first to arrive at the scene of an accident. Someone is unconscious. Which of the following should be given urgent priority to help them?

Mark three answers

- [ ] A. Try to get them to drink water
- [ ] B. Look for any witnesses
- [ ] C. Clear the airway and keep it open
- [ ] D. Check that they are breathing
- [ ] E. Stop any bleeding
- [ ] F. Take the numbers of any vehicles involved

614 PCV/LGV

What must you do if you are involved in an accident?

Mark one answer

- [ ] A. Drive on for help
- [ ] B. Inform the police within seven days
- [ ] C. Stop at the scene of the accident
- [ ] D. Drive to the nearest police station

615 PCV/LGV

Your vehicle has been involved in an accident where someone is injured. You do not produce the required insurance certificate at the time of the accident. You must report the accident to the police as soon as possible, or in any case within

Mark one answer

NI

- [ ] A. 24 hours
- [ ] B. 48 hours
- [ ] C. 72 hours
- [ ] D. seven days

616 PCV/LGV

At the scene of an accident you see a plain orange rectangle displayed on one of the vehicles. This tells you that the vehicle

Mark one answer

- [ ] A. is carrying dangerous goods
- [ ] B. is carrying a First Aid kit
- [ ] C. is carrying medical supplies
- [ ] D. is unladen

617 PCV/LGV

You arrive at an accident where someone is suffering from severe burns. Which of the following would help?

Mark one answer

- [ ] A. Douse the burns with cold water
- [ ] B. Remove anything stuck to the burns
- [ ] C. Burst blisters that form on the burns
- [ ] D. Apply ointment to the burns

618 PCV/LGV

You arrive at the scene of an accident. A pedestrian is bleeding heavily from a leg wound. What should you do?

Mark one answer

- [ ] A. Apply firm pressure to the wound
- [ ] B. Dab the wound to stop the bleeding
- [ ] C. Keep both legs flat on the ground
- [ ] D. Wrap an ice pack near the wound

619
PCV/LGV
An accident has just happened. An injured person is lying in the busy road. What is the first thing you should do to help?

Mark one answer
- A. Treat the person for shock
- B. Warn other traffic
- C. Place them in the recovery position
- D. Make sure the injured person is kept warm

620
PCV/LGV
You are the first person to arrive at an accident where people are badly injured. Which THREE should you do?

Mark three answers
- A. Switch on your own hazard warning lights
- B. Make sure that someone telephones for an ambulance
- C. Try and get people who are injured to drink something
- D. Move the people who are injured clear of their vehicles
- E. Get people who are not injured clear of the scene

621
PCV/LGV
You arrive at a serious motorcycle accident. The motorcyclist is unconscious and bleeding. Your main priorities should be to

Mark three answers
- A. try to stop the bleeding
- B. make a list of witnesses
- C. check the casualty's breathing
- D. take the numbers of the vehicles involved
- E. sweep up any loose debris
- F. check the casualty's airways

622
PCV/LGV
You arrive at an accident. A motorcyclist is unconscious. Your first priority is the casualty's

Mark one answer
- A. breathing
- B. bleeding
- C. broken bones
- D. bruising

623
PCV/LGV
You arrive at the scene of an accident. It has just happened, and someone is unconscious. Which of the following should be given urgent priority to help them?

Mark three answers
- A. Clear the airway and keep it open
- B. Try to get them to drink water
- C. Check that they are breathing
- D. Look for any witnesses
- E. Stop any heavy bleeding
- F. Take the numbers of vehicles involved

624
PCV/LGV
You have stopped at the scene of an accident to give help. Which THREE things should you do?

Mark three answers
- A. Keep injured people warm and comfortable
- B. Keep injured people calm by talking to them reassuringly
- C. Keep injured people on the move by walking them around
- D. Give injured people a warm drink
- E. Make sure that injured people are not left alone

625 PCV/LGV
You arrive at the scene of an accident. It has just happened and someone is injured. Which of the following should be given urgent priority?

Mark three answers
- A. Stop any severe bleeding
- B. Get them a warm drink
- C. Check that their breathing is OK
- D. Take numbers of vehicles involved
- E. Look for witnesses
- F. Clear their airway and keep it open

626 PCV/LGV
You are at the scene of an accident. Someone is suffering from shock. You should

Mark four answers
- A. reassure them constantly
- B. offer them a cigarette
- C. keep them warm
- D. avoid moving them if possible
- E. loosen any tight clothing
- F. give them a warm drink

627 PCV/LGV
Which of the following should you not do at the scene of an accident?

Mark one answer
- A. Warn other traffic by switching on your hazard warning lights
- B. Call the emergency services immediately
- C. Offer someone a cigarette to calm them down
- D. Ask drivers to switch off their engines

628 PCV/LGV
When treating someone for shock you should

Mark two answers
- A. reassure them
- B. loosen tight clothes
- C. walk them around
- D. give them a hot drink
- E. offer them an alcoholic drink

629 PCV/LGV
There has been an accident. The driver is suffering from shock. You should

Mark two answers
- A. give them a drink
- B. reassure them
- C. not leave them alone
- D. offer them a cigarette
- E. ask who caused the accident

630 PCV/LGV
You have to treat someone for shock at the scene of an accident. You should

Mark one answer
- A. reassure them constantly
- B. walk them around to calm them down
- C. give them something cold to drink
- D. cool them down as soon as possible

631 PCV/LGV
You arrive at the scene of a motorcycle accident. No other vehicle is involved. The rider is unconscious, lying in the middle of the road. The first thing you should do is

Mark one answer
- A. move the rider out of the road
- B. warn other traffic
- C. clear the road of debris
- D. give the rider reassurance

632 PCV/LGV
You are giving mouth to mouth to a casualty. They are still not breathing on their own. You should

Mark one answer
- A. give up if you think they are dead
- B. only keep trying for up to two minutes
- C. carry on until an ambulance arrives
- D. only keep trying for up to four minutes

633 PCV/LGV
When you are giving mouth to mouth you should only stop when

Mark one answer
- A. you think the casualty is dead
- B. the casualty can breathe without help
- C. the casualty has turned blue
- D. you think the ambulance is coming

634 PCV/LGV
You arrive at an accident where someone is suffering from severe burns. You should

Mark one answer
- A. apply lotions to the injury
- B. burst any blisters
- C. remove anything stuck to the burns
- D. douse the burns with cool liquid

635 PCV/LGV
You arrive at the scene of an accident. A pedestrian has a severe bleeding wound on their leg, although it is not broken. What should you do?

Mark two answers
- A. Dab the wound to stop bleeding
- B. Keep both legs flat on the ground
- C. Apply firm pressure to the wound
- D. Raise the leg to lessen bleeding
- E. Fetch them a warm drink

636 PCV/LGV
You arrive at the scene of an accident. A passenger is bleeding badly from an arm wound. What should you do?

Mark one answer
- A. Apply pressure over the wound and keep the arm down
- B. Dab the wound
- C. Get them a drink
- D. Apply pressure over the wound and raise the arm

637 PCV/LGV
You arrive at the scene of an accident. A pedestrian is bleeding heavily from a leg wound, but the leg is not broken. What should you do?

Mark one answer
- A. Dab the wound to stop the bleeding
- B. Keep both legs flat on the ground
- C. Apply firm pressure to the wound
- D. Fetch them a warm drink

638 PCV/LGV
At an accident a casualty is unconscious but still breathing. You should only move them if

Mark one answer

- [ ] A. an ambulance is on its way
- [ ] B. bystanders advise you to
- [ ] C. there is further danger
- [ ] D. bystanders will help you to

639 PCV/LGV
At an accident you suspect a casualty has back injuries. The area is safe. You should

Mark one answer

- [ ] A. offer them a drink
- [ ] B. not move them
- [ ] C. raise their legs
- [ ] D. offer them a cigarette

640 PCV/LGV
At an accident it is important to look after the casualty. When the area is safe, you should

Mark one answer

- [ ] A. get them out of the vehicle
- [ ] B. give them a drink
- [ ] C. give them something to eat
- [ ] D. keep them in the vehicle

641 PCV/LGV
You are stopped by a police officer. Which of the following documents are the police most likely to ask you to produce?

Mark three answers

- [ ] A. Insurance certificate
- [ ] B. Vehicle registration document
- [ ] C. Road fund licence
- [ ] D. Theory test certificate
- [ ] E. Driving licence
- [ ] F. Test certificate (MOT)

642 PCV/LGV
At the scene of an accident a person has become hysterical. You should calm them by

Mark one answer

- [ ] A. leaving them to quietly recover
- [ ] B. shouting at them loudly
- [ ] C. giving them a hot drink
- [ ] D. talking quietly and firmly to them

643 PCV/LGV
You are at an accident. Why may it be unwise to move a casualty?

Mark one answer

- [ ] A. You could damage your back
- [ ] B. You could get blood on your hands
- [ ] C. You could be accused of an assault
- [ ] D. You could cause more injury

644 PCV/LGV

There has been an accident. The driver is in contact with live electrical cables. Do not touch the driver unless you can use

Mark one answer

- A. a metal pole
- B. your bare hands
- C. a damp piece of cloth
- D. a length of wood

645 PCV/LGV

You are at the scene of an accident and someone's arm is bleeding heavily. How could you help stop the bleeding?

Mark two answers

- A. Raise the arm
- B. Lower the arm
- C. Place firm pressure on the wound
- D. Keep the wound free from pressure

646 PCV/LGV

When using an emergency telephone on a motorway where should you stand?

Mark one answer

- A. In front of the barrier
- B. Facing the oncoming traffic
- C. With your back to the traffic
- D. Looking towards the grass verge

647 PCV/LGV

Which type of fire extinguisher should NOT be used on flammable liquids?

Mark one answer

- A. Water (red)
- B. Foam (cream)
- C. Dry powder (blue)
- D. Carbon Dioxide (black)

648 PCV/LGV

You have a breakdown on a motorway. You cannot get fully onto the hard shoulder. What should you do?

Mark one answer

- A. Stand at the edge of the carriageway to warn others
- B. Place a warning triangle in the lane behind your vehicle
- C. Wear a bright jacket and stand in the lane behind your vehicle
- D. Go straight to the nearest emergency telephone

649 PCV/LGV

Your engine catches fire. Before attempting to put the fire out you should

Mark one answer

- A. shut off the fuel supply
- B. open the engine housing wide
- C. drive to the nearest fire station
- D. empty the air tanks

650 PCV/LGV
Before driving through a tunnel what should you do?

Mark one answer

- A. Switch your radio off
- B. Remove your sunglasses
- C. Close your sunroof
- D. Switch on windscreen wipers

651 PCV/LGV
You are driving through a tunnel and the traffic is flowing freely. What should you do?

Mark one answer

- A. Use parking lights
- B. Use front spot lights
- C. Use dipped headlights
- D. Use rear fog lights

652 PCV/LGV
Before entering a tunnel it is good advice to

Mark one answer

- A. put on your sunglasses
- B. check tyre pressures
- C. change to a lower gear
- D. tune your radio to a local channel

653 PCV/LGV
You are driving through a congested tunnel and have to stop. What should you do?

Mark one answer

- A. Pull up very close to the vehicle in front to save space
- B. Ignore any message signs as they're never up to date
- C. Keep a safe distance from the vehicle in front
- D. Do not switch on your hazard warning lights

654 PCV/LGV
You are driving through a tunnel. Your vehicle breaks down. What should you do?

Mark one answer

- A. Switch on hazard warning lights
- B. Remain in your vehicle
- C. Wait for the police to find you
- D. Rely on CCTV cameras seeing you

655 PCV/LGV
Your vehicle catches fire while driving through a tunnel. It is still driveable. What should you do?

Mark one answer

- A. Leave it where it is with the engine running
- B. Pull up, then walk to an emergency telephone point
- C. Park it away from the carriageway
- D. Drive it out of the tunnel if you can do so

656 PCV/LGV
You are driving through a tunnel in heavy traffic and it is very busy. What should you do?

Mark one answer

- A. stay close to the vehicle in front to reduce congestion
- B. switch off your dipped headlights to reduce dazzle
- C. closely follow the tail lights of other vehicles
- D. follow instructions given by variable message signs

657 PCV/LGV

A vehicle has rolled over and caught fire. The driver's hands and arms have been burned. You should NOT

Mark one answer

- A. douse the burns with cold water
- B. lay the casualty down
- C. remove smouldering clothing
- D. remove anything sticking to the burns

658 PCV/LGV

At an accident a casualty has stopped breathing. You should

Mark two answers

- A. remove anything that is blocking the mouth
- B. keep the head tilted forwards as far as possible
- C. raise the legs to help with circulation
- D. try to give the casualty something to drink
- E. tilt the head back very gently

659 PCV/LGV

To start mouth to mouth on a casualty you should

Mark three answers

- A. tilt the head forward
- B. clear the airway
- C. turn them on their side
- D. tilt their head back very gently
- E. pinch the nostrils together
- F. put their arms across their chest

660 PCV/LGV

You arrive at the scene of an accident. There has been an engine fire and someone's hands and arms have been burnt. You should NOT

Mark one answer

- A. douse the burn thoroughly with cool liquid
- B. lay the casualty down
- C. remove anything sticking to the burn
- D. remove smouldering clothing

661 PCV/LGV

You have been involved in an accident and damaged some property. Your vehicle is still roadworthy. Nobody else is present. What should you do?

Mark one answer   **NI**

- A. Stop, then report the accident to the police within 24 hours
- B. Leave the scene. Do not report the accident if there are no witnesses
- C. Stop, then report the accident to the police after 48 hours
- D. Leave the scene. Do not report the accident if there were no injuries

662 PCV/LGV

You have an accident while driving through a tunnel. You are not injured but your vehicle CANNOT be driven. What should you do first?

Mark one answer

- A. Rely on other drivers phoning for the police
- B. Switch off the engine and switch on hazard lights
- C. Take the names of witnesses and other drivers
- D. Sweep up any debris that is in the road

663 PCV/LGV
While driving through a tunnel your vehicle catches fire. It cannot be driven. What should you do first?

Mark one answer
- [ ] A. Wait for the police, tunnels are regularly patrolled
- [ ] B. Stay with your vehicle, you will be seen by the CCTV cameras
- [ ] C. Pull over to the side and switch off the engine
- [ ] D. Do not put out the fire, wait for the emergency services

664 PCV/LGV
You are at the scene of an accident. Which of these is a symptom of shock?

Mark one answer
- [ ] A. Flushed complexion
- [ ] B. Alertness
- [ ] C. Rapid pulse
- [ ] D. Slow breathing

665 PCV/LGV
You are driving in a tunnel and your vehicle catches fire. What should you try to do FIRST?

Mark one answer
- [ ] A. Drive out of the tunnel
- [ ] B. Pull over to the side of the tunnel
- [ ] C. Stop and extinguish the fire
- [ ] D. Stop and leave the vehicle immediately

666 PCV/LGV
What will be the likely result of incidents at work?

Mark one answer
- [ ] A. More vehicles off the road
- [ ] B. Lower running costs
- [ ] C. Fewer missed customer orders
- [ ] D. Fewer workdays lost

667 PCV/LGV
You arrive at the scene of an incident, someone is hysterical. What should you do?

Mark one answer
- [ ] A. Talk to them quietly and firmly
- [ ] B. Let them wander off to calm down
- [ ] C. Restrain them physically
- [ ] D. Shout loudly to get their attention

668 PCV/LGV
You are at the scene of a traffic incident. Someone seems to be in shock. What are the symptoms?

Mark one answer
- [ ] A. Rapid pulse and sweating
- [ ] B. Flushed complexion and deep breathing
- [ ] C. Slow pulse and dry skin
- [ ] D. Muscle spasms and an itchy rash

669 PCV/LGV
Your vehicle breaks down in a tunnel. What should you do?

Mark one answer

- [ ] A. Stay in your vehicle and wait for the police
- [ ] B. Stand in the lane behind your vehicle to warn others
- [ ] C. Stand in front of your vehicle to warn oncoming drivers
- [ ] D. Switch on hazard lights then go and call for help immediately

670 PCV/LGV
At a traffic incident a casualty is unconscious. Which THREE of the following should you check urgently?

Mark three answers

- [ ] A. Circulation
- [ ] B. Airway
- [ ] C. Shock
- [ ] D. Breathing
- [ ] E. Broken bones

671 PCV/LGV
You are at the scene of a collision. Some people are injured. Which TWO should you do IMMEDIATELY?

Mark two answers

- [ ] A. Pull people who are hurt out of their vehicles
- [ ] B. Check the casualties for signs of bleeding
- [ ] C. Make sure the emergency services have been called
- [ ] D. Get the casualties to drink something sweet
- [ ] E. Clear a parking area for the emergency services

672 LGV
There is a fire in your engine compartment. Which TWO of the following should you do?

Mark two answers

- [ ] A. Open all windows
- [ ] B. Disconnect electrical leads
- [ ] C. Flag down a passing motorist
- [ ] D. Cut off the fuel supply
- [ ] E. Try to remove the load

673 LGV
Before driving a lorry loaded with toxic substances you MUST take training in

Mark one answer

- [ ] A. using fire-fighting equipment
- [ ] B. operating a fork lift truck
- [ ] C. operating a lorry mounted crane
- [ ] D. using breathing apparatus

674
PCV

You are driving a three-axle double-deck bus and using full steering lock. Why should you take extra care?

Mark one answer

- **A.** Passengers might alter the angle of tilt
- **B.** The power steering might fail
- **C.** You may damage the air suspension
- **D.** You may scrub the rear tyres

675
PCV

You are driving a three-axle double-deck bus and using full steering lock. To avoid rear tyre scrub you should use

Mark one answer

- **A.** the highest gear possible
- **B.** a very low speed
- **C.** the exhaust brake (retarder)
- **D.** a steering ball

676
PCV

On a double-deck bus, what is the minimum depth of tyre tread required over three-quarters of its width?

Mark one answer

- **A.** 0.8mm
- **B.** 1mm
- **C.** 1.6mm
- **D.** 2mm

677
PCV

During your journey you notice that your coach's right rear indicator is not working. You should

Mark one answer

- **A.** continue your journey using arm signals
- **B.** get it repaired before continuing
- **C.** get it repaired on your return to the depot
- **D.** get your passengers to their destination then repair it

678
PCV

Before each journey you should check all warning lights. What should you do if a warning light remains lit?

Mark one answer

- **A.** Report the fault when you return
- **B.** Have the fault checked before setting off
- **C.** Have the fault checked at the next service
- **D.** Ignore it until the fault shows up

679
PCV

Why should you check your tyres more frequently on a coach with three axles?

Mark one answer

- **A.** Because punctures can be more difficult to detect
- **B.** Because air pressure is more easily lost
- **C.** The wheels will need balancing more often
- **D.** You have no room for a spare wheel

580 PCV

Some buses have different size wheels on the front and rear. When driving at high speeds on long journeys what do you need to be aware of?

Mark one answer

- **A.** The larger wheels are more likely to overheat
- **B.** The smaller wheels are more likely to overheat
- **C.** The larger wheels are more likely to lose pressure
- **D.** The smaller wheels are more likely to lose pressure

581 PCV

How frequently should a walk-round check be done?

Mark one answer

- **A.** Daily
- **B.** Weekly
- **C.** Every 100 miles
- **D.** Every 1,000 miles

582 PCV

Your vehicle has a turbo engine. What should you do before switching it off?

Mark one answer

- **A.** Release the air suspension valve
- **B.** Allow the engine to idle
- **C.** Select reverse gear
- **D.** Rev the engine up sharply

683 PCV

One of your passengers tells you they have noticed a wheel nut is missing. How often should you check them?

Mark one answer

- **A.** At the end of every week
- **B.** At the start of every week
- **C.** Every day before starting out
- **D.** Only at every service interval

684 PCV

You are parking your vehicle. It is fitted with a turbo engine. You should

Mark one answer

- **A.** rev the engine up then switch it off
- **B.** switch the engine off immediately
- **C.** allow the engine to idle then switch it off
- **D.** switch the engine off and on repeatedly

685 PCV

You are on a very busy road and it is dark. Your headlights fail suddenly. The fuse box is on the outside of the bus on the right-hand side. What should you do?

Mark one answer

- **A.** Ask a passenger to watch for traffic
- **B.** Drive on without lights
- **C.** Fix the problem yourself
- **D.** Wait for the breakdown services

686
PCV

Your coach often tows a trailer. How often should you check the trailer tyres for pressure?

Mark one answer

- A. at least once a week when they are cold
- B. at least once a month when they are hot
- C. at least once a week when they are hot
- D. at least once a month when fully laden

687
PCV

The bus you are driving is fitted with an automatic gearbox. When would you use kickdown?

Mark one answer

- A. When stopping in an emergency
- B. When changing to a higher gear
- C. When driving at slow speed
- D. When needing brisk acceleration

688
PCV

Your coach is fully laden. You notice the steering feels heavy. What is the most likely reason?

Mark one answer

- A. An icy road
- B. A burst rear tyre
- C. Faulty power steering
- D. Too many passengers

689
PCV

Frequent tyre checks are advised on tri-axle double-deck vehicles because

Mark one answer

- A. their tyres are more likely to deflate
- B. punctures can be difficult to detect
- C. blow-outs are more common on these vehicles
- D. their tyre air pressures are difficult to maintain

690
PCV

The driver of a coach should always wear gloves when

Mark one answer

- A. loading and stowing passengers' luggage
- B. operating a disabled passenger lift
- C. checking the fuel cut-off switch
- D. topping up the oil or water levels

691
PCV

The driver of a coach should always wear gloves when

Mark two answers

- A. emptying the ticket machines
- B. emptying waste systems
- C. driving in cold weather
- D. driving a vehicle without power steering
- E. checking the fuel gauge
- F. checking battery levels

692 PCV
On a six-wheel double-deck bus, rear wheel punctures are

Mark one answer

- [ ] **A.** much easier to detect
- [ ] **B.** more likely to happen
- [ ] **C.** more difficult to detect
- [ ] **D.** less likely to happen

693 PCV
You must inspect all tyres on your bus for

Mark four answers

- [ ] **A.** signs of wear
- [ ] **B.** overheating
- [ ] **C.** maker's details
- [ ] **D.** correct pressure
- [ ] **E.** 'dust cap' in place
- [ ] **F.** objects between twin tyres

694 PCV
Tyres which are over-inflated will

Mark one answer

- [ ] **A.** give better acceleration
- [ ] **B.** wear unevenly and quicker
- [ ] **C.** give much better grip
- [ ] **D.** last much longer

695 PCV
When you are uncoupling a trailer you should

Mark two answers

- [ ] **A.** disconnect the electrical line first
- [ ] **B.** unload at least some of the cargo
- [ ] **C.** choose a well-lit location
- [ ] **D.** apply the trailer brake first
- [ ] **E.** choose a firm level surface

696 PCV
It is dark and you are on a very busy road. Your headlights have failed. The fuse box is on the outside of the bus on the right-hand side. What should you do?

Mark one answer

- [ ] **A.** Pull up on the left and call for assistance
- [ ] **B.** Drive on using sidelights at front and rear
- [ ] **C.** Try to fix the problem on your own
- [ ] **D.** Get a passenger to hold a torch for you

697 PCV/LGV
You are checking your vehicle's tyres before starting a long motorway drive. Each tyre should be checked for

Mark three answers

- [ ] **A.** air pressure
- [ ] **B.** tracking
- [ ] **C.** tread wear
- [ ] **D.** tread pattern
- [ ] **E.** bulges
- [ ] **F.** valve clearance

698 PCV/LGV
You notice that two wheel nuts are missing from one of the wheels. What should you do?

Mark one answer

- [ ] **A.** Continue your journey
- [ ] **B.** Drive to the nearest tyre depot
- [ ] **C.** Use a nut from another wheel
- [ ] **D.** Park and phone for assistance

699 PCV/LGV

Which THREE of the following items would make a tyre illegal for a large vehicle?

Mark three answers
- [ ] **A.** Different makes of tyres on the same axle
- [ ] **B.** A lump or bulge
- [ ] **C.** A deep cut more than 25mm (1 inch) long
- [ ] **D.** An exposed ply or cord
- [ ] **E.** Recut tyres
- [ ] **F.** A tread depth of 1.3mm

700 PCV/LGV

In very cold weather moisture may freeze in your vehicle's air storage tanks. Which of the following would help to prevent this?

Mark one answer
- [ ] **A.** Covering the air tanks with a blanket
- [ ] **B.** Draining the tanks daily
- [ ] **C.** Using the brakes frequently
- [ ] **D.** Pumping the brakes

701 PCV/LGV

What does this warning light on the instrument panel mean?

Mark one answer
- [ ] **A.** Low oil pressure
- [ ] **B.** Battery discharge
- [ ] **C.** Braking system fault
- [ ] **D.** Door open

702 PCV/LGV

You are driving along a motorway. The brake low-pressure warning device starts to operate. What should you do?

Mark one answer
- [ ] **A.** Stop immediately in the lane you are in
- [ ] **B.** Continue slowly to the next service area
- [ ] **C.** Pull up on the hard shoulder as soon as possible
- [ ] **D.** Leave the motorway at the next exit

703 PCV/LGV

Your vehicle has broken down at night on a two-way road. You should try to park your vehicle

Mark one answer
- [ ] **A.** on the left of the road
- [ ] **B.** partly on the pavement
- [ ] **C.** on a grass verge
- [ ] **D.** on the right of the road

704 PCV/LGV

Whilst driving, your power-assisted steering suddenly fails. What should you do?

Mark one answer
- [ ] **A.** Continue driving to the nearest repair centre
- [ ] **B.** Return to the depot
- [ ] **C.** Continue your journey at a slower speed
- [ ] **D.** Park and seek assistance

705 PCV/LGV
Whilst driving your steering suddenly becomes heavy to turn. What could this indicate?

Mark two answers

- A. A puncture in a front tyre
- B. Loss of air brake pressure
- C. A faulty parking brake
- D. A failure of power-assisted steering

706 PCV/LGV
What should you do if the brake pedal becomes 'hard'?

Mark one answer

- A. Continue to drive and report it at the end of the day
- B. Pump the brake pedal continuously
- C. Drain the air tanks and then continue
- D. Park and telephone for assistance

707 PCV/LGV
Air tanks on brake systems require draining because

Mark one answer

- A. excess coolant may collect in them
- B. rain water can often seep in
- C. any engine leakages are directed here
- D. of moisture drawn in from the atmosphere

708 PCV/LGV
Whilst checking your vehicle you discover an air leak in the braking system. What should you do?

Mark one answer

- A. Drive slowly to the nearest garage
- B. Check the leak from time to time on your journey
- C. Leave it parked and report it immediately
- D. Start your journey and report it on your return

709 PCV/LGV
You are driving a large vehicle. A loud buzzer sounds in the cab. This is most likely to indicate low

Mark one answer

- A. oil pressure
- B. air pressure
- C. tyre pressure
- D. fuel level

710 PCV/LGV
How much of the width of a tyre must have the legal limit of tread depth?

Mark one answer

- A. One-quarter
- B. One-half
- C. Five-eighths
- D. Three-quarters

711 PCV/LGV
As a professional driver of large vehicles, why should you carry spare bulbs?

Mark two answers

- A. To fix any fault for the safety of yourself
- B. Because bulbs are more likely to blow when your vehicle is loaded
- C. To repair the lights for the sake of other road users
- D. Because bulbs are more likely to blow when your vehicle is empty

712 PCV/LGV
At very low temperatures diesel fuel will become less effective unless

Mark one answer
- [ ] **A.** anti-freeze is added
- [ ] **B.** anti-waxing additives are added
- [ ] **C.** petrol is added
- [ ] **D.** paraffin is added

713 PCV/LGV
You are about to start a long journey midway through the day. You find that your headlights are not working but you still have sidelights. What should you do?

Mark one answer
- [ ] **A.** Don't drive until they are mended
- [ ] **B.** Drive only until light begins to fade
- [ ] **C.** Avoid driving on motorways after dark
- [ ] **D.** Drive only if the weather is good

714 PCV/LGV
Before starting a journey you want to check your brake system warning lights. On some vehicles these are not operated by the ignition switch. What else can you do?

Mark one answer
- [ ] **A.** Look for a 'check' switch on the dashboard
- [ ] **B.** Get someone behind to check your brake lights
- [ ] **C.** Check them at the end of your journey
- [ ] **D.** Pump the brake pedal a number of times

715 PCV/LGV
On motorways you are usually driving at higher speeds for long distances. What effect can this have on your tyres?

Mark one answer
- [ ] **A.** They may overheat and disintegrate
- [ ] **B.** They will be more liable to punctures
- [ ] **C.** They will lose air pressure more quickly
- [ ] **D.** They will become very slippery

716 PCV/LGV
You notice one of your tyres has a bulge in the side. Why should you not drive the vehicle?

Mark one answer
- [ ] **A.** Your tachograph reading will not be accurate
- [ ] **B.** Your speedometer will give an incorrect reading
- [ ] **C.** It will make the vehicle unsteady on corners
- [ ] **D.** At speed, the tyre could overheat and burst

717 PCV/LGV
The purpose of a pre-heating device is to heat the

Mark one answer
- [ ] **A.** cab
- [ ] **B.** gearbox
- [ ] **C.** engine
- [ ] **D.** seat

718 PCV/LGV
A high-pressure fuel injector delivers fuel into the

Mark one answer
- A. carburettors
- B. cylinders
- C. camshaft
- D. crankshaft

719 PCV/LGV
Why is it most important to avoid overfilling the engine oil level?

Mark one answer
- A. It could leave an oil stain on the road
- B. It will increase the amount of exhaust gases
- C. It could increase oil pressure and cause damage
- D. It will damage the exhaust system

720 PCV/LGV
Why should you use an approved coolant solution in your engine?

Mark one answer
- A. To prevent the engine freezing
- B. For easier starting from cold
- C. To prevent the air tank from freezing
- D. For effective cab heating

721 PCV/LGV
When replacing a tubeless tyre it is good practice to

Mark one answer
- A. fit the same valve
- B. replace the valve
- C. have the valve checked
- D. clean the valve

722 PCV/LGV
You should check the oil level when your engine is

Mark one answer
- A. running
- B. cold
- C. warm
- D. hot

723 PCV/LGV
When should anti-freeze be used in the cooling system?

Mark one answer
- A. In winter only
- B. All year round
- C. In summer only
- D. When starting from cold

724 PCV/LGV
What does this warning light on the instrument panel mean?

Mark one answer
- A. Low fuel pressure
- B. Low oil pressure
- C. Low water pressure
- D. Low air pressure

725 PCV/LGV
As you are driving the ignition warning light comes on. What does it warn of?

Mark one answer
- A. Low oil pressure
- B. An electrical fault
- C. Low air pressure
- D. A hydraulic fault

726 PCV/LGV
Codes are shown on the side walls of bus and lorry tyres. What do these refer to?

Mark one answer
- A. Tread pattern
- B. Minimum temperature
- C. Maximum load
- D. Running pressure

727 PCV/LGV
Regular maintenance and servicing will

Mark one answer
- A. prevent unnecessary breakdowns
- B. increase fuel bills
- C. allow heavier loads to be carried
- D. reduce insurance premiums

728 PCV/LGV
Before changing a wheel on your vehicle you should

Mark one answer
- A. leave the parking brake off
- B. use chocks if available
- C. dismantle the wheel and tyre
- D. get someone to check the other tyres

729 PCV/LGV
You have had to change a wheel on your vehicle. When should you next check the wheel nuts?

Mark one answer
- A. At the next service interval
- B. When they are cold
- C. When they are hot
- D. Shortly afterwards

730 PCV/LGV
A new engine has just been fitted to your vehicle. Why may it be necessary to bleed the fuel system?

Mark one answer
- A. To increase the speed of your vehicle
- B. To remove any trapped air
- C. Because it is illegal not to do so
- D. Because it may cause the tank to freeze

731 PCV/LGV
When may it become necessary to bleed the fuel system to remove any trapped air?

Mark one answer
- A. When the engine has not been run for some time
- B. When you intend to carry unusually heavy loads
- C. When the engine keeps overheating
- D. When you wish to change the taxation on your vehicle

732 PCV/LGV
Using poor quality diesel fuel may lead to

Mark one answer
- [ ] A. better fuel economy
- [ ] B. lower exhaust emissions
- [ ] C. longer service intervals
- [ ] D. early blockage of a fuel injector

733 PCV/LGV
Which of these components are generally found in an internal combustion engine?

Mark three answers
- [ ] A. crankshaft
- [ ] B. propshaft
- [ ] C. crown wheel
- [ ] D. cylinder
- [ ] E. differential
- [ ] F. piston

734 PCV/LGV
Breakdowns can be reduced by

Mark one answer
- [ ] A. driving slowly
- [ ] B. regular servicing
- [ ] C. regular cleaning
- [ ] D. avoiding bad weather

735 PCV/LGV
Why should your engine oil be changed at the recommended intervals?

Mark one answer
- [ ] A. To reduce friction and wear
- [ ] B. For better steering control
- [ ] C. To prevent oil leaks
- [ ] D. To improve clutch wear

736 PCV/LGV
Where should you check your engine oil level?

Mark one answer
- [ ] A. On sloping ground
- [ ] B. On a steep gradient
- [ ] C. On level ground
- [ ] D. On a downhill slope

737 PCV/LGV
You overfill your engine with oil. What could this cause?

Mark one answer
- [ ] A. Better handling
- [ ] B. Lower emissions
- [ ] C. Damaged gaskets
- [ ] D. Longer service intervals

738 PCV/LGV
When uncoupling a trailer the very FIRST thing you must do is

Mark one answer
- [ ] A. lower the trailer legs to the ground
- [ ] B. apply the parking brake
- [ ] C. release the brake air lines
- [ ] D. uncouple the electrical lines

739 PCV/LGV
You are uncoupling a trailer. Before disconnecting any of the airlines, you MUST

Mark one answer
- [ ] A. drain the air tanks
- [ ] B. apply the trailer parking brake
- [ ] C. lower the landing gear
- [ ] D. disconnect the electrical line

740 PCV/LGV
When should you check the wheel nuts on your vehicle?

Mark one answer

- [ ] **A.** Just before any journey
- [ ] **B.** Only before long trips
- [ ] **C.** Only every 1000 miles (1600km)
- [ ] **D.** Just before a major service

741 PCV/LGV
In your vehicle the oil pump is usually driven directly from the

Mark one answer

- [ ] **A.** oil filter
- [ ] **B.** prop shaft
- [ ] **C.** piston valves
- [ ] **D.** engine

742 PCV/LGV
Thick black smoke is coming from the exhaust of your vehicle. You should

Mark one answer

- [ ] **A.** continue on to the nearest garage
- [ ] **B.** return to your depot and report the problem
- [ ] **C.** stop in a safe place and get help
- [ ] **D.** drive slowly with your hazard warning lights on

743 PCV/LGV
You hit the kerb at speed. You should, as soon as possible, check your vehicle for any damage to the

Mark two answers

- [ ] **A.** exhaust
- [ ] **B.** brakes
- [ ] **C.** tyres
- [ ] **D.** steering
- [ ] **E.** lights

744 PCV/LGV
Which of the following is most likely to cause a burst tyre when driving?

Mark one answer

- [ ] **A.** Frequent gear changing in varying conditions
- [ ] **B.** Running at a constant high speed
- [ ] **C.** Always operating in cool weather
- [ ] **D.** Mixing tyres with different tread depth

745 PCV/LGV
When can a 'selective' or 'block' gear change be used?

Mark one answer

- [ ] **A.** To change gear down only
- [ ] **B.** To change gear up only
- [ ] **C.** To change gear to a low speed only
- [ ] **D.** To change gear either up or down

746 PCV/LGV
You are driving a vehicle which has a two-speed axle. This

Mark one answer

- [ ] **A.** halves the number of gears
- [ ] **B.** doubles the number of gears
- [ ] **C.** engages the diff-lock
- [ ] **D.** releases the diff-lock

747 PCV/LGV
On a vehicle with automatic transmission you would use 'kickdown' to

Mark one answer

- [ ] **A.** give quicker acceleration
- [ ] **B.** apply the emergency brakes
- [ ] **C.** stop more smoothly
- [ ] **D.** go down a steep hill

748 PCV/LGV
You are driving a modern vehicle. You notice the steering feels heavy. What is the most likely cause?

Mark one answer
- A. Faulty power steering
- B. An icy road
- C. A burst rear tyre
- D. A wet road

749 PCV/LGV
Your vehicle suffers a tyre blow-out. What is likely to create a hazard for other road users?

Mark one answer
- A. Scattered debris
- B. Skid marks
- C. Suspension failure
- D. Axle damage

750 PCV/LGV
The Vehicle and Operator Services Agency (VOSA) and the police carry out spot checks of vehicle condition. If serious defects are found the vehicle is

Mark one answer **NI**
- A. impounded until a new driver is found
- B. restricted to 30mph for the remainder of the journey
- C. prohibited from further use until the defects are rectified
- D. ordered back to the depot to unload goods or passengers

751 PCV/LGV
A vehicle is found to have serious defects at a Vehicle and Operator Services Agency (VOSA) spot-check. It is prohibited from further use. Who will be notified of the details?

Mark one answer **NI**
- A. The Driver and Vehicle Licencing Agency
- B. The Traffic Commissioner
- C. The Road Transport Industry Training Body
- D. The bus, coach and commercial vehicle council

752 PCV/LGV
You should check your engine oil level regularly. Failure to do this could cause your engine to

Mark one answer
- A. run faster
- B. break down
- C. use less fuel
- D. produce more power

753 PCV/LGV
While driving, your engine oil warning light comes on. Why could it be dangerous to continue driving?

Mark one answer
- A. The engine will get hot
- B. The engine may be damaged
- C. You will need to have the vehicle serviced
- D. You will need to replace the carburettor

754 PCV/LGV
Bus and lorry tyres have codes on the side wall. What do these refer to?

Mark one answer
- [ ] A. Running pressure
- [ ] B. Speed capability
- [ ] C. Minimum temperature
- [ ] D. Tread depth

755 PCV/LGV
Energy-saving tyres have

Mark one answer
- [ ] A. increased tread depth
- [ ] B. reduced rolling resistance
- [ ] C. reduced tread depth
- [ ] D. increased rolling resistance

756 PCV/LGV
You have replaced a tyre. What precautions should you take when tightening the wheel nuts?

Mark two answers
- [ ] A. Only use a wheel brace
- [ ] B. Fully tighten each wheel nut before going on to the next
- [ ] C. Use a calibrated torque wrench
- [ ] D. Only use an air-operated power tool
- [ ] E. Fit and tighten the wheel nuts gradually and diagonally

757 PCV/LGV
Using poor-quality diesel fuel may lead to

Mark one answer
- [ ] A. better fuel economy
- [ ] B. increased wear of the injection pump
- [ ] C. longer service intervals
- [ ] D. lower exhaust emissions

758 PCV/LGV
Energy-saving tyres work because they

Mark three answers
- [ ] A. have reduced rolling resistance
- [ ] B. cost less to produce
- [ ] C. have no tread pattern
- [ ] D. never puncture at high speed
- [ ] E. increase fuel efficiency
- [ ] F. improve grip

759 PCV/LGV
Advice about carrying out minor repairs can be obtained from

Mark one answer
- [ ] A. DVLA guidance notes
- [ ] B. EC and UK Directives
- [ ] C. the Health and Safety Executive
- [ ] D. the owner's handbook

760 PCV/LGV
Where can you get advice about carrying out minor repairs?

Mark one answer
- [ ] A. Workshop manuals
- [ ] B. DVLA guidance notes
- [ ] C. EC and UK Directives
- [ ] D. The Health and Safety Executive

761 PCV/LGV
Overfilling your engine with oil could result in

Mark one answer
- [ ] A. loss of power
- [ ] B. lower emissions
- [ ] C. better handling
- [ ] D. longer service intervals

762 PCV/LGV
What is the purpose of the oil filter?

Mark one answer
- [ ] A. To prevent the engine overheating
- [ ] B. To give better fuel consumption
- [ ] C. To prevent the engine over-revving
- [ ] D. To collect sediment from the oil

763 PCV/LGV
The oil level in your engine should normally be checked when the engine is

Mark one answer
- [ ] A. hot
- [ ] B. revving
- [ ] C. cold
- [ ] D. idling

764 PCV/LGV
When fitting a road wheel which tool is essential?

Mark one answer
- [ ] A. Torque wrench
- [ ] B. Ring spanner
- [ ] C. Open-end spanner
- [ ] D. Adjustable wrench

765 PCV/LGV
You are driving a diesel-engined vehicle. The weather conditions suddenly turn very cold. The engine begins to run erratically. What is the most likely cause of this?

Mark one answer
- [ ] A. The endurance brake coming on
- [ ] B. The air conditioning not working
- [ ] C. The speed limiter operating
- [ ] D. The fuel partly solidifying

766 PCV/LGV
Your vehicle is fitted with heated fuel lines. This is especially useful in cold conditions to prevent the

Mark one answer
- [ ] A. cab temperature dropping
- [ ] B. radiator from freezing
- [ ] C. windows becoming misty
- [ ] D. diesel from partially solidifying

767 PCV/LGV
Before setting off you should do a daily walk-round check. What is this for?

Mark one answer
- [ ] A. To check your route
- [ ] B. To check for any parking violations
- [ ] C. To check your schedule
- [ ] D. To check for any defects

768 PCV/LGV
What happens to diesel fuel when it gets hot?

Mark one answer
- [ ] A. It expands
- [ ] B. It liquefies
- [ ] C. It shrinks
- [ ] D. It waxes

769 PCV/LGV
Vehicle operators MUST have an effective system in place for drivers to

Mark one answer
- [ ] A. report vehicle defects
- [ ] B. report all motorway hold ups
- [ ] C. inform operators of their progress
- [ ] D. inform operators about traffic delays

770
PCV/LGV
Your oil pressure warning light comes on while you are driving. What should you do?

Mark one answer
- [ ] **A.** Wait until your next service interval and tell the mechanic
- [ ] **B.** Ignore the light, it is not the driver's responsibility
- [ ] **C.** Stop and check the oil level as soon as it is safe to do so
- [ ] **D.** Continue with your journey but have it checked on your arrival

771
LGV
What is the main reason for cleaning your wheels and tyres when leaving a building site?

Mark one answer
- [ ] **A.** It helps to keep the tyres in good condition
- [ ] **B.** So that the tyres will not cause damage to the road surface
- [ ] **C.** So that air pressure will not leak from the tyre valves
- [ ] **D.** It is illegal for you to spread mud on the road

772
LGV
You should look at the rear wheels before leaving a building site to check that

Mark one answer
- [ ] **A.** the diff-lock is engaged
- [ ] **B.** the diff-lock is disengaged
- [ ] **C.** the load-sensing valve is working
- [ ] **D.** bricks are not wedged between them

773
LGV
You are driving on a muddy building site. Before driving on normal road surfaces you should

Mark one answer
- [ ] **A.** disengage the diff-lock
- [ ] **B.** engage the diff-lock
- [ ] **C.** apply the steering lock
- [ ] **D.** disengage the twist lock

774
LGV
You are driving a lorry along a motorway. You notice that tread is coming away from one of your tyres. What should you do?

Mark one answer
- [ ] **A.** Stop on the hard shoulder and phone for assistance
- [ ] **B.** Stop on the hard shoulder and change the wheel
- [ ] **C.** Continue driving to the next service station
- [ ] **D.** Continue driving and leave by the next exit

775
LGV
What is the MINIMUM depth of tread required over three-quarters of the breadth of a lorry tyre?

Mark one answer
- [ ] **A.** 1mm
- [ ] **B.** 1.5mm
- [ ] **C.** 2.5mm
- [ ] **D.** 5mm

776
LGV
After recoupling a trailer, which of the following should you do LAST?

Mark one answer
- [ ] **A.** Connect the brake lines
- [ ] **B.** Release the trailer parking brake
- [ ] **C.** Connect the electrical lines
- [ ] **D.** Raise the trailer legs

777 LGV
Your lorry coupling system (fifth wheel) should be checked and lubricated

Mark one answer
- A. only prior to an MOT
- B. every 6 months
- C. yearly
- D. regularly

778 LGV
You are driving a new articulated lorry which is fully laden. You notice the steering feels heavy. What is the most likely reason?

Mark one answer
- A. The road is icy
- B. Faulty power steering
- C. A tyre on the trailer has burst
- D. The load on the trailer has shifted

779 LGV
Wheel nuts should be checked shortly after

Mark one answer
- A. driving down a steep hill
- B. initial tightening
- C. driving on a motorway
- D. unloading

780 LGV
A fifth wheel coupling relies on which of the following connecting devices?

Mark one answer
- A. Suzie
- B. Kingpin
- C. D link
- D. Eyelet

781 LGV
What would you secure with a dog-clip?

Mark one answer
- A. Kingpin release handle
- B. Electric cables
- C. Parking brake
- D. Differential lock

782 LGV
How frequently should the components of a fifth wheel coupling be inspected?

Mark one answer
- A. Daily
- B. Weekly
- C. Monthly
- D. Yearly

783 LGV
On a draw-bar unit which of these should you check for wear or damage?

Mark one answer
- A. Dog-clip
- B. Fifth wheel
- C. Kingpin release handle
- D. Eyelet coupling

784 LGV
What is the fifth wheel coupling used for?

Mark one answer
- A. To connect a tractor unit to the trailer
- B. To support the trailer when detached
- C. To prevent the trailer from jack-knifing
- D. To attach air lines to the trailer

785 LGV
Fifth wheel coupling components should be inspected monthly or every

Mark one answer
- A. 5,000km
- B. 10,000km
- C. 15,000km
- D. 20,000km

786 LGV
When diesel fuel is hot it

Mark one answer
- A. expands
- B. liquefies
- C. shrinks
- D. waxes

787 LGV
Your vehicle is fitted with a synchromesh gearbox. Double-declutching will have the effect of

Mark one answer
- A. reducing clutch wear
- B. increasing clutch wear
- C. increasing the number of gear changes
- D. reducing the number of gear changes

788 PCV

When you intend to open your right-hand door you should check

Mark one answer
- A. the mirror
- B. that all other doors are closed
- C. the air pressure
- D. that the interior is clear of passengers

789 PCV

Many buses have a separate door on the offside for the driver. When leaving the bus by this door you should always

Mark three answers
- A. jump down from the cab
- B. check for traffic which may be passing
- C. apply the parking brake
- D. climb down facing the bus using the footholds
- E. climb down facing away from the bus using the footholds

790 PCV

When getting out of the driver's door on this bus you should

Mark two answers
- A. look out for overtaking vehicles before opening the door
- B. climb down facing away from the bus
- C. climb down facing the bus
- D. signal your intentions to other traffic
- E. open the door to get a good view of approaching traffic

791 PCV

This bus has a separate door for the driver, opening onto the offside. What should you do when getting out of such a vehicle?

Mark two answers
- A. Climb down facing away from the vehicle
- B. Check for passing traffic
- C. Climb down facing towards the vehicle
- D. Jump down carefully, flexing the knees on landing
- E. Climb down holding the steering wheel rim tightly

792 PCV

As a bus driver, on which FOUR occasions should you use your hazard warning lights?

Mark four answers
- A. When you are temporarily obstructing traffic
- B. To thank a driver who has let you pull in
- C. To warn of an obstruction when driving on the motorway
- D. When parking in a restricted area
- E. When you have broken down
- F. When stationary and children are getting off a school bus

793 PCV
Damage can be caused when parking close to another vehicle if your coach is fitted with

Mark one answer
- A. air brakes
- B. hydraulic suspension
- C. air suspension
- D. hydraulic brakes

794 PCV
As a driver, when getting out of your bus you must make sure that

Mark three answers
- A. the parking brake is on
- B. the vehicle has stopped in a safe place
- C. the engine is switched off
- D. the air pressure gauges read full
- E. you have parked at a bus stop
- F. you always change the destination board

795 PCV
When leaving the cab of your bus, which of the following is NOT important?

Mark one answer
- A. Applying the parking brake
- B. Switching off the engine
- C. Watching for approaching traffic
- D. Operating the fuel cut-off switch

796 PCV
You are going to park your bus. What must you check before leaving it?

Mark one answer
- A. The ticket dispenser
- B. Litter left under seats
- C. The parking brake is applied
- D. The intercom is working

797 PCV/LGV
As a driver you should use your mirrors

Mark two answers
- A. as you signal
- B. to check the blind spot
- C. when driving along
- D. before opening your door

798 PCV/LGV
Before you get out of your cab, you must

Mark one answer
- A. empty the air tanks
- B. adjust your mirrors
- C. apply the parking brake
- D. check if the warning lights are working

799 PCV/LGV
Before you leave your vehicle you must always

Mark one answer
- A. empty the air tanks
- B. apply the parking brake
- C. adjust your mirrors
- D. switch on your hazard warning lights

800 PCV/LGV
Before leaving the cab you should make sure that

Mark three answers
- A. you remove your tachograph chart
- B. the engine has stopped
- C. all warning lights are operating
- D. the parking brake is on
- E. all documents are safely stowed
- F. you will not endanger people when opening the door

801 PCV/LGV
Before opening your cab door you should be aware of

Mark one answer

- A. vehicles passing close by
- B. the height of your cab from the ground
- C. loose grab rails near the door
- D. people crossing the road behind you

802 PCV/LGV
When should you use hazard warning lights?

Mark one answer

- A. To warn other drivers that you are towing
- B. Approaching queuing traffic on a motorway
- C. When parked illegally on a busy road
- D. To thank a driver for giving way to you

803 PCV/LGV
You need to stop and get out of your vehicle. The parking brake should be used

Mark one answer

- A. with the service brake
- B. only on uneven ground
- C. at all times when leaving the vehicle
- D. unless the vehicle is in gear

804 PCV/LGV
Before leaving your vehicle cab you should make sure that

Mark three answers

- A. the engine is running smoothly
- B. the engine has stopped
- C. the parking brake is on
- D. you have removed your personal things
- E. the ignition system is switched off

805 PCV/LGV
Before leaving your vehicle cab you should make sure that

Mark two answers

- A. your seat is correctly adjusted
- B. the ignition system is switched on
- C. the engine has stopped
- D. the keys are in the starter switch
- E. the parking brake is on

806 PCV/LGV
Hazard warning lights may be used in which TWO of these situations?

Mark two answers

- A. To thank a driver who has let you pull in after overtaking
- B. As a warning to drivers that you are towing another vehicle
- C. To show your intention to go ahead at a junction when your position might suggest otherwise
- D. When driving on motorways or dual carriageways to warn drivers behind you of a hazard ahead
- E. When your vehicle has stopped to warn others of an obstruction

807 LGV
When pulling up on the left in busy places you should be careful that

Mark one answer

- A. there is good access to unload
- B. you have disconnected all air lines
- C. your nearside mirror does not strike the head of a pedestrian
- D. you change your tachograph mode

808 LGV
You have just parked a lorry at a roadside in very heavy traffic. Before dismounting from the cab you should be particularly careful to do which one of the following?

Mark one answer
- [ ] A. Make sure the radio is turned down
- [ ] B. Check the rear view mirrors
- [ ] C. Make sure the hazard warning lights are on
- [ ] D. Check that all windows are closed

809 LGV
You are driving a long, rigid vehicle. Where must you NOT park?

Mark one answer
- [ ] A. On a pedestrian crossing
- [ ] B. In a lay-by
- [ ] C. In a loading bay
- [ ] D. On a service area

810 LGV
You want to park a semi-trailer and leave it unattended. Where should you NOT do this?

Mark one answer
- [ ] A. In a lorry park
- [ ] B. On level ground
- [ ] C. In a factory
- [ ] D. In a lay-by

811 LGV
Which ONE of the following is NOT important when getting out of a lorry cab?

Mark one answer
- [ ] A. Watching for approaching traffic
- [ ] B. Using the mirrors
- [ ] C. Applying the parking brake
- [ ] D. Disconnecting the air lines

812 LGV
You are the driver of a tanker vehicle. When opening the tank hatches, what dangers should you be aware of?

Mark three answers
- [ ] A. Low air pressure
- [ ] B. Speed limiters
- [ ] C. Slippery walkways
- [ ] D. Emergency air lines
- [ ] E. Overhead cables
- [ ] F. Overhead pipeways

813 PCV
You have arrived at your destination. All your passengers want to leave the bus. Ideally their valuables should be

Mark one answer
- [ ] A. placed on luggage racks
- [ ] B. taken with them
- [ ] C. placed on the seats
- [ ] D. left with you

814 PCV
You are unloading luggage from your coach. Which of these should you wear?

Mark one answer
- [ ] A. High-visibility vest
- [ ] B. Heat-proof gloves
- [ ] C. Safety goggles
- [ ] D. Ear protectors

815 PCV/LGV
You are about to lift a heavy box or suitcase. What should you try to avoid while doing this?

Mark one answer
- A. Bending your knees
- B. Twisting your back
- C. Changing your position
- D. Moving your feet

816 PCV/LGV
When lifting a heavy box or suitcase manually, what should you try to do?

Mark one answer
- A. Lift and twist together
- B. Look down all the time
- C. Lean sideways and lift
- D. Look ahead when the load is secure

817 PCV/LGV
You are lifting a heavy object. What is recognised as good technique?

Mark one answer
- A. Twisting your back while lifting
- B. Having a stable position
- C. Holding the load at arm's length
- D. Lifting the load as quickly as possible

818 PCV/LGV
You are lifting a heavy object. Which THREE things should you do?

Mark three answers
- A. Adopt a stable position
- B. Get a good hold on the object
- C. Move smoothly
- D. Twist your back
- E. Lean sideways
- F. Keep your legs straight

819 LGV
You are working on the platform of a flat-bed lorry. What is the safest way to get down to the ground?

Mark one answer
- A. Use a suitable set of steps
- B. Jump down wearing non-slip shoes
- C. Use ropes to lower yourself down
- D. Climb down facing away from the vehicle

820 LGV
You are transporting a high-value load of cigarettes. What do you need to consider?

Mark one answer
- A. The possibility of a theft or hijack incident
- B. There will be more Customs and Excise checks
- C. You will be allowed to take fewer rest breaks
- D. You will need to maintain your regular route

821 LGV
About 3000 trucks are stolen every year. For added security, what should you consider having on your vehicle?

Mark one answer
- A. Roof markings
- B. Diff-locks
- C. Air horns
- D. Tinted windows

822
LGV
Which may need to be transported at controlled temperatures?

Mark one answer
- A. Perishable foods
- B. Barrels of beer
- C. Cement
- D. Silage

823
LGV
You are driving a loaded skip lorry. The skip should be covered. What is the main reason for this?

Mark one answer
- A. To prevent spillages
- B. To stop children climbing in
- C. To keep the contents dry
- D. To prevent theft

824
LGV
Why is it important to distribute the weight evenly over the axles when loading a lorry?

Mark one answer
- A. To ensure easy unloading
- B. To make it easier to sheet up
- C. To ensure maximum ground clearance
- D. To ensure maximum stability

825
LGV
Which of the following is most important when loading a vehicle?

Mark one answer
- A. Spreading the load evenly
- B. Loading it towards the rear
- C. Loading it towards the front
- D. Easy access for unloading

826
LGV
You are driving a lorry with an ISO container on a trailer. You must make sure that

Mark one answer
- A. the container is secured by ropes
- B. all locking levers are secured
- C. the trailer has a flat-bed platform
- D. the container is sealed

827
LGV
You are loading a steel ISO container. Which statement is true?

Mark one answer
- A. Its own weight will hold it in place
- B. It can be loaded onto any flat-bed lorry
- C. The locking levers must be secured
- D. The container should be roped in place

828
LGV
You are using three sheets to cover your load. Which of the following shows the correct overlap?

Mark one answer
- A.
- B.
- C.
- D.

329 LGV

You are covering a load using more than one sheet. You should start with the rearmost sheet first, then work forwards. This will

Mark one answer

- [ ] **A.** stop you tripping over when walking on the load
- [ ] **B.** stop wind and rain getting under the sheets
- [ ] **C.** make it much easier to fold up the sheets
- [ ] **D.** make it easier to carry longer loads

330 LGV

When roping down a load on your lorry what is the best knot to use?

Mark one answer

- [ ] **A.** A dolly knot
- [ ] **B.** A reef knot
- [ ] **C.** A slip knot
- [ ] **D.** A bow-line knot

331 LGV

Ropes are unsuitable to tie down a load of scrap metal because they

Mark one answer

- [ ] **A.** are hard to tie
- [ ] **B.** will loosen in rain
- [ ] **C.** are hard to untie
- [ ] **D.** wear and snap

332 LGV

You are driving a tipper lorry carrying loose dry sand. Why should you sheet this load?

Mark one answer

- [ ] **A.** To stop handling being affected
- [ ] **B.** To stop the load from shifting
- [ ] **C.** To stop the load from blowing away
- [ ] **D.** To aid your rearward vision

833 LGV

The load on a lorry becomes insecure on a journey. The driver should

Mark one answer

- [ ] **A.** continue at a slower speed to ensure the load does not fall off
- [ ] **B.** attach 'hazard' boards to warn other road users
- [ ] **C.** park and re-secure the load before continuing
- [ ] **D.** inform base at the earliest opportunity

834 LGV

Which of the following would reduce the 'wave effect' when driving tankers?

Mark one answer

- [ ] **A.** Spray guards
- [ ] **B.** Harsh braking
- [ ] **C.** Baffle plates
- [ ] **D.** Wind deflectors

835 LGV

You are driving an articulated tanker vehicle on a straight road. When braking to a stop the liquid load will tend to

Mark one answer

- [ ] **A.** push the vehicle forward
- [ ] **B.** push the vehicle to the side
- [ ] **C.** make the trailer wheels bounce
- [ ] **D.** make the trailer wheels skid

836 LGV
You are driving a tanker that is half full. The inside of the tank is not divided into compartments. When braking to a stop you should

Mark one answer
- A. avoid relaxing the footbrake
- B. relax the footbrake
- C. pump the footbrake rapidly
- D. use the footbrake and parking brake together

837 LGV
Which type of load would most benefit from being carried on a lorry fitted with road-friendly suspension?

Mark one answer
- A. Steel
- B. Timber
- C. Glass
- D. Cables

838 LGV
An attendant must accompany you when your load is wider than

Mark one answer
- A. 2.6 metres (8 feet 5 inches)
- B. 3.0 metres (9 feet 9 inches)
- C. 3.3 metres (10 feet 9 inches)
- D. 3.5 metres (11 feet 5 inches)

839 LGV
Jack-knifing of an articulated lorry is more likely to occur when the trailer is

Mark one answer
- A. loaded at the front
- B. loaded at the rear
- C. unloaded
- D. fully loaded

840 LGV
After recoupling, how should you make sure that the tractor and trailer are secure?

Mark one answer
- A. Try to move forward with the trailer parking brake on
- B. Reverse with the trailer parking brake on
- C. Try to move forward with the trailer parking brake off
- D. Reverse with the trailer parking brake off

841 LGV
When uncoupling or recoupling your trailer, what must you check first?

Mark one answer
- A. The lights are working
- B. The tilt cab mechanism is secure
- C. The trailer brake is applied
- D. The air lines are safely stowed

842 LGV
You are uncoupling a lorry and trailer. After disconnecting the electric line you should

Mark one answer
- A. stow it away safely
- B. drive forward slowly
- C. lower the landing gear
- D. apply the trailer brake

843 LGV
Your lorry has a demountable body. Before demounting the body you should ensure that

Mark one answer
- A. the rear doors are open
- B. the legs are up
- C. the body is unloaded and empty
- D. the surface is firm and level

844
LGV

After recoupling your trailer you should adjust your mirrors to enable you to see

Mark one answer

- [ ] **A.** the full view of your load
- [ ] **B.** both pairs of rear wheels
- [ ] **C.** down each side of the trailer
- [ ] **D.** the road on the other side

845
LGV

Which one of the following vehicles is most likely to be affected by 'vehicle bounce'?

Mark one answer

- [ ] **A.** A long wheel-base empty vehicle
- [ ] **B.** A short wheel-base laden vehicle
- [ ] **C.** A short wheel-base empty vehicle
- [ ] **D.** A long wheel-base laden vehicle

846
LGV

Ropes should NOT be used to tie down a load of

Mark one answer

- [ ] **A.** timber planks
- [ ] **B.** hay bales
- [ ] **C.** steel plates
- [ ] **D.** canvas sacks

847
LGV

Which of the following loads is most likely to move forward with some force if you brake sharply?

Mark one answer

- [ ] **A.** Heavy material in canvas sacks
- [ ] **B.** Loose sand
- [ ] **C.** Timber secured with dolly knots
- [ ] **D.** Tubular metal

848
LGV

When part loading a lorry with an empty ISO container you should position it

Mark one answer

- [ ] **A.** close to the fifth wheel
- [ ] **B.** over the front axle
- [ ] **C.** close to the trailer edge
- [ ] **D.** over the rear axles

849
LGV

When carrying spare sheets and ropes on your trailer you MUST make sure that they are

Mark one answer

- [ ] **A.** laid out flat
- [ ] **B.** visible from the cab
- [ ] **C.** tied down securely
- [ ] **D.** stacked loosely

850
LGV

Jack-knifing is more likely to occur when driving

Mark one answer

- [ ] **A.** a flat-bed lorry
- [ ] **B.** a laden lorry
- [ ] **C.** a high-sided lorry
- [ ] **D.** an unladen lorry

851
LGV

Short wheel-base vehicles will bounce more noticeably than some long wheel-base vehicles particularly when

Mark one answer

- [ ] **A.** laden
- [ ] **B.** turning
- [ ] **C.** empty
- [ ] **D.** unloading

852
LGV

What are the main causes of a lorry shedding its load?

Mark four answers

- [ ] **A.** Driving on motorways
- [ ] **B.** Sudden change of direction
- [ ] **C.** Driving over a level crossing
- [ ] **D.** Harsh use of brakes
- [ ] **E.** Driving too fast
- [ ] **F.** Sudden change of speed

853
LGV

You are driving a double-deck bodied lorry. What could happen if the top deck is loaded and the lower deck is empty?

Mark one answer

- [ ] **A.** The lorry will become unstable under normal braking
- [ ] **B.** The brakes will be less effective
- [ ] **C.** The lorry may overturn when cornering
- [ ] **D.** You will need to change gear more often

854
LGV

Your lorry has a double-deck body. The top tier is loaded and the lower deck is empty. When will this cause the most danger?

Mark one answer

- [ ] **A.** In heavy fog
- [ ] **B.** In high winds
- [ ] **C.** In hot weather
- [ ] **D.** In heavy rain

855
LGV

You are carrying another vehicle piggy-back on your lorry. Chocks should be used to secure the wheels. What else should you use?

Mark one answer

- [ ] **A.** A trolley jack
- [ ] **B.** Axle stands
- [ ] **C.** Restraining straps
- [ ] **D.** A scaffolding bar

856
LGV

The lorry you are driving is heavily laden. Approaching a bend too fast may cause the load to

Mark one answer

- [ ] **A.** push your lorry to the left
- [ ] **B.** pull your lorry to the right
- [ ] **C.** push your lorry straight on
- [ ] **D.** pull your lorry back

857
LGV

You are driving a vehicle with an unladen trailer. You change into a low gear while travelling at speed. What could happen?

Mark one answer

- [ ] **A.** Your vehicle may suddenly accelerate
- [ ] **B.** The endurance brake will come on
- [ ] **C.** You will not be able to brake
- [ ] **D.** Your vehicle could go out of control

358 LGV
Your lorry has a crane fitted. You are loading very heavy items. You feel that the ropes or straps may break. You should

Mark one answer
- **A.** reposition the load
- **B.** use chains and tensioners
- **C.** tie two straps together
- **D.** continue loading carefully

359 LGV
You are carrying other vehicles piggy-back. You should use restraints and the parking brake on each. What else should you do?

Mark one answer
- **A.** Make sure the vehicles are sheeted
- **B.** Place chocks under the wheels
- **C.** Put the heavy vehicles at the top
- **D.** Rope the vehicles together

360 LGV
An articulated car transporter will be least stable when

Mark one answer
- **A.** only the lower deck is loaded
- **B.** only the top deck is loaded
- **C.** it is fully laden
- **D.** it is unladen

361 LGV
What do the legs on a demountable body allow you to do?

Mark one answer
- **A.** Load and unload the body without stopping
- **B.** Stack one body on top of another
- **C.** Drive under and out from the body
- **D.** Alter the overall height of the vehicle

862 LGV
The legs on a demountable body allow you to

Mark one answer
- **A.** load and unload the body without stopping
- **B.** stack one body on top of another
- **C.** alter the overall height of the vehicle
- **D.** demount the body without a crane or lift

863 LGV
What shape are hazardous cargo labels?

Mark one answer
- **A.** Diamond
- **B.** Triangle
- **C.** Circle
- **D.** Oval

864 LGV
Baffle plates help reduce the load movement in lorries that are carrying

Mark one answer
- **A.** containers
- **B.** cars
- **C.** animals
- **D.** liquids

865 LGV
Baffle plates are fitted to tankers to help

Mark one answer
- **A.** reduce wind resistance
- **B.** reduce the 'wave effect'
- **C.** stop the brakes from locking
- **D.** make the steering lighter

866 LGV
Which of these vehicles will be most at risk of 'roll-over' when laden?

Mark one answer

A.

B.

C.

D.

867 LGV
You are unloading an end-tipper lorry. Before tipping the body what should you do?

Mark one answer

- A. Ensure the vehicle is on a firm level surface
- B. Park facing uphill to make unloading easy
- C. Ensure the vehicle is on a soft sloping surface
- D. Park downhill for easier unloading

868 LGV
The load on your trailer hits a railway bridge. You must report it to

Mark two answers N

- A. The police
- B. The Transport Police
- C. The Highways Agency
- D. The railway authority
- E. The local authority

869 LGV
When loading you should NOT exceed axle weight limits. Overloading an axle can result in

Mark one answer

- A. reduced fuel consumption
- B. increased service intervals
- C. a shorter stopping distance
- D. prosecution

870 LGV
Which of these best describes the vehicle's payload?

Mark one answer

- A. The maximum load the vehicle can carry
- B. The maximum load over each axle
- C. The maximum load plus the weight of the vehicle
- D. The maximum load each tyre can take

871 LGV
You are transporting frozen foods. What important additional training do you need specific to the food industry?

Mark one answer

- A. Packaging procedures
- B. Weight distribution procedures
- C. Waste handling procedures
- D. Hygiene procedures

872
LGV
You are delivering a load of building materials on pallets. Before unloading what should you ensure FIRST?

Mark one answer
- A. The engine is switched off
- B. You are parked on firm level ground
- C. The stabilising legs are lowered
- D. You have warning cones set out

873
LGV
You are loading goods of varying weights. How should these be distributed over the width of the vehicle?

Mark one answer
- A. Heavy items at the front, light items at the rear
- B. Light items near the centre line, heavy items towards the sides
- C. Heavy items near the centre line, light items towards the sides
- D. Light items at the front, heavy items at the rear

874
LGV
You are working on a vehicle platform. What should you NOT do?

Mark one answer
- A. Wear brightly coloured clothing
- B. Walk forward near the edges
- C. Wear non-slip footwear
- D. Walk backwards near the edges

875
LGV
Which THREE may need to be transported at controlled temperatures?

Mark three answers
- A. Frozen foods
- B. Chemicals
- C. Chilled foods
- D. Cement
- E. Bulk grain
- F. Timber

876
LGV
You are about to transport livestock. You will need

Mark one answer
- A. to have practical experience to care for animals
- B. to be a member of the RSPCA
- C. to have no driving convictions
- D. to drive for long periods without a break

877
LGV
You need to transport a small herd of pigs. They will only partially fill the vehicle. What should you do?

Mark one answer
- A. Allow no direct access to the animals
- B. Check them for disease before you load
- C. Give the animals plenty of space
- D. Create compartments using moveable panels

878

LGV

You have to transport a flock of sheep. The journey will take longer than eight hours. You MUST make sure

Mark one answer

- [ ] **A.** you only use a vehicle with air conditioning
- [ ] **B.** there is no loose bedding on the floor
- [ ] **C.** you only drive during daylight hours
- [ ] **D.** there is direct access to the animals

879

LGV

You have to transport a flock of sheep. The journey will take longer than eight hours. You MUST make sure

Mark one answer

- [ ] **A.** there is sufficient bedding material on the floor
- [ ] **B.** there is no direct access to the animals
- [ ] **C.** you do not take your normal rest breaks
- [ ] **D.** you do not drive through the night

880

LGV

Your vehicle has a maximum authorised mass (MAM) of 40 tonnes. The kerbside weight is 15 tonnes. What would your maximum payload be?

Mark one answer

- [ ] **A.** 15 tonnes
- [ ] **B.** 25 tonnes
- [ ] **C.** 35 tonnes
- [ ] **D.** 45 tonnes

881

LGV

You are making several deliveries. What problems may this increasingly smaller payload cause?

Mark one answer

- [ ] **A.** You might overload an axle
- [ ] **B.** You will always have heavy items remaining
- [ ] **C.** You might exceed your kerbside weight
- [ ] **D.** You will damage the rest of the load

882

LGV

Axle weight limits should NOT be exceeded. Overloading an axle can result in

Mark one answer

- [ ] **A.** reduced braking efficiency
- [ ] **B.** reduced braking distance
- [ ] **C.** increased kerbside weight
- [ ] **D.** increased fuel efficiency

883

LGV

You are loading a lorry. What could be the result of overloading an axle

Mark one answer

- [ ] **A.** Reduced tyre temperature
- [ ] **B.** Damage to the road surface
- [ ] **C.** Damage to the tachograph
- [ ] **D.** Increased tyre life

884

LGV

You are transporting a skip carrying loose waste. The material should be

Mark one answer

- [ ] **A.** covered
- [ ] **B.** shrink-wrapped
- [ ] **C.** visible
- [ ] **D.** kept dry

885 LGV

You are securing a very heavy load with a ratchet strap. What type of anchorage point should NOT be used?

Mark one answer

- [ ] **A.** Rope hook
- [ ] **B.** Eye bolt
- [ ] **C.** Shackle
- [ ] **D.** 'D' link

886 LGV

You are securing a load using wire ropes. What is the minimum diameter of rope that should be used?

Mark one answer

- [ ] **A.** 4mm
- [ ] **B.** 8mm
- [ ] **C.** 12mm
- [ ] **D.** 16mm

887 LGV

You are securing a load using chains. What type of chain should NOT be used?

Mark one answer

- [ ] **A.** Short link
- [ ] **B.** Round link
- [ ] **C.** Oval link
- [ ] **D.** Split link

888 LGV

You are using chains to secure a load. What type of chain should NOT be used?

Mark one answer

- [ ] **A.** Square link
- [ ] **B.** Round link
- [ ] **C.** Iron
- [ ] **D.** Steel

889 LGV

You are securing a load using ropes. What is the minimum diameter that should be used?

Mark one answer

- [ ] **A.** 5mm
- [ ] **B.** 10mm
- [ ] **C.** 15mm
- [ ] **D.** 20mm

890 LGV

You are loading timber onto a flat-bed lorry. You want to cover it with sheets. Which sheet should be positioned first?

Mark one answer

- [ ] **A.** Front
- [ ] **B.** Middle
- [ ] **C.** Rear
- [ ] **D.** Side

891 LGV

Which of these may need to be transported at controlled temperatures?

Mark one answer

- [ ] **A.** Chemicals
- [ ] **B.** Bulk grain
- [ ] **C.** Sugar
- [ ] **D.** Beer barrels

892 LGV
Which symbol on a lorry means it is likely to be carrying compressed gases?

Mark one answer

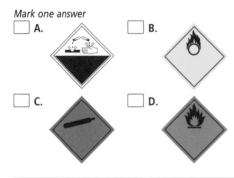

- [ ] A.
- [ ] B.
- [ ] C.
- [ ] D.

893 LGV
You see this symbol on a lorry. What is it carrying?

Mark one answer
- [ ] A. Corrosive materials
- [ ] B. Compressed gases
- [ ] C. Oxidising agents
- [ ] D. Radioactive materials

894 LGV
Which symbol on the back of a lorry means it is carrying corrosives?

Mark one answer

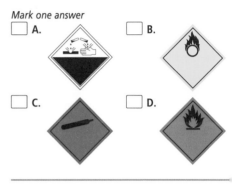

- [ ] A.
- [ ] B.
- [ ] C.
- [ ] D.

895 LGV
Which symbol on a lorry shows its load is dangerous when wet?

Mark one answer

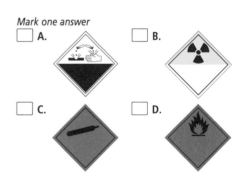

- [ ] A.
- [ ] B.
- [ ] C.
- [ ] D.

896 LGV
You are driving a loaded lorry with curtain sides. You can see the curtain bulging on one side. What should you do?

Mark one answer

- A. Check the load by carefully entering by the rear door or opposite curtain
- B. Check the load by carefully opening the curtain in the affected area
- C. Continue driving as this is normal for these types of vehicles
- D. Continue driving at a much reduced speed

897 LGV
You are loading a curtain-sided vehicle. What should you NOT use the curtains for?

Mark one answer

- A. Restraint
- B. Protection from the weather
- C. Security
- D. Advertising the company name

898 LGV
You are using a lorry-mounted crane to unload building materials. What safety features should you use?

Mark one answer

- A. Wheel-clamps
- B. Kingpin locks
- C. Jockey wheels
- D. Vehicle stabilisers

899 LGV
You intend to move a heavy object using a barrow or trolley. What is the best position for the handle height?

Mark one answer

- A. Between the shoulder and waist
- B. As high as you can reach
- C. Between the knee and waist
- D. As low as possible for comfort

900 LGV
Your vehicle has a maximum authorised mass (MAM) of 40 tonnes. The tare weight is 10 tonnes. What would your maximum payload be?

Mark one answer

- A. 20 tonnes
- B. 30 tonnes
- C. 40 tonnes
- D. 50 tonnes

901
PCV/LGV
Your vehicle is fitted with a reverse warning bleeper. When driving backwards you

Mark one answer
- **A.** do not need to look round
- **B.** should only use the offside mirror
- **C.** still need to take all-round observation
- **D.** should only use the nearside mirror

902
PCV/LGV
Large vehicles have many blind spots. What does 'blind spot' mean?

Mark one answer
- **A.** An area of road covered by your right-hand mirror
- **B.** An area of road covered by your left-hand mirror
- **C.** An area of road that cannot be seen in your mirrors
- **D.** An area of road that is not lit by your headlights

903
PCV/LGV
Because of its size and design a large vehicle will have

Mark one answer
- **A.** less blind spots than smaller vehicles
- **B.** more blind spots than smaller vehicles
- **C.** the same blind spots as smaller vehicles
- **D.** no blind spots at all

904
PCV/LGV
The audible warning device is operating as you reverse. You should be

Mark one answer
- **A.** relying on a clear path behind
- **B.** expecting others to be aware of your course
- **C.** taking continuous, all-round observation
- **D.** concentrating solely on your blind areas

905
PCV/LGV
Many modern vehicles are fitted with an additional nearside mirror. This is positioned so that the driver can see

Mark one answer
- **A.** the front wheel in relation to the kerb
- **B.** the exhaust to check for excessive emissions
- **C.** the rear of the vehicle when reversing
- **D.** the distance the following vehicle is behind

906
LGV
Your lorry has a sleeper cab. A quick sideways glance would be helpful especially

Mark two answers
- **A.** after driving over a pedestrian crossing
- **B.** when traffic is merging from the right or left
- **C.** before climbing a steep hill
- **D.** when driving round sharp bends
- **E.** before changing lanes on a motorway

907 PCV
Some coaches have a mirror on their nearside angled down to show the front nearside wheel. This should be used when you are

Mark two answers
- A. pulling in after overtaking
- B. pulling up to park at the kerb
- C. moving close to the left in normal driving
- D. changing lanes on a motorway

908 PCV
In a bus with a high driving position you may have to look out for

Mark one answer
- A. cyclists close in front
- B. cyclists close behind
- C. large vehicles close in front
- D. large vehicles close behind

909 PCV
On a coach with high side windows it can be difficult to see either side. What should you do before you pull away?

Mark one answer
- A. Get out of your vehicle and stop the traffic
- B. Ask a passenger to make sure it is safe to move off
- C. Indicate before checking all of your mirrors
- D. Open the window and look down and round to the right

910 PCV
Your bus has a high seating position. Which of these may be out of sight below the windscreen line?

Mark one answer
- A. Following vehicles
- B. Overtaking vehicles
- C. Cyclists and pedestrians
- D. Other buses

911 PCV/LGV
What should you first check before moving to the LEFT?

Mark one answer
- A. The nearside mirror
- B. The offside mirror
- C. Behind, over your right shoulder
- D. Behind, over your left shoulder

912 PCV/LGV
What should you first check before moving to the RIGHT?

Mark one answer
- A. The nearside mirror
- B. Behind, over your left shoulder
- C. Behind, over your right shoulder
- D. The offside mirror

913 PCV/LGV
You are about to move off. You should always

Mark one answer

- [ ] **A.** extend your right arm as far as you can out of the window
- [ ] **B.** use only the offside mirror and move away quickly
- [ ] **C.** signal right with indicator and arm together
- [ ] **D.** use your mirrors and look behind

914 PCV/LGV
In which THREE of the following situations would you FIRST need to check your nearside mirror?

Mark three answers

- [ ] **A.** Before moving out to pass a car parked on your left
- [ ] **B.** After passing cars on your left
- [ ] **C.** Before moving to the left
- [ ] **D.** After passing pedestrians standing on the nearside kerb
- [ ] **E.** Before moving out to the right

915 PCV/LGV
The MSM routine is used to negotiate a hazard. What do the initials MSM stand for?

Mark one answer

- [ ] **A.** Mirror, signal, manoeuvre
- [ ] **B.** Manoeuvre, speed, mirror
- [ ] **C.** Mirror, speed, manoeuvre
- [ ] **D.** Manoeuvre, signal, mirror

916 PCV/LGV
What does this sign mean?

Mark one answer

- [ ] **A.** Contraflow bus and cycle lane
- [ ] **B.** With-flow bus and cycle lane
- [ ] **C.** No buses or cycles
- [ ] **D.** Priority to buses or cycles

917 PCV/LGV
To have good all-round vision you should make sure that

Mark one answer

- [ ] **A.** windows are open
- [ ] **B.** a sun visor is fitted
- [ ] **C.** your seat is properly adjusted
- [ ] **D.** all lights are clean

918 PCV/LGV
Some large vehicles with restricted vision to the rear may be fitted with an audible warning device for reversing. In areas with a 30mph restriction the device may be used

Mark one answer

- [ ] **A.** between 7am and 11.30pm only
- [ ] **B.** between 11.30pm and 7am only
- [ ] **C.** during hours of daylight only
- [ ] **D.** at any time

919
PCV/LGV
Driving too close to the vehicle in front will

Mark one answer

- **A.** decrease your view ahead
- **B.** increase your view ahead
- **C.** increase the view of following drivers
- **D.** decrease the view of following drivers

920
PCV/LGV
At junctions it is difficult to see motorcyclists because they

Mark two answers

- **A.** are easily hidden in blind spots
- **B.** always ride in the gutter
- **C.** always wear black leathers
- **D.** are smaller than other vehicles

921
PCV/LGV
Just before turning right from a main road to a side road, you should check your right-hand mirror. This is because

Mark one answer

- **A.** there may be pedestrians stepping off the kerb
- **B.** you need to check your position
- **C.** a motorcyclist may be overtaking you
- **D.** your rear view to the left is blocked

922
PCV/LGV
Before turning left you should have a final look into the

Mark one answer

- **A.** left-hand mirror
- **B.** interior mirror
- **C.** right-hand mirror
- **D.** overtaking mirror

923
PCV/LGV
You are driving a long vehicle. Before turning left onto a main road you should be ESPECIALLY careful of

Mark two answers

- **A.** cyclists alongside you on the left
- **B.** motorcyclists alongside you on the left
- **C.** motorcyclists coming from your left
- **D.** cyclists coming from your left

924
PCV/LGV
You want to turn right at a roundabout marked with two right-turn lanes. There is ample room for your vehicle in either lane. You should

Mark one answer

- **A.** use the right-hand of the two lanes
- **B.** use the left-hand of the two lanes
- **C.** use the left-hand lane then move to the right as you enter the roundabout
- **D.** use the right-hand lane then move to the left as you enter the roundabout

925 PCV/LGV
You are turning right at a T-junction. Your view to the right and left is blocked due to parked vehicles. You should

Mark one answer
- A. lean forward to get a better view without crossing the 'give way' lines
- B. edge out until you are about 1 metre (3 feet 3 inches) over the 'give way' lines
- C. ease forward until you can see clearly past the vehicles
- D. ask a passenger to assist by waving you out when clear

926 LGV
Some lorries have an extra mirror angled down towards the nearside front wheel. This mirror is ESPECIALLY useful when

Mark two answers
- A. moving off
- B. parking
- C. checking your trailer
- D. turning right
- E. overtaking

927 LGV
You wish to park your trailer. The site you choose should be

Mark three answers
- A. firm
- B. downhill
- C. uphill
- D. legal
- E. grassed
- F. level

928 LGV
You are driving a lorry. You are about to move off from behind a stationary car. What should you do?

Mark three answers
- A. Start to signal when moving
- B. Signal before moving, if necessary
- C. Check the blind spot before moving
- D. Use both mirrors before moving
- E. Use both mirrors only after moving

929 LGV
You are driving this lorry. Emerging at this junction needs extra care because of the

Mark one answer
- A. bollards in the middle of the road
- B. traffic from the right
- C. motorcycle on the left
- D. grass verge on the left

930 LGV
You are driving this lorry (arrowed). An emergency vehicle is trying to emerge from the side road. You should

Mark one answer

- **A.** brake hard to a stop and wave it out
- **B.** brake smoothly and allow it to emerge
- **C.** drive on, you are on the major road
- **D.** turn left quickly to give it a clear view

931 LGV
You are unable to see clearly when reversing into a loading bay. You should

Mark one answer

- **A.** get someone to guide you
- **B.** use an audible warning signal
- **C.** back into the bay until your bumper touches
- **D.** open your door and lean well out.

932 LGV
You are driving this lorry and turning right from this minor road. What should you be ESPECIALLY aware of?

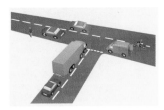

Mark one answer

- **A.** Motorcyclist from the right passing the parked van
- **B.** Vehicles coming from the left along the main road
- **C.** Pedestrians on the footpath on the main road
- **D.** Vehicles coming from the rear on the minor road

933 LGV
You are parking your lorry at night. In which of these places must you use parking lights?

Mark one answer

- **A.** On the road
- **B.** In a motorway service area
- **C.** In a factory entrance
- **D.** In dock authority areas

934 LGV
You are turning right in this lorry (arrowed). The main dangers to be aware of are

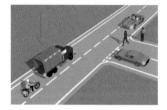

Mark two answers
- [ ] **A.** the pedestrian stepping out
- [ ] **B.** the following motorcyclist
- [ ] **C.** the oncoming car
- [ ] **D.** the 'give way' lines

935 LGV
You have a sleeper cab fitted to your lorry. This could make your driving more difficult because it

Mark one answer
- [ ] **A.** increases your blind spots
- [ ] **B.** increases your view of the road ahead
- [ ] **C.** reduces your view in the right-hand mirror
- [ ] **D.** reduces your view in the left-hand mirror

936 LGV
You are waiting to turn right in this lorry (arrowed). What dangers shoul you be most aware of?

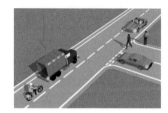

Mark two answers
- [ ] **A.** The oncoming car
- [ ] **B.** The pedestrians
- [ ] **C.** The hazard line
- [ ] **D.** The motorcycle
- [ ] **E.** The car waiting to emerge
- [ ] **F.** The 'give way' lines

937 PCV/LGV
Before reversing you MUST always

Mark one answer
- [ ] **A.** remove your seat belt
- [ ] **B.** look all around
- [ ] **C.** use an audible warning device
- [ ] **D.** change the tachograph setting

938 PCV
Which category licence do you need to drive a tri-axle double-deck coach?

Mark one answer
- A. D1
- B. D
- C. D1+E
- D. C

939 PCV
At international ports, why may coaches be subject to a search by immigration authorities?

Mark one answer
- A. For national security
- B. To check for red diesel
- C. For tachograph regulations
- D. To check vehicle condition

940 PCV
You are returning from Europe with a coach. Why should you search the vehicle at the port?

Mark one answer
- A. To look for missing property
- B. To ensure duty-free limits are not exceeded
- C. To prevent the carriage of illegal immigrants
- D. To ensure the vehicle has the correct documentation

941 PCV
You are making a journey which crosses international borders. Which document should you produce at immigration control?

Mark one answer
- A. A list of passengers
- B. A breakdown insurance certificate
- C. A route plan
- D. A list of alcohol on board

942 PCV
What licence category do you need to drive an articulated bus ('bendi-bus')?

Mark one answer
- A. D1+E
- B. D
- C. D+E
- D. D1

943 PCV
The holder of a full category D licence can tow a trailer with a maximum authorised mass (MAM) NOT exceeding

Mark one answer
- A. 750kg
- B. 1000kg
- C. 1250kg
- D. 1500kg

944 PCV
You hold a full category D licence. This means you

Mark one answer
- A. cannot tow a trailer at all
- B. can tow a trailer not exceeding 750kg
- C. can tow a trailer of any weight
- D. cannot tow a trailer with more than one axle

945 PCV
You are the driver of a coach. You are loading luggage before a long continental tour. In the interests of security and passenger confidence, what should you do?

Mark one answer
- [ ] **A.** Load the luggage before allowing any passengers on board
- [ ] **B.** Make sure all passengers are seated and then load the luggage
- [ ] **C.** Make sure the passengers load their luggage as they arrive
- [ ] **D.** Allow passengers to load their luggage in accordance with the seating plan

946 PCV
You intend to drive a midibus for hire or reward. It will have more than 16 passenger seats. What is the minimum licence entitlement you need?

Mark one answer
- [ ] **A.** C
- [ ] **B.** C1
- [ ] **C.** D
- [ ] **D.** D1

947 PCV
Which licence category do you need to drive a bus with 25 passenger seats?

Mark one answer
- [ ] **A.** D
- [ ] **B.** D1
- [ ] **C.** D+E
- [ ] **D.** D1+E

948 PCV
Which authority has the power to impose conditions on a passenger carrying vehicle (PCV) operators licence?

Mark one answer
- [ ] **A.** The Traffic Commissioner
- [ ] **B.** DVLA
- [ ] **C.** VOSA
- [ ] **D.** The Highways Agency

949 PCV/LGV
You will be driving your vehicle in Europe. Which of these documents MUST you carry?

Mark one answer
- [ ] **A.** The vehicle service record
- [ ] **B.** Your medical examination form
- [ ] **C.** Your national driving licence
- [ ] **D.** The vehicle workshop manual

950 PCV/LGV
You may be prevented from obtaining a lorry or bus licence if you have

Mark one answer
- [ ] **A.** dyslexia
- [ ] **B.** partial blindness
- [ ] **C.** skin problems
- [ ] **D.** stomach problems

951

PCV/LGV

You have been convicted of a drink-drive offence while driving your car, and banned from driving. This ban will affect

Mark one answer

- **A.** all your driving entitlements
- **B.** only your car entitlement
- **C.** only your lorry entitlement
- **D.** only your bus entitlement

952

PCV/LGV

You are two and a half times over the legal alcohol limit. You are disqualified from driving. Before regaining your licence who will you have to satisfy that you do NOT have an alcohol problem?

Mark one answer   **NI**

- **A.** The local hospital
- **B.** Drivers' Medical Branch, DVLA
- **C.** Alcoholics Anonymous
- **D.** Vehicle and Operator Services Agency

953

PCV/LGV

How long will a Statutory Off Road Notification (SORN) last for?

Mark one answer

- **A.** 12 months
- **B.** 24 months
- **C.** 3 years
- **D.** 10 years

954

PCV/LGV

What is a Statutory Off Road Notification (SORN) declaration?

Mark one answer   **NI**

- **A.** A notification to tell VOSA that a vehicle does not have a current MOT
- **B.** Information kept by the police about the owner of the vehicle
- **C.** A notification to tell DVLA that a vehicle is not being used on the road
- **D.** Information held by insurance companies to check the vehicle is insured

955

PCV/LGV

A Statutory Off Road Notification (SORN) declaration is

Mark one answer   **NI**

- **A.** to tell DVLA that your vehicle is being used on the road but the MOT has expired
- **B.** to tell DVLA that you no longer own the vehicle
- **C.** to tell DVLA that your vehicle is not being used on the road
- **D.** to tell DVLA that you are buying a personal number plate

956

PCV/LGV

A Statutory Off Road Notification (SORN) is valid

Mark one answer

- **A.** for as long as the vehicle has an MOT
- **B.** for 12 months only
- **C.** only if the vehicle is more than 3 years old
- **D.** provided the vehicle is insured

957
PCV/LGV
A Statutory Off Road Notification (SORN) will last

Mark one answer
- [ ] **A.** for the life of the vehicle
- [ ] **B.** for as long as you own the vehicle
- [ ] **C.** for 12 months only
- [ ] **D.** until the vehicle warranty expires

958
PCV/LGV
What is the maximum specified fine for driving without insurance?

Mark one answer
- [ ] **A.** £50
- [ ] **B.** £500
- [ ] **C.** £1000
- [ ] **D.** £5000

959
PCV/LGV
It is an offence to bring an illegal immigrant into the UK. The current fine can be up to

Mark one answer
- [ ] **A.** £1000
- [ ] **B.** £2000
- [ ] **C.** £3000
- [ ] **D.** £4000

960
PCV/LGV
Drivers can be fined for bringing illegal immigrants into the UK. Who else can be fined?

Mark two answers
- [ ] **A.** The vehicle repairer
- [ ] **B.** The vehicle insurer
- [ ] **C.** The vehicle owner
- [ ] **D.** The vehicle hirer

961
PCV/LGV
Operators should operate an 'effective system' to prevent the carriage of illegal immigrants. What are the three main elements of this?

Mark three answers
- [ ] **A.** Vehicle security
- [ ] **B.** Vehicle tracking devices
- [ ] **C.** Vehicle checks
- [ ] **D.** Mobile communications
- [ ] **E.** Documentation

962
PCV/LGV
You are returning to the UK and about to board a ferry. An immigration officer asks to see your documentation. What must you produce immediately?

Mark one answer
- [ ] **A.** The vehicle registration book
- [ ] **B.** The driver's hours record
- [ ] **C.** Operator documentation
- [ ] **D.** Your driving licence

963
PCV/LGV
For a driver convicted of bringing illegal immigrants into the UK, a fine of up to £2,000 can be imposed for each

Mark one answer
- [ ] **A.** family group they bring in
- [ ] **B.** court attendance they make
- [ ] **C.** person they bring in
- [ ] **D.** journey they made in the last year

964

PCV/LGV
The Driver Certificate of Professional Competence (CPC) requires you to take training every five years. What is the MINIMUM number of hours training required?

Mark one answer
- [ ] **A.** 30 hours
- [ ] **B.** 35 hours
- [ ] **C.** 40 hours
- [ ] **D.** 45 hours

965

PCV/LGV
You wish to maintain your Driver Certificate of Professional Competence (CPC). To do this you will need to take a minimum of 35 hours training within a period of

Mark one answer
- [ ] **A.** one year
- [ ] **B.** three years
- [ ] **C.** five years
- [ ] **D.** ten years

966

PCV/LGV
The holder of a Driver Certificate of Professional Competence (CPC) is required to take 35 hours of training every five years. This training must be taken in blocks of at least

Mark one answer
- [ ] **A.** one hour
- [ ] **B.** seven hours
- [ ] **C.** twelve hours
- [ ] **D.** thirty-five hours

967

PCV/LGV
You hold a Driver Certificate of Professional Competence (CPC). Every five years you MUST complete a minimum training period of

Mark one answer
- [ ] **A.** 25 hours
- [ ] **B.** 30 hours
- [ ] **C.** 35 hours
- [ ] **D.** 40 hours

968

PCV/LGV
A driver is applying for a LGV or PCV licence for the first time. They need UNCORRECTED visual acuity in each eye of at least

Mark one answer
- [ ] **A.** 3/60
- [ ] **B.** 6/9
- [ ] **C.** 6/12
- [ ] **D.** 9/60

969

LGV
You have been asked to drive a fully loaded petrol tanker back to the depot. It has a Maximum Authorised Mass (MAM) of 10 tonnes. What MUST you do?

Mark one answer
- [ ] **A.** Notify the police that you are moving a dangerous load
- [ ] **B.** Have a fully qualified tanker driver with you for the journey
- [ ] **C.** Carry a valid DVLA 'approved course' certificate
- [ ] **D.** Complete the whole journey avoiding built-up areas

970 LGV
As a driver of a goods vehicle it is your responsibility to ensure that

Mark one answer
- A. you are correctly paid for the goods after unloading
- B. the goods arrive in the same condition as when loaded
- C. the goods reach their destination ahead of schedule
- D. your return load is at least as heavy as the outward load

971 LGV
The CMR consignment note is generally required for carrying goods overseas for hire or reward. How many copies of this note are required?

Mark one answer
- A. Two
- B. Three
- C. Four
- D. Five

972 LGV
You hold a full category C licence. This means that you

Mark one answer
- A. can tow a trailer of any weight
- B. cannot tow a trailer with more than one axle
- C. can tow a trailer up to 750kg
- D. cannot tow a trailer at all

973 LGV
You are delivering boxes of chilled food to a supermarket. In which area may you require additional specific training?

Mark one answer
- A. Hygiene procedures
- B. ADR procedures
- C. Waste-handling procedures
- D. Eco-safe driving procedures

974 PCV/LGV
Your vehicle is fitted with a reverse warning bleeper. You MUST switch it off between the hours of 11.30pm and 7am on a road with a

Mark one answer
- [ ] **A.** 30mph speed limit
- [ ] **B.** temporary speed limit
- [ ] **C.** national speed limit
- [ ] **D.** 40mph speed limit

975 PCV
You are waiting at a terminus for some time. You will reduce pollution by

Mark one answer
- [ ] **A.** revving your engine
- [ ] **B.** switching off your engine
- [ ] **C.** leaving your engine on tickover
- [ ] **D.** keeping your engine at high revs

976 PCV
You are waiting for some time in a stationary traffic queue. Why should you switch your engine off?

Mark three answers
- [ ] **A.** To reduce noise levels
- [ ] **B.** To save on vehicle air pressure
- [ ] **C.** To reduce exhaust fumes
- [ ] **D.** To reduce television interference
- [ ] **E.** To prevent local annoyance

977 PCV
You have been waiting in a traffic queue for several minutes. The road in front is blocked. What should you do?

Mark one answer
- [ ] **A.** Keep your engine at tickover speed
- [ ] **B.** Rev your engine occasionally
- [ ] **C.** Switch off your engine
- [ ] **D.** Run the engine at a constant higher speed

978 PCV
Using air conditioning systems continuously will usually increase fuel consumption by about

Mark one answer
- [ ] **A.** 15%
- [ ] **B.** 30%
- [ ] **C.** 50%
- [ ] **D.** 75%

979 PCV
The occupants of about how many cars can be carried by one double-deck bus?

Mark one answer
- [ ] **A.** 20
- [ ] **B.** 30
- [ ] **C.** 40
- [ ] **D.** 50

980 PCV
After refuelling your bus, what MUST you check before driving?

Mark one answer
- [ ] **A.** Your filler caps are securely shut
- [ ] **B.** Your tank is full to the top
- [ ] **C.** The position of the emergency fuel cut-off switch
- [ ] **D.** The low-fuel warning light is working

981 PCV/LGV
Which of the following would be most affected by a vehicle with faulty suspension?

Mark two answers
- [ ] A. Underground pipes
- [ ] B. Road surfaces
- [ ] C. Tyre pressures
- [ ] D. Road tunnels
- [ ] E. Overhead gantries

982 PCV/LGV
The pictured vehicle is 'environmentally friendly' because it

Mark three answers
- [ ] A. reduces noise pollution
- [ ] B. uses diesel fuel
- [ ] C. uses electricity
- [ ] D. uses unleaded fuel
- [ ] E. reduces parking places
- [ ] F. reduces town traffic

983 PCV/LGV
Which of the following vehicles are MOST likely to cause severe damage to road surfaces?

Mark two answers
- [ ] A. Lorries
- [ ] B. Cars
- [ ] C. Motorcycles
- [ ] D. Bicycles
- [ ] E. Buses

984 PCV/LGV
Air suspension can reduce damage to

Mark three answers
- [ ] A. the fuel system
- [ ] B. the road surface
- [ ] C. passengers
- [ ] D. bridges
- [ ] E. the tachograph
- [ ] F. underground services

985 PCV/LGV
You can help to reduce the impact of road transport on the environment by

Mark two answers
- [ ] A. avoiding high gears
- [ ] B. reducing rest periods
- [ ] C. braking in good time
- [ ] D. increasing your overall speed
- [ ] E. avoiding over-acceleration

986 PCV/LGV
As a driver you can help to protect the environment by

Mark one answer
- [ ] A. driving faster to reduce travelling time
- [ ] B. avoiding town centres and using bypasses
- [ ] C. filling your fuel tank with red diesel fuel
- [ ] D. leaving your engine running in traffic jams

987 PCV/LGV
As a professional driver you should

Mark one answer
- [ ] A. keep to maximum speeds for shorter journeys
- [ ] B. plan routes to avoid busy times and congestion
- [ ] C. avoid route-planning because of the time it takes
- [ ] D. drive at a faster speed through hazardous areas

988 PCV/LGV
You have just refilled your fuel tank. You MUST make sure that the

Mark one answer
- [ ] A. tank is completely full up to the filler neck
- [ ] B. filler cap is vented correctly by keeping it loose
- [ ] C. filler cap is properly closed and secure
- [ ] D. tank is nearly full and the filler cap is slightly loose

989 PCV/LGV
To prevent fuel spillages it is important to

Mark one answer
- [ ] A. stop refuelling when half full
- [ ] B. use a filtered system
- [ ] C. close and secure all filler caps
- [ ] D. place the drip tray correctly

990 PCV/LGV
You are following a lorry with a leaking fuel tank. What should you be especially aware of?

Mark one answer
- [ ] A. The road may be very slippery
- [ ] B. The fuel may splash your vehicle
- [ ] C. Your brake linings will become slippery
- [ ] D. Your spray reducers will not be effective

991 PCV/LGV
The road surface is more likely to be damaged by large vehicles with

Mark one answer
- [ ] A. a mixture of tyre makes
- [ ] B. a mixture of re-cut and new tyres
- [ ] C. faulty spray-suppression equipment
- [ ] D. faulty suspension

992 PCV/LGV
How could you save fuel when driving?

Mark three answers
- [ ] A. By reducing overall speed
- [ ] B. By braking as late as you can
- [ ] C. By planning routes to avoid congestion
- [ ] D. By having properly inflated tyres
- [ ] E. By extending vehicles' service times

993 PCV/LGV
Vehicles have damaged the environment. This has resulted in

Mark three answers
- [ ] A. air pollution
- [ ] B. reduced traffic noise
- [ ] C. building deterioration
- [ ] D. less road surface damage
- [ ] E. using up of natural resources

994 PCV/LGV
In a diesel engine which of the following fuels would most improve vehicle emissions?

Mark one answer
- [ ] A. High sulphur diesel
- [ ] B. Red diesel
- [ ] C. Low sulphur diesel
- [ ] D. Blue diesel

995
PCV/LGV
Using which of the following fuels in a diesel engine would most help the environment?

Mark one answer
- **A.** Anti-waxing diesel
- **B.** Low sulphur diesel
- **C.** Red diesel
- **D.** Anti-foaming diesel

996
PCV/LGV
What must you do after filling your fuel tanks?

Mark two answers
- **A.** Return the pump keys to the office
- **B.** Check your tachograph
- **C.** Clean up any fuel that has spilled
- **D.** Check that the filler caps are closed
- **E.** Complete the fuel log sheets
- **F.** Check your fuel gauge

997
PCV/LGV
Your vehicle is fitted with a reverse warning bleeper. You must switch the bleeper off when reversing

Mark one answer
- **A.** after 11.30pm at night along a 30mph road
- **B.** after 11.30pm at night along a 40mph road
- **C.** near a school entrance
- **D.** near a hospital entrance

998
PCV/LGV
Fuel consumption could be made worse by continuous use of

Mark one answer
- **A.** air suspension
- **B.** heated mirrors
- **C.** air conditioning
- **D.** electrical retarder

999
PCV/LGV
You are driving a vehicle fitted with 'road-friendly' suspension. This helps the environment by reducing damage to

Mark three answers
- **A.** the driver's seat
- **B.** historical buildings
- **C.** the road surface
- **D.** overhead cables
- **E.** river banks
- **F.** bridges

1000
PCV/LGV
As a driver you can help to ease traffic congestion by

Mark one answer
- **A.** planning journeys to avoid the busy times
- **B.** planning journeys to avoid driving at quiet times
- **C.** driving on motorways for all journeys
- **D.** avoiding using motorways for all journeys

1001 PCV/LGV
You are parked for a short period in a town while you plan a route. You should

Mark one answer
- A. keep the engine running on tickover
- B. rev the engine occasionally for air pressure
- C. never turn off the engine for short periods
- D. switch off the engine

1002 PCV/LGV
Which three of the following could cause unnecessary pollution to the environment?

Mark three answers
- A. Excessive exhaust fumes
- B. Regular servicing
- C. Vehicles driven poorly
- D. Poorly maintained vehicles
- E. High level exhaust systems

1003 PCV/LGV
Diesel fuel has been spilled on the road. This will be particularly dangerous for

Mark one answer
- A. lorries
- B. motorcycles
- C. horses
- D. cars

1004 PCV/LGV
Members of the public are encouraged to report any vehicle with

Mark one answer
- A. excessive exhaust fumes
- B. an unsheeted load
- C. different makes of tyres
- D. no contact address visible

1005 PCV/LGV
You should only sound your horn in a built-up area between 11.30pm and 7am when

Mark one answer
- A. you are parked
- B. your vehicle is moving
- C. you are stationary
- D. another vehicle poses a danger

1006 PCV/LGV
You should take great care to avoid spilling diesel. It is very slippery and causes a serious risk on the road, particularly to

Mark one answer
- A. motorcycles
- B. tractors
- C. buses
- D. lorries

1007 LGV
Your lorry has been fitted with wind deflectors. When driving in windy conditions these will help to

Mark two answers
- A. increase the amount of fuel you will use
- B. increase the wind resistance on your vehicle
- C. increase the pressure in the tyres
- D. reduce the wind resistance on your vehicle
- E. reduce the amount of fuel you will use

1008 LGV
Cab-mounted wind deflectors can reduce

Mark one answer
- [ ] **A.** journey times
- [ ] **B.** load capacity
- [ ] **C.** tyre wear
- [ ] **D.** fuel consumption

1009 LGV
Fuel consumption for lorries can be reduced by fitting

Mark two answers
- [ ] **A.** single axles only
- [ ] **B.** a high-level exhaust pipe
- [ ] **C.** side skirts
- [ ] **D.** wind deflectors

1010 LGV
You are a driver who is certified to carry dangerous goods. The certificate is valid for

Mark one answer
- [ ] **A.** one year
- [ ] **B.** two years
- [ ] **C.** five years
- [ ] **D.** ten years

1011 LGV
Which of the following would help to reduce the impact that your lorry has on the environment?

Mark three answers
- [ ] **A.** Driving through town centres
- [ ] **B.** Braking in good time
- [ ] **C.** Planning routes to avoid busy times
- [ ] **D.** Racing to make up time
- [ ] **E.** Anticipating well ahead

1012 LGV
The purpose of a fly sheet tightly fastened over a tipper body is to reduce the

Mark one answer
- [ ] **A.** drag effect
- [ ] **B.** steering effort
- [ ] **C.** legal load weight
- [ ] **D.** load capacity

1013 LGV
How could you improve the fuel consumption of your lorry?

Mark two answers
- [ ] **A.** Brake late as often as you can
- [ ] **B.** Fit a cab-mounted wind deflector
- [ ] **C.** Avoid sheeting any bulky loads
- [ ] **D.** Try to increase your overall speed
- [ ] **E.** Make regular checks on tyre pressures

1014 LGV
Red diesel is

Mark one answer
- [ ] **A.** only used by private cars
- [ ] **B.** for authorised purposes only
- [ ] **C.** available at all garages
- [ ] **D.** very environmentally friendly

1015 LGV
You are driving a lorry with a loaded skip. The skip should be covered with a net to

Mark one answer
- [ ] **A.** prevent rubbish from falling out of it
- [ ] **B.** protect the contents from the weather
- [ ] **C.** make it more visible to other traffic
- [ ] **D.** stop others from adding to the load

1016 LGV
You may park a lorry over 7.5 tonnes on a verge for essential loading, but it must have

Mark one answer
- [ ] A. a collection note
- [ ] B. an orange badge
- [ ] C. the owner's permission
- [ ] D. an attendant

1017 LGV
You must not park any unattended lorry over 7.5 tonnes on a verge without

Mark one answer
- [ ] A. police permission
- [ ] B. warning lights
- [ ] C. the owner's permission
- [ ] D. a loading permit

1018 LGV
Cab-mounted wind deflectors are fitted to

Mark one answer
- [ ] A. increase wind buffeting
- [ ] B. increase engine power
- [ ] C. reduce exhaust emissions
- [ ] D. reduce fuel consumption

1019 PCV
Air pressure should be built up with the

Mark one answer
- [ ] A. engine switched off
- [ ] B. service brake on
- [ ] C. engine ticking over
- [ ] D. engine revving up

1020 PCV/LGV
Vehicles are fitted with air suspension to

Mark one answer
- [ ] A. reduce wear to roads
- [ ] B. reduce tyre wear
- [ ] C. improve fuel consumption
- [ ] D. help the driver stay awake

1021 PCV/LGV
Your vehicle is fitted with a warning device, which sounds when reversing. When should you NOT use it in a built-up area?

Mark one answer
- [ ] A. Between 10.30pm and 6.30am
- [ ] B. Between 11pm and 6.30am
- [ ] C. Between 11.30pm and 7am
- [ ] D. Between 12.30am and 8am

1022 PCV/LGV
You are driving a vehicle with excessive exhaust smoke. Which of the following is correct?

Mark two answers
- [ ] A. You risk being reported
- [ ] B. You risk reducing your vision ahead
- [ ] C. You could cause the brakes to fade
- [ ] D. You are breaking the law

1023 PCV/LGV
A vehicle 'reverse warning bleeper' must NOT be used

Mark one answer
- [ ] A. in parking bays
- [ ] B. between 11pm and 7.30am
- [ ] C. between 11.30pm and 7am in 30mph limits
- [ ] D. near hospitals

1024 PCV/LGV
You have lost the filler cap to your diesel tank. You should

Mark one answer
- A. get a replacement before driving
- B. push a rag into the filler pipe
- C. drive slowly back to your depot
- D. only fill the tank half-full

1025 PCV/LGV
Why can it be an advantage for traffic speed to stay constant over a longer distance?

Mark one answer
- A. You will do more stop-start driving
- B. You will use far more fuel
- C. You will be able to use more direct routes
- D. Your overall journey time may normally improve

1026 PCV/LGV
Before starting a journey it is wise to plan your route. How can you do this?

Mark one answer
- A. Look at a map
- B. Contact your local garage
- C. Look in your vehicle service record
- D. Check your vehicle registration document

1027 PCV/LGV
It can help to plan your route before starting a journey. You can do this by contacting

Mark one answer   NI
- A. your local filling station
- B. a motoring organisation
- C. the Driver Vehicle Licensing Agency
- D. your vehicle manufacturer

1028 PCV/LGV
How can you plan your route before starting a long journey?

Mark one answer
- A. Check your vehicle's workshop manual
- B. Ask your local garage
- C. Use a route planner on the internet
- D. Consult your travel agents

1029 PCV/LGV
Planning your route before setting out can be helpful. How can you do this?

Mark one answer
- A. Look in a motoring magazine
- B. Only visit places you know
- C. Try to travel at busy times
- D. Print or write down the route

1030 PCV/LGV
Why is it a good idea to plan your journey to avoid busy times?

Mark one answer
- A. You will have an easier journey
- B. You will have a more stressful journey
- C. Your journey time will be longer
- D. It will cause more traffic congestion

1031 PCV/LGV
Planning your journey to avoid busy times has a number of advantages. One of these is

Mark one answer
- A. your journey will take longer
- B. you will have a more pleasant journey
- C. you will cause more pollution
- D. your stress level will be greater

1032
PCV/LGV
It is a good idea to plan your journey to avoid busy times. This is because

Mark one answer
- A. your vehicle will use more fuel
- B. you will see less roadworks
- C. it will help to ease congestion
- D. you will travel a much shorter distance

1033
PCV/LGV
By avoiding busy times when travelling

Mark one answer
- A. you are more likely to be held up
- B. your journey time will be longer
- C. you will travel a much shorter distance
- D. you are less likely to be delayed

1034
PCV/LGV
It can help to plan your route before starting a journey. Why should you also plan an alternative route?

Mark one answer
- A. Your original route may be blocked
- B. Your maps may have different scales
- C. You may find you have to pay a congestion charge
- D. Because you may get held up by a tractor

1035
PCV/LGV
You will find that driving smoothly can

Mark one answer
- A. reduce journey times by about 15%
- B. increase fuel consumption by about 15%
- C. reduce fuel consumption by about 15%
- D. increase journey times by about 15%

1036
PCV/LGV
You can save fuel when conditions allow by

Mark one answer
- A. using lower gears as often as possible
- B. accelerating sharply in each gear
- C. using each gear in turn
- D. missing out some gears

1037
PCV/LGV
The rev counter on most vehicles has colour-coded bands. For optimum fuel efficiency which band should you try to stay in?

Mark one answer
- A. Amber
- B. Blue
- C. Green
- D. Red

1038
PCV/LGV
Usually a rev counter is divided into coloured bands. Which band should you stay in for maximum fuel economy?

Mark one answer
- A. Blue
- B. Green
- C. Amber
- D. Red

1039
PCV/LGV
Your vehicle is fitted with an engine management system. When starting the engine why should you NOT press the accelerator?

Mark one answer
- [ ] A. The vehicle will surge forward
- [ ] B. It will stall the engine
- [ ] C. The endurance brake will be activated
- [ ] D. It will waste fuel

1040
PCV/LGV
Driving with the rev counter in the red band could

Mark one answer
- [ ] A. give optimum fuel economy
- [ ] B. improve engine efficiency
- [ ] C. damage the engine
- [ ] D. falsify the tachograph reading

1041
PCV/LGV
It's expected that a driver who holds a Driver Certificate of Professional Competence (CPC) will drive in a manner that leads to

Mark one answer
- [ ] A. increased downtime
- [ ] B. increased fuel consumption
- [ ] C. reduced traffic volume
- [ ] D. reduced emissions

1042
PCV/LGV
Energy-saving tyres contribute to better fuel economy because they

Mark one answer
- [ ] A. have a reduced rolling resistance
- [ ] B. are much easier to manufacture
- [ ] C. allow you to travel at higher speeds
- [ ] D. allow heat to disperse more quickly

1043
PCV/LGV
Your vehicle is fitted with an engine management system. Pressing the accelerator when starting the engine will

Mark one answer
- [ ] A. use an excessive amount of fuel
- [ ] B. cause an excessive build up of air pressure
- [ ] C. decrease exhaust emissions
- [ ] D. decrease oil consumption

1044
PCV/LGV
A benefit of the Driver Certificate of Professional Competence (CPC) qualification is expected to be enhanced professionalism. What other adavantage is expected?

Mark one answer
- [ ] A. A reduction in fuel consumption
- [ ] B. An exemption from tachograph regulations
- [ ] C. A reduction in road tax charges
- [ ] D. An exemption from all congestion charges

1045 PCV/LGV
You have been stopped at a roadside check. What would staff from environmental health departments be looking for?

Mark one answer

A. Licence entitlement

B. Exhaust emissions

C. Tachograph changes

D. Illegal immigrants

1046 PCV/LGV
What will help you to become an eco-safe driver?

Mark one answer

A. being aware of hazards

B. avoiding block changing

C. accelerating rapidly

D. using air conditioning

1047 PCV/LGV
Which of these can help to maximise fuel economy?

Mark one answer

A. Cruise control

B. Air suspension

C. Re-grooved tyres

D. Diff-lock

1048 PCV/LGV
What is a benefit of forward planning and early recognition of potential hazards?

Mark one answer

A. Eco-safe driving

B. Increased fuel consumption

C. Late braking

D. Rapid acceleration

1049 PCV/LGV
What will help you to achieve eco-safe driving?

Mark one answer

A. keeping in the lower gears

B. planning well ahead

C. keeping close to a vehicle ahead

D. braking as late as possible

1050 PCV/LGV
Which of these will cause the greatest increase in your vehicles fuel consumption?

Mark one answer

A. Electric windows

B. Manual sun roof

C. Air conditioning

D. Power steering

1051 PCV/LGV
Some ancillary equipment can increase fuel consumption. Which will cause the greatest increase?

Mark one answer

A. Air suspension

B. Air brakes

C. Air bags

D. Air conditioning

1052 LGV
All drivers need to consider the environment. Which of these can help to reduce fuel consumption?

Mark one answer

A. Changing filters regularly

B. Keeping tyres under-inflated

C. Always using gears in sequence

D. Keeping the rev counter in the amber band

1053 LGV
What will a correctly adjusted air deflector do?

Mark one answer

- [ ] **A.** Save fuel
- [ ] **B.** Reduce tyre wear
- [ ] **C.** Reduce road surface wear
- [ ] **D.** Cut loading time

1054 LGV
You are at a roadside check. What would staff from HM Revenue and Customs be looking for?

Mark one answer

- [ ] **A.** Red diesel
- [ ] **B.** Vehicle defects
- [ ] **C.** Driver's hours records
- [ ] **D.** Exhaust emissions

1055 LGV
Why should the height of a load be kept to a minimum?

Mark one answer

- [ ] **A.** To reduce aerodynamic drag
- [ ] **B.** To increase rolling resistance
- [ ] **C.** To increase momentum
- [ ] **D.** To reduce unloading time

1056 PCV
When driving through a bus station you should

Mark one answer

- A. ensure that your destination boards are correct
- B. drive only in first gear
- C. look out for people leaving the buses
- D. use your mirrors more than usual

1057 PCV/LGV
While driving at night you see a pedestrian wearing reflective clothing and carrying a red light. This means you are approaching

Mark one answer

- A. men at work
- B. an organised walk
- C. an accident blackspot
- D. slow-moving vehicles

1058 PCV/LGV
Which road users are more vulnerable at night in built-up areas?

Mark one answer

- A. Runners
- B. Drivers of black taxi cabs
- C. Double-deck vehicle drivers
- D. Ambulance drivers

1059 PCV/LGV
Which road users are more vulnerable at night in built-up areas?

Mark one answer

- A. Drivers of black taxi cabs
- B. Pedestrians in dark clothing
- C. Double-deck vehicle drivers
- D. Ambulance drivers

1060 PCV/LGV
Which road users are more vulnerable at night in built-up areas?

Mark one answer

- A. Drivers of black taxi cabs
- B. Double-deck vehicle drivers
- C. Cyclists
- D. Ambulance drivers

1061 PCV/LGV
You are about to overtake a motorcyclist. They look over their right shoulder. It is most likely that

Mark one answer

- A. the rider intends moving to the right
- B. something has fallen from the machine
- C. the drive chain is slack
- D. the rear tyre is flat

1062 PCV/LGV
You are driving behind a moped. You want to turn left at a junction just ahead. You should

Mark one answer

- A. stay behind until the moped has passed the junction
- B. overtake the moped before the junction
- C. pull alongside the moped and stay level until just before the junction
- D. sound your horn as a warning and pull in front of the moped

1063 PCV/LGV
Why should you allow EXTRA room to motorcyclists who are riding through roadworks?

Mark one answer
- [ ] **A.** There may be a reduced speed limit
- [ ] **B.** There may be temporary traffic lights
- [ ] **C.** They may swerve to avoid potholes
- [ ] **D.** The traffic may be in single file

1064 PCV/LGV
At roadworks motorcyclists might swerve to avoid potholes. You should

Mark one answer
- [ ] **A.** give them extra room
- [ ] **B.** keep alongside them
- [ ] **C.** try to pass them
- [ ] **D.** stay close behind them

1065 PCV/LGV
You should be careful NOT to allow your vehicle to spill diesel fuel onto the road. It can be a serious risk ESPECIALLY to

Mark one answer
- [ ] **A.** motorcycles
- [ ] **B.** empty tankers
- [ ] **C.** towed vehicles
- [ ] **D.** fire engines

1066 PCV/LGV
You are driving in a town. Ahead is a stationary bus showing this sign. You should

Mark one answer
- [ ] **A.** accelerate quickly
- [ ] **B.** stop behind the bus and wait until it moves off
- [ ] **C.** drive past slowly
- [ ] **D.** drive normally, the driver will look after the children

1067 PCV/LGV
You are following this scooter on a poor road surface. You should

Mark three answers
- [ ] **A.** overtake without any delay
- [ ] **B.** stay close behind until you can pass
- [ ] **C.** make sure you stay well back
- [ ] **D.** look out as they may wobble
- [ ] **E.** sound your horn as you get close
- [ ] **F.** be aware they may suddenly swerve

1068 PCV/LGV
You should be extra careful when following riders of scooters as they may suddenly

Mark one answer

- A. look down
- B. give signals
- C. swerve
- D. accelerate

1069 PCV/LGV
You are following a scooter. The rider has left it too late to avoid potholes in the road. You should be aware that the rider may suddenly

Mark one answer

- A. accelerate
- B. slow down
- C. overtake
- D. turn left

1070 PCV/LGV
At a toucan crossing you should look out for pedestrians and

Mark one answer

- A. horse riders
- B. cyclists
- C. motorcyclists
- D. trams

1071 PCV/LGV
You are driving on a dual carriageway. Ahead you see a vehicle with an amber flashing light. What may this be?

Mark one answer

- A. An ambulance
- B. A fire engine
- C. A doctor's car on call
- D. A disabled person's vehicle

1072 PCV/LGV
You are driving near a school in busy traffic. A group of children are walking close to the kerb on your side of the road. What should you do?

Mark one answer

- A. Move to the other side of the road
- B. Wave at them to move back from the kerb
- C. Stop for a moment to see what they do
- D. Drive slowly until you are clear of the area

1073 PCV/LGV
You are following a scooter on an uneven road. You should

Mark one answer

- A. allow extra room, they may swerve to avoid pot holes
- B. leave less room so they can see you in their mirrors
- C. drive closely behind and get ready to overtake
- D. drive close to shield them

1074 PCV/LGV
You wish to turn left into a side road. In front of you is a cyclist. You should

Mark one answer

- A. overtake the cyclist before the turning
- B. wait until the cyclist has passed the turning
- C. sound your horn, the cyclist will give way to you
- D. drive alongside and check for the cyclist in the mirrors

1075 PCV/LGV

You are waiting to turn left at a junction. In your mirror you can see a cyclist moving up between the kerb and nearside of your vehicle. You should

Mark one answer

- A. allow them to move in front of you
- B. move off and make them wait for you
- C. steer to the left to make them dismount
- D. tell them to move out of your way

1076 PCV/LGV

You are approaching a roundabout. You see a cyclist signal right. Why is the cyclist keeping to the left?

Mark one answer

- A. It is a quicker route for the cyclist
- B. The cyclist is going to turn left
- C. The cyclist is more vulnerable
- D. The Highway Code does not apply to cyclists

1077 PCV/LGV

You are entering a roundabout. A cyclist in front of you is signalling to turn right. What should you do?

Mark one answer

- A. Overtake on the right
- B. Sound the horn
- C. Overtake on the left
- D. Allow plenty of room

1078 PCV/LGV

As you are driving a group of horse riders comes towards you. The leading rider's horse suddenly becomes nervous of your presence. What should you do?

Mark one answer

- A. Brake gently to a stop until they have passed
- B. Brake quickly to a stop, applying the parking brake
- C. Continue driving, keeping well in to the nearside
- D. Increase speed to pass the riders quickly

1079 PCV/LGV

You are emerging from a side road into a queue of traffic. Which of these vehicles are especially hard to see?

Mark one answer

- A. Cycles
- B. Tractors
- C. Milk floats
- D. Cars

1080 PCV/LGV

Motorcycle riders are more at risk from other road users. This is because they

Mark one answer

- A. are easier for other road users to see
- B. are more likely to break down
- C. cannot give arm signals
- D. are more difficult for other road users to see

1081 PCV/LGV
What is the MAIN cause of motorcycle collisions?

Mark one answer
- [ ] A. Other drivers
- [ ] B. Other motorcyclists
- [ ] C. Wet roads
- [ ] D. Icy roads

1082 PCV/LGV
Motorcyclists often filter between lines of slow-moving vehicles. Which of the following will cause them particular danger?

Mark two answers
- [ ] A. The queuing vehicles
- [ ] B. Vehicles changing lanes
- [ ] C. Vehicles emerging from junctions
- [ ] D. Traffic lights
- [ ] E. Zebra crossings

1083 PCV/LGV
At road junctions, which of the following are most at risk?

Mark three answers
- [ ] A. Motorcyclists
- [ ] B. Pedestrians
- [ ] C. Car drivers
- [ ] D. Cyclists
- [ ] E. Lorry drivers

1084 PCV/LGV
Drivers should be aware that motorcyclists are more vulnerable ESPECIALLY

Mark three answers
- [ ] A. to emerging vehicles
- [ ] B. in gusting winds
- [ ] C. on poor road surfaces
- [ ] D. at traffic lights
- [ ] E. near zebra crossings
- [ ] F. when exiting motorways

1085 PCV/LGV
Your vehicle leaks diesel fuel on a roundabout. This will most affect

Mark one answer
- [ ] A. three-wheel vehicle drivers
- [ ] B. motorcyclists
- [ ] C. towed vehicles
- [ ] D. car drivers

1086 PCV/LGV
Which THREE of these vehicles are most likely to be affected by strong winds?

Mark three answers
- [ ] A. Flat-bed lorries
- [ ] B. Double-deck buses
- [ ] C. Motorcycles
- [ ] D. Horse boxes
- [ ] E. Tractors
- [ ] F. Estate cars

1087 PCV/LGV

The vehicle ahead is being driven by a learner. You should

Mark one answer

- [ ] A. keep calm and be patient
- [ ] B. drive up close behind
- [ ] C. put your headlights on full beam
- [ ] D. sound your horn and overtake

1088 PCV/LGV

You are about to overtake horse riders. Which TWO of the following could scare the horses?

Mark two answers

- [ ] A. Sounding your horn
- [ ] B. Giving arm signals
- [ ] C. Driving slowly
- [ ] D. Revving your engine

1089 PCV/LGV

You have stopped at a pelican crossing. A disabled person is crossing slowly in front of you. The lights have now changed to green. You should

Mark two answers

- [ ] A. allow the person to cross
- [ ] B. drive in front of the person
- [ ] C. drive behind the person
- [ ] D. sound your horn
- [ ] E. be patient
- [ ] F. edge forward slowly

1090 PCV/LGV

Which sign means that there may be people walking along the road?

Mark one answer

- [ ] A.
- [ ] B.
- [ ] C.
- [ ] D.

1091 PCV/LGV

You are turning left at a junction. Pedestrians have started to cross the road. You should

Mark one answer

- [ ] A. go on, giving them plenty of room
- [ ] B. stop and wave at them to cross
- [ ] C. sound your horn and proceed
- [ ] D. give way to them

1092 PCV/LGV

You are turning left from a main road into a side road. People are already crossing the road into which you are turning. You should

Mark one answer

- [ ] A. continue, as it is your right of way
- [ ] B. signal to them to continue crossing
- [ ] C. wait and allow them to cross
- [ ] D. sound your horn to warn them of your presence

1093 PCV/LGV
You are at a road junction, turning into a minor road. There are pedestrians crossing the minor road. You should

Mark one answer

- A. stop and wave the pedestrians across
- B. sound your horn to let the pedestrians know that you are there
- C. give way to the pedestrians who are already crossing
- D. carry on, the pedestrians should give way to you

1094 PCV/LGV
You intend to turn right into a side road. Just before turning you should check for motorcyclists who might be

Mark one answer

- A. overtaking on your left
- B. following you closely
- C. emerging from the side road
- D. overtaking on your right

1095 PCV/LGV
A toucan crossing is different from other crossings because

Mark one answer

- A. moped riders can use it
- B. it is controlled by a traffic warden
- C. it is controlled by two flashing lights
- D. cyclists can use it

1096 PCV/LGV
At toucan crossings

Mark two answers

- A. there is no flashing amber light
- B. cyclists are not permitted
- C. there is a continuously flashing amber beacon
- D. pedestrians and cyclists may cross
- E. you only stop if someone is waiting to cross

1097 PCV/LGV
Where would you see this sign?

Mark one answer

- A. In the window of a car taking children to school
- B. At the side of the road
- C. At playground areas
- D. On the rear of a school bus or coach

1098 PCV/LGV
What does this sign mean?

Mark one answer

- A. No route for pedestrians and cyclists
- B. A route for pedestrians only
- C. A route for cyclists only
- D. A route for pedestrians and cyclists

1099 PCV/LGV
What action would you take when elderly people are crossing the road?

Mark one answer

- A. Wave them across so they know that you have seen them
- B. Be patient and allow them to cross in their own time
- C. Rev the engine to let them know that you are waiting
- D. Tap the horn in case they are hard of hearing

1100 PCV/LGV
You see two elderly pedestrians about to cross the road ahead. You should

Mark one answer

- A. expect them to wait for you to pass
- B. speed up to get past them quickly
- C. stop and wave them across the road
- D. be careful, they may misjudge your speed

1101 PCV/LGV
You are coming up to a roundabout. A cyclist is signalling to turn right. What should you do?

Mark one answer

- A. Overtake on the right
- B. Give a horn warning
- C. Signal the cyclist to move across
- D. Give the cyclist plenty of room

1102 PCV/LGV
You are approaching this roundabout and see the cyclist signal right. Why is the cyclist keeping to the left?

Mark one answer

- A. It is a quicker route for the cyclist
- B. The cyclist is going to turn left instead
- C. The cyclist thinks The Highway Code does not apply to bicycles
- D. The cyclist is slower and more vulnerable

1103 PCV/LGV
You are waiting to come out of a side road. Why should you watch carefully for motorcycles?

Mark one answer

- A. Motorcycles are usually faster than cars
- B. Police patrols often use motorcycles
- C. Motorcycles are small and hard to see
- D. Motorcycles have right of way

1104 PCV/LGV
In daylight, an approaching motorcyclist is using a dipped headlight. Why?

Mark one answer

- A. So that the rider can be seen more easily
- B. To stop the battery overcharging
- C. To improve the rider's vision
- D. The rider is inviting you to proceed

1105 PCV/LGV
Motorcyclists should wear bright clothing mainly because

Mark one answer
- [ ] **A.** they must do so by law
- [ ] **B.** it helps keep them cool in summer
- [ ] **C.** the colours are popular
- [ ] **D.** drivers often do not see them

1106 PCV/LGV
Motorcyclists will often look round over their right shoulder just before turning right. This is because

Mark one answer
- [ ] **A.** they need to listen for following traffic
- [ ] **B.** motorcycles do not have mirrors
- [ ] **C.** looking around helps them balance as they turn
- [ ] **D.** they need to check for traffic in their blind area

1107 PCV/LGV
You are approaching a roundabout. There are horses just ahead of you. You should

Mark two answers
- [ ] **A.** be prepared to stop
- [ ] **B.** treat them like any other vehicle
- [ ] **C.** give them plenty of room
- [ ] **D.** accelerate past as quickly as possible
- [ ] **E.** sound your horn as a warning

1108 PCV/LGV
Which THREE should you do when passing sheep on a road?

Mark three answers
- [ ] **A.** Allow plenty of room
- [ ] **B.** Drive very slowly
- [ ] **C.** Pass quickly but quietly
- [ ] **D.** Be ready to stop
- [ ] **E.** Briefly sound your horn

1109 PCV/LGV
At night you see a pedestrian wearing reflective clothing and carrying a bright red light. What does this mean?

Mark one answer
- [ ] **A.** You are approaching roadworks
- [ ] **B.** You are approaching an organised walk
- [ ] **C.** You are approaching a slow-moving vehicle
- [ ] **D.** You are approaching an accident black spot

1110 PCV/LGV
There are flashing amber lights under a school warning sign. What action should you take?

Mark one answer
- [ ] **A.** Reduce speed until you are clear of the area
- [ ] **B.** Keep up your speed and sound the horn
- [ ] **C.** Increase your speed to clear the area quickly
- [ ] **D.** Wait at the lights until they change to green

1111 PCV/LGV
You are approaching this crossing. You should

Mark one answer
- A. prepare to slow down and stop
- B. stop and wave the pedestrians across
- C. speed up and pass by quickly
- D. drive on unless the pedestrians step out

1112 PCV/LGV
These road markings must be kept clear to allow

Mark one answer
- A. school children to be dropped off
- B. for teachers to park
- C. school children to be picked up
- D. a clear view of the crossing area

1113 PCV/LGV
You must not stop on these road markings because you may obstru

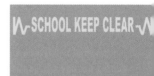

Mark one answer
- A. childrens' view of the crossing area
- B. teachers' access to the school
- C. delivery vehicles' access to the school
- D. emergency vehicles' access to the school

1114 PCV/LGV
Stopping on these road markings may obstruct

Mark one answer
- A. emergency vehicles' access to the school
- B. drivers' view of the crossing area
- C. teachers' access to the school
- D. delivery vehicles' access to the school

1115 PCV/LGV

You are following two cyclists. They approach a roundabout in the left-hand lane. In which direction should you expect the cyclists to go?

Mark one answer

- **A.** Left
- **B.** Right
- **C.** Any direction
- **D.** Straight ahead

1116 PCV/LGV

You are travelling behind a moped. You want to turn left just ahead. You should

Mark one answer

- **A.** overtake the moped before the junction
- **B.** pull alongside the moped and stay level until just before the junction
- **C.** sound your horn as a warning and pull in front of the moped
- **D.** stay behind until the moped has passed the junction

1117 PCV/LGV

You see a horse rider as you approach a roundabout. They are signalling right but keeping well to the left. You should

Mark one answer

- **A.** proceed as normal
- **B.** keep close to them
- **C.** cut in front of them
- **D.** stay well back

1118 PCV/LGV

How would you react to drivers who appear to be inexperienced?

Mark one answer

- **A.** Sound your horn to warn them of your presence
- **B.** Be patient and prepare for them to react more slowly
- **C.** Flash your headlights to indicate that it is safe for them to proceed
- **D.** Overtake them as soon as possible

1119 PCV/LGV

You are following a learner driver who stalls at a junction. You should

Mark one answer

- **A.** be patient as you expect them to make mistakes
- **B.** stay very close behind and flash your headlights
- **C.** start to rev your engine if they take too long to restart
- **D.** immediately steer around them and drive on

1120 PCV/LGV

You are on a country road. What should you expect to see coming towards you on YOUR side of the road?

Mark one answer

- **A.** Motorcycles
- **B.** Bicycles
- **C.** Pedestrians
- **D.** Horse riders

1121
PCV/LGV
You are turning left into a side road. Pedestrians are crossing the road near the junction. You should

Mark one answer

- **A.** wave them on
- **B.** sound your horn
- **C.** switch on your hazard lights
- **D.** wait for them to cross

1122
PCV/LGV
You are following a car driven by an elderly driver. You should

Mark one answer

- **A.** expect the driver to drive badly
- **B.** flash your lights and overtake
- **C.** be aware that the driver's reactions may not be as fast as yours
- **D.** stay very close behind but be careful

1123
PCV/LGV
You are following a cyclist. You wish to turn left just ahead. You should

Mark one answer

- **A.** overtake the cyclist before the junction
- **B.** pull alongside the cyclist and stay level until after the junction
- **C.** hold back until the cyclist has passed the junction
- **D.** go around the cyclist on the junction

1124
PCV/LGV
A horse rider is in the left-hand lane approaching a roundabout. You should expect the rider to

Mark one answer

- **A.** go in any direction
- **B.** turn right
- **C.** turn left
- **D.** go ahead

1125
PCV/LGV
You are at the front of a queue of traffic waiting to turn right into a side road. Why is it important to check your right mirror just before turning?

Mark one answer

- **A.** To look for pedestrians about to cross
- **B.** To check for overtaking vehicles
- **C.** To make sure the side road is clear
- **D.** To check for emerging traffic

1126
PCV/LGV
You are driving past a line of parked cars. You notice a ball bouncing out into the road ahead. What should you do?

Mark one answer
- **A.** Continue driving at the same speed and sound your horn
- **B.** Continue driving at the same speed and flash your headlights
- **C.** Slow down and be prepared to stop for children
- **D.** Stop and wave the children across to fetch their ball

1127
PCV/LGV
You want to turn right from a main road into a side road. Just before turning you should

Mark one answer
- **A.** cancel your right-turn signal
- **B.** select first gear
- **C.** check for traffic overtaking on your right
- **D.** stop and set the handbrake

1128
PCV/LGV
You are driving in town. There is a bus at the bus stop on the other side of the road. Why should you be careful?

Mark one answer
- **A.** The bus may have broken down
- **B.** Pedestrians may come from behind the bus
- **C.** The bus may move off suddenly
- **D.** The bus may remain stationary

1129
PCV/LGV
How should you overtake horse riders?

Mark one answer
- **A.** Drive up close and overtake as soon as possible
- **B.** Speed is not important but allow plenty of room
- **C.** Use your horn just once to warn them
- **D.** Drive slowly and leave plenty of room

1130
PCV/LGV
Where in particular should you look out for motorcyclists?

Mark one answer
- **A.** In a filling station
- **B.** At a road junction
- **C.** Near a service area
- **D.** When entering a car park

1131
PCV/LGV
You are driving towards a zebra crossing. A person in a wheelchair is waiting to cross. You should

Mark one answer
- **A.** continue on your way
- **B.** wave to the person to cross
- **C.** wave to the person to wait
- **D.** be prepared to stop

1132
PCV/LGV
How will a school crossing patrol signal you to stop?

Mark one answer
- **A.** By pointing to children on the opposite pavement
- **B.** By displaying a red light
- **C.** By displaying a 'stop' sign
- **D.** By giving you an arm signal

1133 PCV/LGV
There is a slow-moving motorcyclist ahead of you. You are unsure what the rider is going to do. What is the first thing you should do?

Mark one answer

- **A.** Pass on the left
- **B.** Pass on the right
- **C.** Stay behind
- **D.** Move closer

1134 PCV/LGV
At road junctions, which of the following are most vulnerable?

Mark three answers

- **A.** Cyclists
- **B.** Motorcyclists
- **C.** Pedestrians
- **D.** Car drivers
- **E.** Lorry drivers

1135 PCV/LGV
You notice horse riders ahead. What should you do FIRST?

Mark one answer

- **A.** Pull out to the middle of the road
- **B.** Be prepared to slow down
- **C.** Accelerate around them
- **D.** Signal right

1136 PCV/LGV
As you approach a pelican crossing the lights change to green. Elderly people are halfway across. You should

Mark one answer

- **A.** wave at them to cross as quickly as they can
- **B.** rev your engine to make them hurry
- **C.** flash your lights in case they have not heard you
- **D.** wait because they will take longer to cross

1137 PCV/LGV
Where would you see this sign?

Mark one answer

- **A.** Near a school crossing
- **B.** At a playground entrance
- **C.** On a school bus
- **D.** In a 'pedestrians only' area

1138
PCV/LGV
You are following a motorcyclist on an uneven road. You should

Mark one answer

- A. allow less room so you can be seen in their mirrors
- B. overtake immediately
- C. allow extra room in case they swerve to avoid potholes
- D. allow the same room as normal because road surfaces do not affect motorcyclists

1139
PCV/LGV
Which THREE of the following are hazards motorcyclists may present in queues of traffic?

Mark three answers

- A. Cutting in just in front of you
- B. Riding in single file
- C. Passing very close to you
- D. Riding with their headlight on dipped beam
- E. Filtering between the lanes

1140
PCV/LGV
You are driving past parked cars. You notice a bicycle wheel sticking out between them. What should you do?

Mark one answer

- A. Accelerate past quickly and sound your horn
- B. Slow down and wave the cyclist across
- C. Brake sharply and flash your headlights
- D. Slow down and be prepared to stop for a cyclist

1141
PCV/LGV
Yellow zigzag lines on the road outside schools mean

Mark one answer

- A. sound your horn to alert other road users
- B. stop to allow children to cross
- C. you must not wait or park on these lines
- D. you must not drive over these lines

1142
PCV/LGV
You are driving on a main road. You intend to turn right into a side road. Just before turning you should

Mark one answer

- A. adjust your interior mirror
- B. flash your headlights
- C. steer over to the left
- D. check for traffic overtaking on your right

1143
PCV/LGV
Where should you take particular care to look out for motorcyclists and cyclists?

Mark one answer

- A. On dual carriageways
- B. At junctions
- C. At zebra crossings
- D. In one-way streets

1144 PCV
Which of the following are most likely to share a bus lane?

Mark two answers
- [ ] **A.** Cyclists
- [ ] **B.** Lorries
- [ ] **C.** Orange badge holders
- [ ] **D.** Cars towing caravans
- [ ] **E.** Taxis

1145 PCV/LGV
What does this sign mean?

Mark one answer
- [ ] **A.** Vehicle carrying dangerous goods in packages
- [ ] **B.** Vehicle broken down ahead
- [ ] **C.** Holiday route
- [ ] **D.** Emergency diversion route for motorway traffic

1146 PCV/LGV
You are driving on a three-lane motorway. There are red reflective studs on your left and white reflective studs on your right. Which lane are you in?

Mark one answer
- [ ] **A.** Hard shoulder
- [ ] **B.** Middle lane
- [ ] **C.** Right-hand lane
- [ ] **D.** Left-hand lane

1147 PCV/LGV
Diamond-shaped signs give instructions to drivers of

Mark one answer
- [ ] **A.** lorries
- [ ] **B.** trams
- [ ] **C.** buses
- [ ] **D.** tractors

1148 PCV/LGV
On which of the following pedestrian crossings can a cyclist ride across without dismounting, as well as pedestrians crossing over?

Mark one answer
- [ ] **A.** Toucan
- [ ] **B.** Pelican
- [ ] **C.** Puffin
- [ ] **D.** Zebra

1149 PCV/LGV
Certain types of crossings are shared by pedestrians and cyclists. Which one of these may a cyclist ride across at?

Mark one answer
- [ ] **A.** Puffin
- [ ] **B.** Zebra
- [ ] **C.** Pelican
- [ ] **D.** Toucan

1150 PCV/LGV
'Red Routes' tell you that

Mark one answer
- A. special waiting restrictions apply
- B. part-time traffic lights operate
- C. drivers have to pay a toll
- D. night-time and weekend weight limits apply

1151 PCV/LGV
On a motorway the colour of reflective studs on the right-hand edge of the carriageway is

Mark one answer
- A. amber
- B. green
- C. red
- D. blue

1152 PCV/LGV
On a motorway, green–yellow fluorescent studs

Mark one answer
- A. mark the lanes in a contraflow system
- B. separate the slip road from the motorway
- C. mark access points for emergency services
- D. separate the edge of the hard shoulder from the grass verge

1153 PCV/LGV
This sign means

Mark one answer
- A. tramway speed limit
- B. distance to level crossing
- C. maximum passenger capacity
- D. goods vehicle weight limit

1154 PCV/LGV
At puffin crossings which light will not show to a driver?

Mark one answer
- A. Flashing amber
- B. Red
- C. Steady amber
- D. Green

1155 PCV/LGV
You are approaching a red light at a puffin crossing. Pedestrians are on the crossing. The red light will stay on until

Mark one answer
- A. you start to edge forward onto the crossing
- B. the pedestrians have reached a safe position
- C. the pedestrians are clear of the front of your vehicle
- D. a driver from the opposite direction reaches the crossing

1156
PCV/LGV
A bus lane on your left shows no times of operation. This means it is

BUS
LANE

Mark one answer
- [ ] **A.** not in operation at all
- [ ] **B.** only in operation at peak times
- [ ] **C.** in operation 24 hours a day
- [ ] **D.** only in operation in daylight hours

1157
PCV/LGV
At a puffin crossing what colour follows the green signal?

Mark one answer
- [ ] **A.** Steady red
- [ ] **B.** Flashing amber
- [ ] **C.** Steady amber
- [ ] **D.** Flashing green

1158
PCV/LGV
You are approaching a pelican crossing. The amber light is flashing. You MUST

Mark one answer
- [ ] **A.** give way to pedestrians who are crossing
- [ ] **B.** encourage pedestrians to cross
- [ ] **C.** not move until the green light appears
- [ ] **D.** stop even if the crossing is clear

1159
PCV/LGV
On the motorway the hard shoulder should be used

Mark one answer
- [ ] **A.** to answer a mobile phone
- [ ] **B.** when an emergency arises
- [ ] **C.** for a short rest when tired
- [ ] **D.** to check a road atlas

1160
PCV/LGV
You are allowed to stop on a motorway when you

Mark one answer
- [ ] **A.** need to walk and get fresh air
- [ ] **B.** wish to pick up hitch hikers
- [ ] **C.** are told to do so by flashing red lights
- [ ] **D.** need to use a mobile phone

1161
PCV/LGV
Usually, on a motorway, how far from the exit is the first sign showing the junction number?

Mark one answer
- [ ] **A.** Half a mile
- [ ] **B.** One mile
- [ ] **C.** Two miles
- [ ] **D.** Three miles

1162
PCV/LGV
You are in an Active Traffic Management area on a motorway. When the hard shoulder is in use as a running lane

Mark one answer
- [ ] **A.** all speed limits are only advisory
- [ ] **B.** the national speed limit will apply
- [ ] **C.** the appropriate speed limit is displayed
- [ ] **D.** the speed limit is always 30mph

1163 PCV/LGV
Motorway emergency telephones are usually linked to the police. In some areas they are now linked to

Mark one answer

A. a Highways Agency Regional Control Centre

B. the Driver Vehicle Licensing Agency

C. the Driving Standards Agency

D. a local district Vehicle Registration Office

1164 PCV/LGV
An Emergency Refuge Area is an area

Mark one answer

A. on a motorway for use in cases of emergency or breakdown

B. for use if you think you will be involved in a road rage incident

C. on a motorway for a police patrol to park and watch traffic

D. for construction and road workers to store emergency equipment

1165 PCV/LGV
What is an Emergency Refuge Area on a motorway for?

Mark one answer

A. An area to park in when you want to use a mobile phone

B. To use in cases of emergency or breakdown

C. For an emergency recovery vehicle to park in a contraflow system

D. To drive in when there is queuing traffic ahead

1166 PCV/LGV
Highways Agency Traffic Officers

Mark one answer

A. cannot assist at a breakdown or emergency

B. cannot stop and direct anyone on a motorway

C. will tow a broken down vehicle and its passengers home

D. are able to stop and direct anyone on a motorway

1167 PCV/LGV
You are on a motorway. A red cross is displayed above the hard shoulder. What does this mean?

Mark one answer

A. Pull up in this lane to answer your mobile phone

B. You may use this lane as a running lane

C. This lane can be used if you need a rest

D. You should not use this lane as a running lane

1168 PCV/LGV

You are on a motorway in an Active Traffic Management (ATM) area. A mandatory speed limit is displayed above the hard shoulder. What does this mean?

Mark one answer

- [ ] **A.** You should not use the hard shoulder as a running lane
- [ ] **B.** The hard shoulder can be used as a running lane between junctions
- [ ] **C.** You can park on the hard shoulder if you feel tired
- [ ] **D.** No service area facilities or fuel are available for fifty miles

1169 PCV/LGV

The aim of an Active Traffic Management scheme on a motorway is to

Mark one answer

- [ ] **A.** prevent overtaking
- [ ] **B.** reduce rest stops
- [ ] **C.** prevent tailgating
- [ ] **D.** reduce congestion

1170 PCV/LGV

You are in an Active Traffic Management area on a motorway. When the Actively Managed mode is operating

Mark one answer

- [ ] **A.** speed limits are only advisory
- [ ] **B.** the national speed limit will apply
- [ ] **C.** the speed limit is always 30mph
- [ ] **D.** all speed limit signals are set

1171 PCV/LGV

You are travelling on a motorway. A red cross is shown above the hard shoulder and mandatory speed limits above all other lanes. This means

Mark one answer

- [ ] **A.** the hard shoulder can be used as a rest area if you feel tired
- [ ] **B.** the hard shoulder is for emergency or breakdown use only
- [ ] **C.** the hard shoulder can be used as a normal running lane
- [ ] **D.** the hard shoulder has a speed limit of 50mph

1172 PCV/LGV

You are travelling on a motorway. A red cross is shown above the hard shoulder. What does this mean?

Mark one answer

- A. Use this lane as a rest area
- B. Use this as a normal travelling lane
- C. Do not use this lane as a running lane
- D. National speed limit applies in this lane

1173 PCV/LGV

You see this sign on a motorway in an Active Traffic Management area. You can use

Mark one answer

- A. any lane except the hard shoulder
- B. the hard shoulder only
- C. the three right-hand lanes only
- D. all the lanes including the hard shoulder

1174 PCV/LGV

You should not normally travel on the hard shoulder of a motorway. When can you use it?

Mark one answer

- A. When taking the next exit
- B. When traffic is stopped
- C. When signs show that you can
- D. When traffic is slow moving

1175 LGV

What is the national speed limit for a lorry over 7.5 tonnes on a motorway?

Mark one answer

- A. 50mph (80kph)
- B. 55mph (88kph)
- C. 60mph (96kph)
- D. 70mph (112kph)

1176 PCV

This sign means

Mark one answer

- A. buses only
- B. bus lane
- C. no buses
- D. bus stop

1177 PCV

You are driving a 12 metres long, fully loaded coach. What should you do when you approach this sign?

Mark one answer

- **A.** Do not proceed past the sign but find another route
- **B.** Set down all your passengers at a safe place before the sign
- **C.** Stop and check the legal lettering on the side panel
- **D.** Proceed as normal, the sign does not apply to you

1178 PCV/LGV

What does this sign mean?

Mark one answer

- **A.** End of restricted speed area
- **B.** End of restricted parking area
- **C.** End of clearway
- **D.** End of cycle route

1179 PCV/LGV

Which sign means 'No stopping'?

Mark one answer

- **A.**
- **B.**
- **C.**
- **D.**

1180 PCV/LGV

What is the meaning of this traffic sign?

Mark one answer

- **A.** End of two-way road
- **B.** Give priority to vehicles coming towards you
- **C.** You have priority over vehicles coming towards you
- **D.** Bus lane ahead

1181 PCV/LGV
What does this sign mean?

Mark one answer
- **A.** No overtaking
- **B.** You are entering a one-way street
- **C.** Two-way traffic ahead
- **D.** You have priority over vehicles from the opposite direction

1182 PCV/LGV
At a junction you see this sign partly covered by snow. What does it mean?

Mark one answer
- **A.** Crossroads
- **B.** Give way
- **C.** Stop
- **D.** Turn right

1183 PCV/LGV
What does this sign mean?

Mark one answer
- **A.** Service area 30 miles ahead
- **B.** Maximum speed 30mph
- **C.** Minimum speed 30mph
- **D.** Lay-by 30 miles ahead

1184 PCV/LGV
Which of these signs means turn left ahead?

Mark one answer

A.   B.

C.   D.

1185 PCV/LGV
What does this sign mean?

Mark one answer
- [ ] **A.** Route for trams
- [ ] **B.** Give way to trams
- [ ] **C.** Route for buses
- [ ] **D.** Give way to buses

1186 PCV/LGV
Which of these signs means that you are entering a one-way street?

Mark one answer
- [ ] **A.**
- [ ] **B.**
- [ ] **C.**
- [ ] **D.**

1187 PCV/LGV
What does this sign mean?

Mark one answer
- [ ] **A.** Bus station on the right
- [ ] **B.** Contraflow bus lane
- [ ] **C.** With-flow bus lane
- [ ] **D.** Give way to buses

1188 PCV/LGV
What does a sign with a brown background show?

Mark one answer
- [ ] **A.** Tourist directions
- [ ] **B.** Primary roads
- [ ] **C.** Motorway routes
- [ ] **D.** Minor routes

1189
PCV/LGV
Which FOUR of these would be indicated by a triangular road sign?

Mark four answers
- [ ] **A.** Road narrows
- [ ] **B.** Ahead only
- [ ] **C.** Low bridge
- [ ] **D.** Minimum speed
- [ ] **E.** Children crossing
- [ ] **F.** T-junction

1190
PCV/LGV
Which sign means that pedestrians may be walking along the road?

Mark one answer
- [ ] **A.**
- [ ] **B.**
- [ ] **C.**
- [ ] **D.**

1191
PCV/LGV
What does this sign mean?

Mark one answer
- [ ] **A.** Crosswinds
- [ ] **B.** Road noise
- [ ] **C.** Airport
- [ ] **D.** Adverse camber

1192
PCV/LGV
What does this traffic sign mean?

Mark one answer
- [ ] **A.** Slippery road ahead
- [ ] **B.** Tyres liable to punctures ahead
- [ ] **C.** Danger ahead
- [ ] **D.** Service area ahead

1193 PCV/LGV
You are about to overtake when you see this sign. You should

Mark one answer

- [ ] **A.** overtake the other driver as quickly as possible
- [ ] **B.** move to the right to get a better view
- [ ] **C.** switch your headlights on before overtaking
- [ ] **D.** hold back until you can see clearly ahead

1194 PCV/LGV
What does this sign mean?

Mark one answer

- [ ] **A.** Uneven road surface
- [ ] **B.** Bridge over the road
- [ ] **C.** Road ahead ends
- [ ] **D.** Water across the road

1195 PCV/LGV
You see this traffic light ahead. Which light(s) will come on next?

Mark one answer

- [ ] **A.** Red alone
- [ ] **B.** Red and amber together
- [ ] **C.** Green and amber together
- [ ] **D.** Green alone

1196 PCV/LGV
These flashing red lights mean STOP. In which THREE of the following places could you find them?

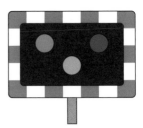

Mark three answers

- [ ] **A.** Pelican crossings
- [ ] **B.** Lifting bridges
- [ ] **C.** Zebra crossings
- [ ] **D.** Level crossings
- [ ] **E.** Motorway exits
- [ ] **F.** Fire stations

1197
PCV/LGV

You see this sign when driving through roadworks. What does it tell you?

Mark one answer

- **A.** Large vehicles must go straight ahead
- **B.** Traffic is joining from the left
- **C.** All traffic must leave at the next exit
- **D.** The distance to the next exit

1198
PCV/LGV

What does this sign mean?

Mark one answer

- **A.** Stop only to pick up passengers
- **B.** No stopping at any time
- **C.** Stop only to set down passengers
- **D.** No stopping at peak times

1199
PCV/LGV

You are driving on a motorway and there is no traffic ahead. You see this sign. Where should you be driving?

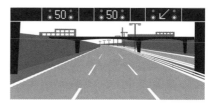

Mark one answer

- **A.** In the right-hand lane
- **B.** Along the hard shoulder
- **C.** In the left-hand lane
- **D.** Along the middle lane

1200
PCV/LGV

Which of these signs shows an uphill gradient?

Mark one answer

- **A.**
- **B.**
- **C.**
- **D.**

1201
PCV/LGV
Which of these signs means uneven road?

Mark one answer

- [ ] **A.**
- [ ] **B.**
- [ ] **C.**
- [ ] **D.**

1202
PCV/LGV
Some junctions are marked with advanced stop lines. What are these for?

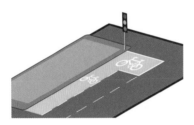

Mark one answer

- [ ] **A.** To allow room for pedestrians to cross the road
- [ ] **B.** To allow space for large vehicles to turn
- [ ] **C.** To allow cyclists to position in front of other traffic
- [ ] **D.** To allow you to select where to stop

1203
PCV/LGV
The driver of the car in front is giving this arm signal. This means the driver

Mark one answer

- [ ] **A.** intends to turn left
- [ ] **B.** is slowing down
- [ ] **C.** wants you to keep back
- [ ] **D.** wants you to go past

1204
PCV/LGV
This motorway sign means

Mark one answer

- [ ] **A.** use the hard shoulder
- [ ] **B.** contraflow system ahead
- [ ] **C.** overhead bridge repairs
- [ ] **D.** all lanes ahead closed

1205 PCV/LGV
This sign warns of

Mark one answer
- [ ] **A.** a slippery road
- [ ] **B.** a double bend
- [ ] **C.** an overhead electric cable
- [ ] **D.** a series of bends

1206 PCV/LGV
You are approaching this sign. Who has priority?

Mark one answer
- [ ] **A.** Larger vehicles
- [ ] **B.** Oncoming traffic
- [ ] **C.** Smaller vehicles
- [ ] **D.** You have right of way

1207 PCV/LGV
What does this sign mean?

Mark one answer
- [ ] **A.** Car lane only
- [ ] **B.** Single file only
- [ ] **C.** Queues likely
- [ ] **D.** Keep your distance

1208 PCV/LGV
What does this sign mean?

Mark one answer
- [ ] **A.** Road flooded
- [ ] **B.** Risk of punctures
- [ ] **C.** Loose chippings
- [ ] **D.** Uneven surface

1209 PCV/LGV
What does this sign mean?

Mark one answer
- [ ] **A.** You are allowed to carry on but only with a police escort
- [ ] **B.** You should continue very slowly if your weight is above the limit
- [ ] **C.** Do not cross unless the bridge is clear of other vehicles
- [ ] **D.** Do not cross the bridge if your weight exceeds the limit

1210 PCV/LGV
This is the first countdown marker to a

Mark one answer
- [ ] **A.** motorway slip road
- [ ] **B.** primary road junction
- [ ] **C.** concealed level crossing
- [ ] **D.** roadside rest area

1211 PCV/LGV
What do DOUBLE red lines at the edge of a road mean?

Mark one answer
- [ ] **A.** Limited loading
- [ ] **B.** No stopping
- [ ] **C.** Bus route
- [ ] **D.** Short term parking

1212 PCV/LGV
Where would you expect to see these road markings?

Mark one answer
- [ ] **A.** At the entrance to a car park
- [ ] **B.** On the approach to an arched bridge
- [ ] **C.** At the start of a cycle lane
- [ ] **D.** On the approach to a lifting barrier

1213 PCV/LGV
You are approaching a red traffic light. What signal or signals will show next?

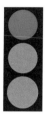

Mark one answer
- **A.** red and amber, then green
- **B.** green, then amber
- **C.** amber, then green
- **D.** green and amber, then green

1214 PCV/LGV
The double white line along the centre of the road is continuous on your side. You may cross the line to

Mark two answers
- **A.** overtake any slower moving vehicle
- **B.** pass a stationary vehicle
- **C.** see if it is safe to overtake
- **D.** overtake a learner driver travelling at 20mph or less
- **E.** pass a pedal cycle travelling at 10mph or less

1215 PCV/LGV
You see this sign ahead. What should you do?

Mark one answer
- **A.** Accelerate because you have priority
- **B.** Slow down, the road may be narrow ahead
- **C.** Stop and give way to oncoming traffic
- **D.** Maintain your speed, it's just an information sign

1216 PCV/LGV
Why should you slow down when you see this sign?

Mark one answer
- **A.** Because pedestrians have right of way
- **B.** There is a 'road race' in progress
- **C.** There are pedestrian crossings ahead
- **D.** Because children may be crossing

1217 PCV/LGV
Which sign means 'No overtaking'?

Mark one answer

A.

B.

C.

D.

1218 PCV/LGV
You might see this sign on a motorway. What does it mean?

Mark one answer
- A. Right-hand lane closed ahead
- B. One tonne weight limit ahead
- C. Left-hand lane closed ahead
- D. T-junction one mile ahead

1219 PCV/LGV
What does this sign mean?

Mark one answer
- A. Accident blackspot ahead
- B. Ancient monument ahead
- C. Humpback bridge ahead
- D. Tunnel ahead

1220 PCV/LGV
What does this sign mean?

Mark one answer
- A. No U-turns
- B. Two-way traffic
- C. One-way system
- D. End of one-way system

1221 PCV/LGV
What does this sign mean?

Mark one answer

- [ ] **A.** Low bridge
- [ ] **B.** Tunnel ahead
- [ ] **C.** Accident blackspot
- [ ] **D.** Speed camera

1222 PCV/LGV
What does this sign mean?

Mark one answer

- [ ] **A.** Rumble strips
- [ ] **B.** Road humps
- [ ] **C.** Uneven road
- [ ] **D.** Double humpback bridge

1223 PCV/LGV
Why should you slow down when you see this sign?

Mark one answer

- [ ] **A.** Your tyres may suffer a blow-out
- [ ] **B.** To avoid splashing others with water
- [ ] **C.** To avoid throwing up loose chippings
- [ ] **D.** There is a road gritter ahead

1224 PCV/LGV
Why should you NOT park on the verge where you see this sign?

Mark one answer

- [ ] **A.** Your wheels will sink into the mud
- [ ] **B.** Only cars may park here
- [ ] **C.** Parking restrictions apply
- [ ] **D.** Fuel and water tanks will leak

1225 LGV

You are driving a 38-tonne lorry on a single carriageway road. You see this sign. You may drive at up to

Mark one answer

- [ ] **A.** 40mph
- [ ] **B.** 50mph
- [ ] **C.** 60mph
- [ ] **D.** 70mph

1226 LGV

You are driving a 38-tonne lorry and trailer on a dual carriageway. This sign means you may drive at up to

Mark one answer

- [ ] **A.** 40mph
- [ ] **B.** 50mph
- [ ] **C.** 60mph
- [ ] **D.** 70mph

1227 LGV

You are driving an articulated lorry. What should you do when you see this sign ahead?

Mark one answer

- [ ] **A.** Turn round and find an alternative route
- [ ] **B.** Park safely and arrange alternative transport for the goods
- [ ] **C.** Inform your vehicle operator and await further instructions
- [ ] **D.** Proceed as normal, the sign does not appl to you

1228 LGV

Which sign must you NOT drive your lorry past?

Mark one answer

- [ ] **A.**
- [ ] **B.**
- [ ] **C.**
- [ ] **D.**

1229 LGV

You are driving a lorry 30 feet long and towing a trailer 15 feet long. You see this sign ahead. What should you do?

Mark one answer

- [ ] **A.** Find an alternative route to your destination
- [ ] **B.** Stop and wait for a police escort
- [ ] **C.** Continue past the sign but reduce your speed
- [ ] **D.** Carry on, as the sign applies to the towing vehicle only

1230 LGV

You are driving a lorry with a heavy load. You see this sign ahead. What should you be prepared to do?

Mark one answer

- [ ] **A.** Brake to a lower speed
- [ ] **B.** Change up to a higher gear
- [ ] **C.** Stop to check your load
- [ ] **D.** Change down to a lower gear

1231 LGV

You are on a motorway. Your lorry has a maximum authorised mass of more than 7.5 tonnes. What does this sign mean to you?

Mark one answer

- [ ] **A.** You must not use the right-hand lane
- [ ] **B.** You can only use the right-hand lane
- [ ] **C.** You cannot leave the motorway at this junction
- [ ] **D.** You can use the middle or right-hand lane

1232 LGV

As a lorry driver, when MUST you use these two signs?

Mark one answer

- [ ] **A.** When the load overhangs the front or rear of the vehicle by more than one metre (3 feet 3 inches)
- [ ] **B.** Whenever your vehicle is being towed
- [ ] **C.** Whenever a police escort is required
- [ ] **D.** When the load overhangs the front or rear of the vehicle by more than two metres (6 feet 6 inches)

1233 LGV
You are driving a 14-tonne lorry on a motorway. What does this sign mean?

Mark one answer
- **A.** Maximum speed 40mph
- **B.** Maximum speed 50mph
- **C.** Maximum speed 60mph
- **D.** Maximum speed 70mph

1234 LGV
You are driving a 14-tonne lorry on a dual carriageway. What does this sign mean?

Mark one answer
- **A.** Maximum speed 40mph
- **B.** Maximum speed 50mph
- **C.** Maximum speed 60mph
- **D.** Maximum speed 70mph

1235 LGV
You are driving a 14-tonne lorry on a single carriageway road. What does this sign mean?

Mark one answer
- **A.** Maximum speed 30mph
- **B.** Maximum speed 40mph
- **C.** Maximum speed 50mph
- **D.** Maximum speed 60mph

1236 LGV
When a Red Route is in operation you must not

Mark one answer
- **A.** stop and park
- **B.** overtake
- **C.** change lanes
- **D.** straddle the lines

Answers to Questions

Answers to Questions – Section 16

VEHICLE WEIGHTS AND DIMENSIONS – SECTION 1

1 B	2 A	3 A	4 C	5 B	6 A	7 C	8 A	9 C
10 B	11 B	12 A	13 D	14 C	15 B	16 D	17 C	18 B
19 C	20 C	21 ABD	22 D	23 A	24 ADF	25 C	26 B	27 D
28 A	29 D	30 ACF	31 A	32 A	33 B	34 C	35 C	36 B
37 C	38 B	39 B	40 ABE	41 C	42 A	43 C	44 A	45 C
46 C	47 C	48 B	49 D	50 D	51 A	52 A	53 B	54 B
55 B	56 B	57 ABE	58 A	59 B	60 A	61 C	62 B	63 B
64 A	65 D	66 B	67 A	68 B	69 C	70 B	71 D	72 A
73 C	74 C	75 D	76 B	77 D	78 C	79 C		

DRIVERS' HOURS AND REST PERIODS – SECTION 2

80 C	81 D	82 B	83 B	84 C	85 B	86 A	87 D	88 C
89 A	90 D	91 A	92 A	93 C	94 C	95 A	96 B	97 D
98 DEF	99 BC	100 AD	101 C	102 D	103 AB	104 D	105 C	106 C
107 C	108 C	109 C	110 B	111 D	112 C	113 C	114 BDF	115 D
116 D	117 ADE	118 A	119 A	120 B	121 CE	122 A	123 C	124 B
125 B	126 D	127 B	128 B	129 B	130 A	131 D	132 C	133 D
134 B	135 B	136 BEF	137 BD	138 A	139 B	140 A	141 C	142 D
143 D	144 B	145 A	146 AC	147 A	148 BCF	149 ADE	150 C	151 D
152 A	153 A	154 B	155 A	156 BDF	157 AB	158 B	159 A	160 D

BRAKING SYSTEMS – SECTION 3

161 B	162 C	163 A	164 C	165 D	166 A	167 B	168 A	169 A
170 A	171 A	172 A	173 C	174 A	175 D	176 D	177 D	178 C
179 D	180 D	181 A	182 ACD	183 B	184 D	185 A	186 B	187 D
188 D	189 B	190 D	191 B	192 C	193 C	194 B	195 BC	196 C
197 A	198 A	199 D	200 C	201 B	202 A	203 D	204 B	205 AB
206 B	207 D	208 D	209 BC	210 B	211 B	212 A	213 A	214 AC
215 A	216 A	217 B	218 C	219 D	220 B	221 C	222 ABC	223 C
224 B	225 A	226 D	227 A	228 D	229 A	230 B	231 DEF	232 A
233 ACE	234 C	235 D	236 A	237 A	238 B	239 B		

THE DRIVER – SECTION 4

240 BC	241 ACEF	242 B	243 A	244 D	245 C	246 ACD	247 BCD	248 CDE
249 C	250 A	251 ABE	252 B	253 A	254 C	255 CD	256 B	257 D
258 B	259 A	260 BD	261 C	262 B	263 A	264 A	265 B	266 B
267 C	268 A	269 BCD	270 A	271 A	272 D	273 A	274 B	275 A
276 CDE	277 BCD	278 AB	279 B	280 D	281 C	282 ABC	283 ACE	284 ABE
285 D	286 B	287 C	288 C	289 CD	290 C	291 D	292 AB	293 C
294 AB	295 A	296 B	297 A	298 B	299 A	300 C	301 A	302 C
303 C	304 C	305 C	306 A	307 C	308 B	309 C	310 D	311 B
312 A	313 B	314 B	315 D	316 B	317 D	318 D	319 ABD	320 B
321 A	322 A	323 C	324 CDF	325 A	326 A	327 A	328 A	329 D
330 B	331 ABE	332 B	333 A	334 B	335 A	336 C	337 A	338 B
339 A	340 A	341 BDE	342 A	343 A	344 A	345 A	346 A	347 A
348 D	349 A	350 A	351 C	352 D	353 AE	354 B	355 A	356 A

CARRYING PASSENGERS – SECTION 5

357 B	358 A	359 AD	360 D	361 AB	362 D	363 A	364 B	365 AB
366 B	367 A	368 C	369 A	370 ABC	371 DE	372 D	373 A	374 BEF
375 A	376 B	377 A	378 BCF	379 ACD	380 BD	381 C	382 A	383 B
384 BC	385 C	386 C	387 C	388 ABC	389 C	390 B	391 D	392 B
393 BC	394 AD	395 BC	396 ADF	397 A	398 B	399 D	400 C	401 C
402 C	403 A	404 B	405 B	406 D	407 AD	408 B	409 D	410 D
411 A	412 D	413 C	414 ABD	415 CD	416 B	417 A	418 C	419 D
420 C	421 A	422 D	423 C	424 B	425 C	426 D	427 D	428 D
429 D	430 DE	431 B	432 B	433 D	434 D	435 B	436 A	437 A
438 C	439 A	440 A	441 A	442 D				

THE ROAD – SECTION 6

443 D	444 C	445 D	446 A	447 BE	448 A	449 C	450 A	451 D
452 D	453 A	454 D	455 A	456 B	457 A	458 C	459 C	460 C
461 D	462 A	463 B	464 A	465 D	466 C	467 D	468 B	469 D
470 BC	471 A	472 BE	473 BCE	474 A	475 B	476 B	477 BC	478 BE
479 B	480 A	481 B	482 A	483 D	484 A	485 C	486 A	487 DEF
488 ABDF	489 BCDF	490 B	491 BCD	492 C	493 D	494 A	495 B	496 BCE
497 D	498 B	499 D	500 C	501 B	502 D	503 B	504 A	505 A
506 A	507 D	508 BCE	509 B	510 D	511 A	512 D	513 BCF	514 B
515 DE	516 C	517 C	518 D	519 D	520 CEF	521 C	522 C	523 A
524 A	525 D	526 D	527 BC	528 BCF	529 C	530 A	531 C	532 B
533 A	534 B	535 BCF	536 B	537 A	538 A	539 B	540 C	541 AB
542 A	543 A	544 B	545 A	546 B	547 BDF	548 ACF	549 A	550 D
551 D	552 A	553 A	554 A	555 D	556 A	557 AB	558 D	559 A
560 CE	561 B	562 A	563 D	564 B	565 D	566 B	567 D	568 A
569 A	570 A	571 D	572 D	573 C	574 C	575 C	576 D	577 B
578 C	579 D	580 C	581 D	582 D	583 A	584 ADF	585 B	586 A
587 C	588 AC	589 B	590 CE	591 C	592 D	593 D	594 A	595 C
596 D	597 B	598 A						

ACCIDENT HANDLING – SECTION 7

599 D	600 B	601 D	602 D	603 A	604 A	605 B	606 D	607 B
608 AD	609 A	610 B	611 D	612 AC	613 CDE	614 C	615 A	616 A
617 A	618 A	619 B	620 ABE	621 ACF	622 A	623 ACE	624 ABE	625 ACF
626 ACDE	627 C	628 AB	629 BC	630 A	631 B	632 C	633 B	634 D
635 CD	636 D	637 C	638 C	639 B	640 D	641 AEF	642 D	643 D
644 D	645 AC	646 B	647 A	648 D	649 A	650 B	651 C	652 D
653 C	654 A	655 D	656 D	657 D	658 AE	659 BDE	660 C	661 A
662 B	663 C	664 C	665 A	666 A	667 A	668 A	669 D	670 ABD
671 BC	672 BD	673 A						

VEHICLE CONDITION – SECTION 8

674 D	675 B	676 B	677 B	678 B	679 A	680 B	681 A	682 B
683 C	684 C	685 D	686 A	687 D	688 C	689 B	690 D	691 BF
692 C	693 ABDF	694 B	695 DE	696 A	697 ACE	698 D	699 BCD	700 B
701 C	702 C	703 A	704 D	705 AD	706 D	707 D	708 C	709 B
710 D	711 AC	712 B	713 A	714 A	715 A	716 D	717 C	718 B
719 C	720 A	721 B	722 B	723 B	724 B	725 B	726 C	727 A
728 B	729 D	730 B	731 A	732 D	733 ADF	734 B	735 A	736 C
737 C	738 B	739 B	740 A	741 D	742 C	743 CD	744 B	745 D
746 B	747 A	748 A	749 A	750 C	751 B	752 B	753 B	754 B
755 B	756 CE	757 B	758 AEF	759 D	760 A	761 A	762 D	763 C
764 A	765 D	766 D	767 D	768 A	769 A	770 C	771 D	772 D
773 A	774 A	775 A	776 B	777 D	778 B	779 B	780 B	781 A
782 C	783 D	784 A	785 B	786 A	787 B			

LEAVING THE VEHICLE – SECTION 9

788 A	789 BCD	790 AC	791 BC	792 ACEF	793 C	794 ABC	795 D	796 C
797 CD	798 C	799 B	800 BDF	801 A	802 B	803 C	804 BCE	805 CE
806 DE	807 C	808 B	809 A	810 D	811 D	812 CEF	813 B	814 A
815 B	816 D	817 B	818 ABC	819 A	820 A	821 A		

VEHICLE LOADING – SECTION 10

822 A	823 A	824 D	825 A	826 B	827 C	828 A	829 B	830 A
831 D	832 C	833 C	834 C	835 A	836 A	837 C	838 D	839 C
840 A	841 C	842 A	843 D	844 C	845 C	846 C	847 D	848 D
849 C	850 D	851 C	852 BDEF	853 C	854 B	855 C	856 C	857 D
858 B	859 B	860 B	861 C	862 D	863 A	864 D	865 B	866 A
867 A	868 AD	869 D	870 A	871 D	872 B	873 C	874 D	875 ABC
876 A	877 D	878 D	879 A	880 B	881 A	882 A	883 B	884 A
885 A	886 B	887 D	888 C	889 B	890 C	891 A	892 C	893 C
894 A	895 D	896 A	897 A	898 D	899 A	900 B		

RESTRICTED VIEW – SECTION 11

901 C	902 C	903 B	904 C	905 A	906 BE	907 BC	908 A	909 D
910 C	911 A	912 D	913 D	914 BCD	915 A	916 B	917 C	918 A
919 A	920 AD	921 C	922 A	923 AB	924 B	925 C	926 AB	927 ADF
928 BCD	929 C	930 B	931 A	932 A	933 A	934 AB	935 A	936 BD
937 B								

DOCUMENTS – SECTION 12

938 B	939 A	940 C	941 A	942 B	943 A	944 B	945 A	946 C
947 A	948 A	949 C	950 B	951 A	952 B	953 A	954 C	955 C
956 B	957 C	958 D	959 B	960 CD	961 ACE	962 C	963 C	964 B
965 C	966 B	967 C	968 A	969 C	970 B	971 C	972 C	973 A

ENVIRONMENTAL ISSUES – SECTION 13

974 A	975 B	976 ACE	977 C	978 A	979 A	980 A	981 AB
982 ACF	983 AE	984 BDF	985 CE	986 B	987 B	988 C	989 C
990 A	991 D	992 ACD	993 ACE	994 C	995 B	996 CD	997 A
998 C	999 BCF	1000 A	1001 D	1002 ACD	1003 B	1004 A	1005 D
1006 A	1007 DE	1008 D	1009 CD	1010 C	1011 BCE	1012 A	1013 BE
1014 B	1015 A	1016 D	1017 A	1018 D	1019 C	1020 A	1021 C
1022 AD	1023 C	1024 A	1025 D	1026 A	1027 B	1028 C	1029 D
1030 A	1031 B	1032 C	1033 D	1034 A	1035 C	1036 D	1037 C
1038 B	1039 D	1040 C	1041 D	1042 A	1043 A	1044 A	1045 B
1046 A	1047 A	1048 A	1049 B	1050 C	1051 D	1052 A	1053 A
1054 A	1055 A						

OTHER ROAD USERS – SECTION 14

1056 C	1057 B	1058 A	1059 B	1060 C	1061 A	1062 A	1063 C
1064 A	1065 A	1066 C	1067 CDF	1068 C	1069 B	1070 B	1071 D
1072 D	1073 A	1074 B	1075 A	1076 C	1077 D	1078 A	1079 A
1080 D	1081 A	1082 BC	1083 ABD	1084 ABC	1085 B	1086 BCD	1087 A
1088 AD	1089 AE	1090 D	1091 D	1092 C	1093 C	1094 D	1095 D
1096 AD	1097 D	1098 D	1099 B	1100 D	1101 D	1102 D	1103 C
1104 A	1105 D	1106 D	1107 AC	1108 ABD	1109 B	1110 A	1111 A
1112 D	1113 A	1114 B	1115 C	1116 D	1117 D	1118 B	1119 A
1120 C	1121 D	1122 C	1123 C	1124 A	1125 B	1126 C	1127 C
1128 B	1129 D	1130 B	1131 D	1132 C	1133 C	1134 ABC	1135 B
1136 D	1137 C	1138 C	1139 ACE	1140 D	1141 C	1142 D	1143 B

TRAFFIC SIGNS – SECTION 15

1144 AE	1145 D	1146 D	1147 B	1148 A	1149 D	1150 A	1151 A
1152 A	1153 A	1154 A	1155 B	1156 C	1157 C	1158 A	1159 B
1160 C	1161 B	1162 C	1163 A	1164 A	1165 B	1166 D	1167 D
1168 B	1169 D	1170 D	1171 B	1172 C	1173 D	1174 C	1175 C
1176 C	1177 D	1178 B	1179 B	1180 C	1181 D	1182 C	1183 C
1184 B	1185 A	1186 B	1187 B	1188 A	1189 ACEF	1190 A	1191 A
1192 C	1193 D	1194 D	1195 A	1196 BDF	1197 D	1198 B	1199 C
1200 C	1201 B	1202 C	1203 A	1204 D	1205 C	1206 B	1207 C
1208 C	1209 D	1210 C	1211 B	1212 B	1213 A	1214 BE	1215 B
1216 D	1217 B	1218 A	1219 D	1220 A	1221 B	1222 C	1223 C
1224 A	1225 A	1226 B	1227 D	1228 B	1229 A	1230 D	1231 A
1232 D	1233 C	1234 B	1235 B	1236 A			

Notes